Between the Wedding & the War

The Bulloch/Roosevelt Letters:
1854-1860

Between the Wedding & the War

The Bulloch/Roosevelt Letters: 1854-1860

Gwendolyn I. Koehler

Gwendolyn I. Koehler
&
Connie M. Huddleston

The Bulloch Letters
Volume 2
Friends of Bulloch, Inc.
Roswell, Georgia

Between the Wedding & the War:
The Bulloch/Roosevelt Letters: 1854-1860

Published by:
Friends of Bulloch, Inc.
Roswell, Georgia

Cover design by Interpreting Time's Past, LLC

ISBN-13: 978-0-692-75963-9

Volume II in The Bulloch Letters Series.
Volume I is *Mittie & Thee: An 1853 Roosevelt Romance*

Table of Contents

List of Figures

Dedications

We dedicate this book to
Roswell's
Magnolia Sampler Guild
and
Friends of Bulloch's
Board of Directors
for all their support.

Acknowledgments

Without the interest and support of many individuals and groups, publication of these letters would never have been possible. The project began with the collection of historian Clarece Martin, now held in the Bulloch Hall Archives. We deeply appreciate her family's donation of the materials and her initial work on the letters.

The generous monetary donations from the Magnolia Sampler Guild of Bulloch Hall, who fell in love with the charm of Mittie and Thee's story, and the Friends of Bulloch, Inc., who matched the Guild's donation, made possible our research at the Houghton Library, Harvard University.

The archivists, curators, and staff of the Houghton Library, Harvard University, in particular Heather Cole, Curator of the Theodore Roosevelt Collection, graciously assisted our research in the Theodore Roosevelt Collection.

Two individuals require a great deal of thanks for their contributions to this project. First, Savannah Wilcy organized all of the letters and associated documents and kept our digital files up to date and protected. Second, Amy C. Davis created our ebook files for this book as well as for the first volume, *Mittie & Thee*. Without her work, ebook versions would never have happened. We applaud both!

We wish to sincerely thank the remarkable and diligent interns from Kennesaw State University and other universities who enabled us to speed up the lengthy transcription process. Their dedication to cataloging the letters and to assisting with accurate transcription has allowed us to proceed far beyond what we could have accomplished on our own.

Two beta readers and our friend and editor began working with our manuscript early in the year. We wish to sincerely thank Rhonda Webb, Ph.D., and Ina Born for their efforts on our behalf. Sherron Lawson edited our series of manuscripts and helped us make the necessary and numerous corrections. Sherron also is able to read cursive and helped us decipher some of the previously illegible words in these letters.

We also wish to thank our three first readers, U. S. Navy Captain Walter E. Wilson (retired), fellow author; Mickey Crowell, Bulloch Hall Docent; and Deborah Prosser, Ph.d., Dean of Libraries, University of North Georgia. Each provided insights (and corrections) to make this book more enjoyable. We count each as a friend.

Preface

This book is the second in the Bulloch Letters Series, if you read *Mittie & Thee: An 1853 Roosevelt Romance*, you may wish to skip this section although some new information is included.

Bulloch Hall, Roswell, Georgia, is the antebellum home of James Stephens Bulloch and Martha Bulloch. Built in the late 1830s, this Greek Revival town home served as one of the Bulloch children's many homes and was their last in the South. Today, Bulloch Hall is operated as a house museum and is owned and administered by the City of Roswell. The Friends of Bulloch, Inc., (501(c)3) actively works to assure Bulloch Hall is well cared for and funded. In addition to the main house, the site features a reproduction farmhouse entrance center and gift shop, a summer house, two reproduction slave quarters (one of which holds administrative offices), a reproduction carriage house, two reproduction privies, two restored well houses, a pond, gardens, a nature trail, and a large pavilion used for events.

In 2008, Bulloch Hall's archives received forty-eight boxes from the estate of a local historian filled with miscellaneous papers, memorabilia, print clippings, and copies of newspaper articles covering a wide variety of topics related to Roswell's history. Copies of Bulloch and Roosevelt family letters, some complete and others simply random pages, were scattered throughout the boxes. After reading through a few of the pages, we (the authors) realized we possessed a treasure trove of family information and stories. Initially, we did not have a clear idea of the letters' source. Later in our search, we found partial lists of letters that had been obtained from the Theodore Roosevelt Collection housed in Harvard University's Houghton Library.

In 2014, we traveled to Harvard to examine that collection and locate additional letters and/or find missing pages. Curator Heather Cole provided invaluable assistance as we explored the entire Bulloch family-related collection and found additional letters and documents that helped complete the story.

At Bulloch Hall, university interns, volunteers, docents, and staff helped sort the contents of each box. They matched pages whenever possible, and the arduous years long task of transcribing began and still continues. The letters were originally written on small, often transparent, paper with pen and ink, which required the transcriber to determine if a mark on the page was intentional punctuation or merely an ink blot. Copies of some letters were faint and high intensity lighting and computer enhancement aided in their interpretation. Some words simply remained indecipherable. A few of the letters were incomplete. We came to every new letter with feelings of anticipation and delight, as each revealed new insights about the family members.

Transcribing letters written in the 19th century poses a fascinating set of problems. There were no standard rules of punctuation or capitalization, and alternate word spellings and meanings were often used. For example Mittie referred to her fiancé as *Thee, Thee-a-te, Thee-ate, Thee a te,* and *Theeate. Myown, atlast,* and *atall* were almost always written as one word, an indication of personal style. Some individuals used hyphens inconsistently. *Grandmother* would also be written as *grand mother* or *grand-mother*. Letter formation varied greatly from writer to writer (if you can't read cursive you can't read old letters). Individual handwriting changed with age, stress, and circumstance. Writers often inserted words above the text (presented here as superscript) and did not capitalize days of the week. It took each transcriber considerable time and patience to become comfortable with individual writing styles. Some writers commonly used dashes between sentences. We found unfamiliar vocabulary words, *quondam* and *philopena*, for instance, which sent us to the dictionary. We thought the word *waitor* was a misspelling of waiter, as it sometimes was, but learned it was "a tray on which something was carried." Our writers did not use periods after Mr, Mrs, or Dr. We have maintained the original spelling of all words as written as well as the original punctuation.

Letter writers of the 19th century used a variety of stationery. Sometimes the writer folded a sheet of paper in half. They might begin writing on the outside left panel, then on the inside right panel, next on the inside left panel, and finally on the outside left panel. When the writer ran out of room, they sometimes turned the paper 90 degrees and continued writing in the margin or even perpendicular to and over their previous words.

Gwen and two additional individuals interpreted each letter. The first interpreter transcribed by hand. Then a second set of eyes proofed the results. The letter was then typed, compared to the original, and proofed again. Gwen performed the fourth and final proofing.

Transcribing many letters from a particular individual is a deeply personal experience. The transcribers came to know the correspondents intimately, imagining each writer was watching to ensure accuracy in content and tone. These

Bulloch and Roosevelt letters provide a singular window into personal lives of the 19th century and a pivotal moment in American history. The courtship letters are the focus of the first book, *Mittie & Thee: An 1853 Roosevelt Romance*.

Additional Bulloch and Roosevelt letters included in the collection have been and are still (2016) being transcribed. This book presents the letters between Mittie and Thee's 1853 wedding and the beginning of the American Civil War in 1861. A final volume of letters will encompass all those from the beginning of the War until the War's end.

To increase reader enjoyment and understanding of these letters, we have researched those individuals mentioned and discussed within each letter. Within the letters, we simply inserted last or full names where necessary for understanding. In order to not interrupt the flow of the original letters, a glossary of individuals is provided after the endnotes. Our intent is to provide the reader with basic birth and death dates, and family relationships, where possible. When we could not identify an individual to great accuracy, we provide no further information than did Mittie and Thee. It should be noted that some individuals did not have middle names, such as Martha *Mittie* Bulloch and Theodore Roosevelt. Middle names are present when applicable. Other individuals had nicknames, often several, such as *Sudie* and *Tudie* for Susan Elliott West. Daniel Stewart (Stuart) Elliot officially changed his name from Stewart to Stuart in December of 1853. It seems he wished to be called Stuart; however, as family will do, his siblings continued to call him *Brother Dan* in many of these letters.

While transcribing the letters, we often felt it necessary to include information within the letter, such as a person's name or translation of a misspelled word. Our intrusions into the letters are always presented in brackets [ ]. A { } set of brackets may contain an underline to represent an illegible word or even letters of a partially recognizable word. When {?} is used, it denotes that we are unsure of the previous word's transcription.

Martha *Mittie* Bulloch Roosevelt, at age 22, about 1856,
Courtesy of the Theodore Roosevelt Collection, Houghton Library,
Harvard University

Theodore *Thee* Roosevelt, at age 31, in 1862,
Courtesy of the Theodore Roosevelt Collection, Houghton Library,
Harvard University

Chapter I
Introduction

*An abridged history of the Bulloch and Roosevelt families,
as presented in "Mittie & Thee: An 1853 Roosevelt Romance" the
first book in the Bulloch Letters Series, is provided in Appendix
A. A list of those persons mentioned more than once in these letters
is provided after the Bibliography. Family trees for the Bulloch,
Roosevelt, Dunwoody, and King families are included in the text
where appropriate. The following section brings the reader up
to date with the writers of these letters and the various family
members. It also includes some historical details not presented in
the first volume of The Bulloch/Roosevelt letters.*

The letters between Mittie and Thee's December
1853 wedding and the beginning of the Civil War found the
family in a period of transition. Martha Bulloch and her two
remaining children by James Bulloch still resided at Bulloch
Hall, Roswell, Georgia. Anna, now 21 years old, became a
lively correspondent keeping Mittie and Thee aware of all of
Roswell society's happenings and her various travels. Irvine
still attended Roswell's Academy and irritated his sister as does
any twelve-year-old. Thirty-four-year-old Susan, Martha's
daughter by her first husband John Elliott, was married to
Hilborne West and resided in Philadelphia. Twenty-eight-
year-old Daniel Stewart (Stuart) Elliott, Martha's son by John
Elliott, remained a bachelor and visited Roswell, Savannah,
and New York when not on a lengthy European venture. His
various romances kept the family letters busy with speculation.

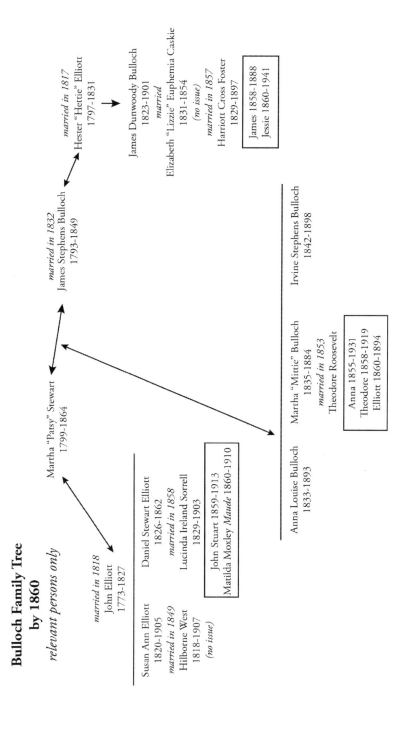

**Bulloch Family Tree
by 1860**
relevant persons only

Martha "Patsy" Stewart
1799-1864

married in 1832
James Stephens Bulloch
1793-1849

married in 1817
Hester "Hettie" Elliott
1797-1831

married in 1818
John Elliott
1773-1827

James Dunwoody Bulloch
1823-1901
married
Elizabeth "Lizzie" Euphemia Caskie
1831-1854
(no issue)
married in 1857
Harriott Cross Foster
1829-1897

James 1858-1888
Jessie 1860-1941

Daniel Stewart Elliott
1826-1862
married in 1858
Lucinda Ireland Sorrell
1829-1903

John Stuart 1859-1913
Matilda Moxley *Maude* 1860-1910

Susan Ann Elliott
1820-1905
married in 1849
Hilborne West
1818-1907
(no issue)

Irvine Stephens Bulloch
1842-1898

Martha "Mittie" Bulloch
1835-1884
married in 1853
Theodore Roosevelt

Anna 1855-1931
Theodore 1858-1919
Elliott 1860-1894

Anna Louise Bulloch
1833-1893

Early 1854 found Mittie and Thee in New York celebrating their 22 December 1853 Georgia wedding with the Roosevelt family, most of whom did not attend the Roswell event. The couple lived with Thee's parents for most of that first year while a home for them was arranged next door to brother Robert, his wife Lizzie, and their children. All of the other Roosevelt brothers lived nearby.

The elder Roosevelts lived on Broadway. However, Cornelius, Sr. bought or built a row of brownstones on East Twentieth Street just off Fifth Avenue and presented each son with a home of his own upon his marriage. Thee and Mittie's new home, which they occupied in late 1854 or early 1855, at 33 East Twentieth lay directly adjacent to that of Robert and Lizzie.[1]

Almost immediately after their arrival in New York, tragedy stuck when Mittie's older half brother Captain James Dunwoody Bulloch's wife, Elizabeth *Lizzie* Caskie, died of tuberculosis in Mobile, Alabama. Doctors had recommended sea travel to ease her illness, and she had often traveled with Captain Bulloch aboard the SS *Black Warrior.* The steamship arrived in Mobile on 20 January. Lizzie died on the 23rd. James returned her body to her family home in Richmond, Virginia, where she was buried on 9 February 1854. The couple had no children.[2]

During this period between 1854 and 1860, financial means, investments, and property were discussed in letters and deeply affected the family members' lives. For example, Susan, who had inherited a great deal of money and nine slaves from her father, Senator John Elliott, had also inherited money in 1848 from her sister Georgia, called *Daisy*. At the time of her wedding in January of 1849, Susan's wealth equaled about

$20,000 according to family friend Robert Hutchison, as revealed in this 1848 letter to his future wife:

> Yesterday when I went down to the Post office I found a letter from Mr. Bulloch of the 12th acquainting me with the welfare of our friends in Roswell and enclosing to me a copy of dear Daisy's will, which I am named coexecutor with himself. It was made out by herself in her own handwriting & phraseology & without allusion to it to any one just one week before she died. She bequeathed her little property (about $13,000) one half to Susan & one fourth each to her mother & brother Daniel all simply & clearly expressed in very concise terms and the divisions are which way both natural & proper.
>
> This unlooked for access into Susan's means will make her worth $20,000. So ample a provision that even if Mr. West's circumstances prove next to Nihil [nil] I shall advise her to conclude her marriage without any further delay thus will be respectful to Georgia's memory and leave scenes which must be full of gloom to her for the cheerful ones of the north.[3]

Robert Hutchison had served as Susan's guardian and trustee since her father's death many years before and would have been very familiar with her financial status. While no copy of Susan's marriage contract has been found, it is quite possible that Robert continued to serve in this capacity even after Susan's marriage to Hilborne, as women were not considered capable of handling their own financial matters. Additionally, it was the practice of the time, when the bride had more wealth than the groom, for her money and property to be retained in trust for her with oversight by a guardian. This would ensure her continual financial well being.[4]

Robert Hutchison's 1848 letter to Mary Edmonia Caskie came just before his second marriage. The Bullochs considered Robert, a wealthy Savannah resident, to be "family" as his first wife was Corinne Elliott, Martha's stepdaughter by John Elliott. Robert and Mary married on 31 October 1848. By 1851, they had two daughters, Mary born in 1849 and Nancy E. *Nannie* born in 1851. His daughter Mary died in November of 1851, and his wife Mary died, of consumption, on 3 July 1852. Robert continued to be very much a part of the Bulloch/Roosevelt family during subsequent years.

Of the Roosevelt's five sons, four were married by the mid-1850s, and three had children. All resided in New York City. Silas Weir, the eldest, and his wife Mary West (sister of Hilborne West) had two sons by this time, Cornelius, born in 1847, and Hilborne Lewis (named for Mary's two brothers) born in 1850. James Alfred and wife, Elizabeth *Lizzie* Emlen, had produced two daughters; Mary, born in 1848, and Cornelia, born in 1850. Robert Barnhill and his wife, Elizabeth *Lizzie* Ellis, had a daughter Margaret Barnhill, born in 1851, and a son John Ellis, born in 1853.

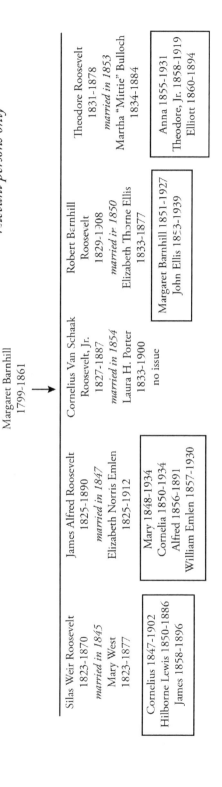

Roosevelt Family
by1860
relevant persons only

Cornelius Van Schaak
Roosevelt
1794-1871
married
Margaret Barnhill
1799-1861

Silas Weir Roosevelt
1823-1870
married in 1845
Mary West
1823-1877

Cornelius 1847-1902
Hilborne Lewis 1850-1886
James 1858-1896

James Alfred Roosevelt
1825-1890
married in 1847
Elizabeth Norris Emlen
1825-1912

Mary 1848-1934
Cornelia 1850-1934
Alfred 1856-1891
William Emlen 1857-1930

Cornelius Van Schaak
Roosevelt, Jr.
1827-1887
married in 1854
Laura H. Porter
1833-1900
no issue

Robert Barnhill
Roosevelt
1829-1908
married in 1850
Elizabeth Thorne Ellis
1833-1877

Margaret Barnhill 1851-1927
John Ellis 1853-1939

Theodore Roosevelt
1831-1878
married in 1853
Martha "Mittie" Bulloch
1834-1884

Anna 1855-1931
Theodore, Jr. 1858-1919
Elliott 1860-1894

Chapter II
1854

The World in 1854

Franklin Pierce took office in 1853 as the 14th President of the United States of America. In 1854, the issues of the nation centered on slavery and the economic consequences and realities of a mechanized industrial North and an agricultural-based South. In Congress and the nation, the admittance of new states and whether they were to be free or slave states intensified the turmoil. The year began on a contentious note when on 4 January Stephen A. Douglas, U.S. Senator from Illinois, introduced a bill to organize the Nebraska Territory. Douglas wanted to enforce law and order in the area to ensure the western railroad and its ensuing economic boom would pass through his state. The original bill allowed the territory to organize and become a free state under the Missouri Compromise of 1820. Later, to gain Southern support for his bill, Douglas proposed the creation of two territories, Kansas and Nebraska, and the repeal of the Missouri Compromise line, leaving to the settlers of the two territories the issue of slave or free. The bill passed Congress as the Kansas-Nebraska Act on 30 May 1854, but prompted severe violence in Kansas in the coming years as the people argued their status as a free or slave territory or state. By the time Kansas was admitted to the Union the Civil War had begun. Additionally, the Midwestern Transcontinental Railroad was constructed but not where Douglas had desired, in his home state.

World events of the year included the 31 March Treaty of Kanagawa in which Commodore Matthew Perry (U.S. Navy) forced Japan to open its ports to United States and world trade. The Crimean War began in October of 1853 and surged to the forefront of world news as Russia fought an alliance of France, the United Kingdom, the Ottoman Empire, and Sardinia. On 21 October, Great Britain sent Florence Nightingale with a staff of 38 nurses to the Crimean War. They did not arrive before the 25 October Charge of Light Brigade during the Battle of Balaclava, where 409 members of the British Light Brigade perished. Later in the year, Alfred, Lord Tennyson published his narrative poem, *The Charge of the Light Brigade*, just six weeks after the event. The poem tells the brave story of the cavalry's valor as they carried out their orders, despite the obvious outcome.

Elisha Graves Otis, an American inventor, demonstrated his first safety elevator, which he called a *safety hoist*, at the New York's Crystal Palace. His successful demonstration included Otis riding the platform high in the air and then ordering the rope cut, which led to widespread use of the elevator.

The U.S. saw the publication of two important novels. Transcendentalist Henry David Thoreau published *Walden; or Life in the Woods* reflecting upon the idea of a simple life in natural surroundings. The second, *The Planter's Northern Bride* by Caroline Lee Hentz, was a response to *Uncle Tom's Cabin* by Harriet Beecher Stowe, published in 1852. Hentz's novel criticized abolitionist and anti-slavery organizations such as the Underground Railroad. The book's protagonist, Eulalia, the daughter of a New England abolitionist, marries a plantation owner and over time observes his benign treatment of his enslaved population. She also uncovers a plot by abolitionists to incite a slave rebellion and to murder both her and her husband, despite their kindness to their slaves.

The letters for 1854 were all from Anna or Martha to either Mittie or Thee. Thus, the family story continued, albeit one-sided. Anna frequently took time to relate the activities of Roswell's inhabitants, her own comings and goings, updates on family and friends, and her constant longing for Mittie. None of Mittie's responses are present in the collection of letters.

Savannah, April 8ᵗʰ 1854

My dearest Sister

How can I thank you for your dear letter - oh Mittie there is nothing I possess I would not give just to hold you to my heart and kiss your sweet baby cheek over and over again - Now darling while I am writing the tears will just keep coming down my face only because I love you so. Ah Mittie dear how sad is retrospection even where there is no guilt to look back upon. This morning how vividly our two lives will keep passing up before me - It's delightful to me to feel that neither of us can remember anything before we remember each other. I have no recollection of the twenty-two months before you were born! On Monday I will leave for dear home under the kind care of Mr Jones. This too, as everything does will make me remember a time when he took care of us both, when we were so inseparable it seemed as if nothing could divide us. Since your letter came to me in Darien I have not been able to answer it first of all I was sick in bed a week at dear Tilly's. Just think of me sick and a Physician attending me. It was a very great surprise to me. I was at the Reeses [plural of *Rees*.] at the breakfast table when suddenly I fainted and would have fallen to the floor if some one had not caught me. I do not know anything more - I think I was a little delirious for several hours. Dʳ Holmes says it was a nervous attack I do not know what could have caused it I had been perfectly prudent for weeks before - Staying quietly out at Hopestill with Carrie where the old people went to bed so early that we had not even lost rest. I am now entirely recovered, I only mentioned it because I tell you everything. I reached Savannah on last monday.

Every day I have been very busy at the Shops for mother Sister and myself. You know how very little I know about shopping at best, then think of not having any one at all to consult about it. I got for Sister a beautiful lawn [soft linen or cotton fabric]. I hope it will please her. Mother sent for a black silk dress this I would not get on my own responsibility, so Cousin Louisa went with me just to chose that and the linen for my chemise, but I had not the heart to ask her to do more for me as she is very delicate you know. She has asked constantly about you and Thee and seems always so pleased at whatever I tell her about you both. If you can I would write to her at some time dearest. You know they have all been very kind to us and are our relations. By the way Mittie I have met Lydia Hunter who calls me Cousin Anna! and seems to like me very much. she says her Sisters called on you in New York and are with you! And that you promised to spend a day with them all - the relationships in Savannah are more bewildering than ever. I would not be at all surprised to find out that Miss Harriet Campbell was my sister. I like Lydia very much. Sarah Potter was to send in their carriage to take us out to drive at Colerane today - but it has rained so incessantly all the morning that we have given up all idea of going out today - I am very sorry as I will not see Sarah again as I leave on Monday. Sarah begs me to give much love to her "dear friend Mittie" for her. She is very lovely, the report is that she is engaged to that Mr Canorn who called with her on us in Philadelphia. I do not know that it is so.

I saw Mary Langhorn. She is more quiet than ever, <u>as large as life</u>!

Mr and Mrs Poullaine inquired most particularly and kindly about you. Sarah invited me to spend two or three weeks with her but I have not the time. Lucy Parkman told me yesterday that Mary Cowper would be married early in May up in Cass. The two Parkmans, Ellen Habersham, Mary Anna, Leila Elliott and Kitty Stiles were all the ladies invited up to attend the wedding. Fred Habersham and one or two beaux are all the visitors invited to attend, as the wedding is to be private, no bridesmaids, the party is invited for ten days or a fortnight. Phoebe Elliott will not go up to the wedding as she will join them here and go to Europe with them - I will be able to write you much oftener dear Mittie after I get home, you know the numerous interruptions while visiting. I have many things I will recall then that will interest you, generally forgotten while writing so hurriedly - Mother wrote to me for her summer bonnet an <u>extra</u> <u>sized</u> black straw, nothing could be found all over Savannah to answer her directions so I ordered a beautiful light black silk bonnet with <u>white</u> ribbon strings. do you think it was rash! You know I had not time to consult her, neither could I wait for any of the milliners to send North for a straw. I did my best, and can but fail as many have done before me - Mittie darling write soon to me tell me all about yourself and Thee, nothing interests me more. I do not know yet if Mother has had any applications for her house. Just think of being so near you! Three hours apart! I am rather skeptical about my being much in Philadelphia. Mother writes me she is much better. Dear darling I will just devote myself to her this summer - And you shall hear of her to your hearts fill through me, You need never fear that I would in any way conceal it from you if she is not well.

Now, Mittie darling do write me candidly how you are if you do not care to enlarge upon your health to all the family, no one you know need see my letters.

Do give much love to dear Mrs. Roosevelt for me. I love her because she is so good to you, love to Mr. and Mrs. Weir, and kind remembrances to all who ever think of me. Give my warm love to Thee. I have been so excited about the Black Warrior affair. Write me something about brother Jimmie, too. And now Goodbye my precious Sister. May God in his mercy bless and keep you as he alone can in happiness and peace.

Your own sister
Anna

Anna wrote from Savannah just before her return to Roswell. She indicated she would be accompanied by Mr. Jones, probably the Reverend Charles Colcock Jones of Liberty County, Georgia, a family friend. During this period, unmarried women rarely traveled alone. Anna had recently traveled from Darien, a small seaport village in Liberty County, Georgia, to Savannah. The Bulloch family homes, before their late 1830s move to upcountry Roswell, had been in Savannah and Liberty County. Martha Stewart Elliott Bulloch, her first husband Senator John Elliott, and her second husband James Stephens Bulloch, all had rich ties to Liberty County and its residents. Their social circle was wide and consisted mostly of wealthy rice and cotton plantation owners and their extended families, many of whom were distant relatives.

In Darien, Anna stayed with Carrie Shackelford at Hopestill Plantation, which belonged to Carrie's maternal grandmother, Elizabeth West Smith (1794-1879), widow of James Dunwoody (1789-1833).[5] After Anna's visit with

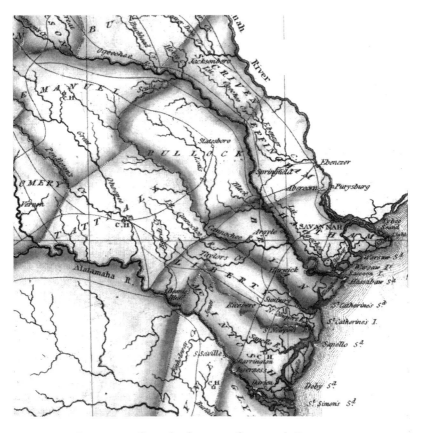

Portion of a relief map of coastal Georgia,
from the *Samuel Lewis Atlas*, dated 1817.
Courtesy of the Library of Congress.

Carrie, she visited the Rees family at their McIntosh County residence. Elizabeth *Lizzie* and Matilda *Tilly* Rees also owned property in Roswell.[6]

Dr. James *Bullie* Holmes (1804-1883) attended Anna during her illness. A resident of nearby Sunbury, Holmes wrote a series of articles about Liberty County's early years that included several references to Anna's mother, Martha Stewart, and her marriage to John Elliott.

The Bulloch, Dunwoody, and Stewart families were all large and intermarried with one another and many of Liberty County's other residents. Most of these families resided in Savannah and/or Liberty County. Anna's cousin Louisa has not been identified. There was only one Louisa born in Anna's generation to a Bulloch; however this daughter of William Berringer Bulloch apparently died soon after birth.

Anna continued to bring Mittie up to date on her social life by mentioning a number of acquaintances. Lydia E. Hunter (1829-1902) called Anna "cousin" because her mother was Anna Glen Bulloch who married Wimberly Jones Hunter.[7] Lydia had two sisters, Martha and Virginia, who called on Mittie in New York. Lydia and Martha never married.

Harriet Tattnall Campbell (1790-1862) was the daughter of Macartan and Sarah Fenwick Campbell of Augusta, Georgia. Harriet's sister was Sarah Jones (1789-1834), widow of Noble Wimberly Jones, a relative of the Bullochs through marriage. Anna's failed visitation occurred when rain prevented a trip to Colerain Plantation to see Sarah Potter.[8] The *Poullaine* family was no doubt Dr. Thomas Poullain and wife Mildred of the Scull Shoals Manufacturing Company, a cotton mill on the Oconee River in north Georgia.[9]

Attendees of Mary Cowper Stiles wedding to Andrew Low II (1812-1886) included, Lucy Parkman (1831-1913), an unknown sibling, Susan Ellen Habersham (1835-1892), and her cousin Frederick Augustus Habersham (1831-1863).[10] Kitty Stiles was Katherine Clay Stiles, sister to Mary and William Henry.

Only four months after Mittie and Thee's wedding, Anna's letter revealed Martha's desire to rent or sell Bulloch

Hall with the line. "I do not know yet if Mother has had any applications for her house." It seems very probable that Martha had planned before Mittie's wedding to move herself, Anna, and Irvine to the north to be nearer her two married daughters.

During a normal United States Mail Steamship run from Mobile to New York City via Havana, Captain James Dunwoody Bulloch became embroiled in a conflict between the United States government and the Cuban government. The *Black Warrior* departed Mobile on 25 February 1854 with its passengers and 1,000 bales of cotton listed as ballast. This was James' first run after the death of his wife Elizabeth. The ship stopped in Havana to pick up passengers and to load coal and light freight before continuing the journey to New York. Conflict with port authorities arose when the bales of cotton, listed by James as ballast, were seized by the inspector who promptly proclaimed the load undeclared cargo, and customs officials seized the vessel.

What was seen by many as a minor customs incident between Cuba and the United States simmered into newspaper headlines as an insult to the reputation of the United States. The threat of war between the two countries loomed as diplomats sought resolution to the conflict. Finally James paid a $6,000 fine, retook the vessel, and continued on to New York City arriving on the 24th of March. This incident is seen by many historians as one of the precursors to the Spanish American War of 1895, which would involve James' nephew Colonel Theodore Roosevelt.[11] Despite the grief of losing his wife on his previous journey, James Bulloch handled the situation with calm reserve and patience.

Anna, whom Thee often called *Annie,* frequently wrote to Thee in the coming years. She now called herself *sister* as was the fashion of the times. Anna often discussed events in her life, and her letters indicate she was receiving letters from Mittie and Thee, which are not available in the archival collection. The following partial letter also contains a page from Martha to Mittie.

Anna Louise Bulloch, date unknown.
Courtesy of the Theodore Roosevelt Collection.

Roswell May 6th

My dear Mittie

      I wanted to write long before this but Mr West kept thinking he would write to you – and as there is so little to interest here after the family affairs have been discovered I told him I would not write by the same mail. The things you sent me of course suited me exactly. The gray hound heads I sent immediately to Savannah to Mrs Bond and by yesterdays mail received a note thanking me most rapturously for them. Both pairs of gloves are an exact fit. I have already lined and trimmed my traveling bonnet it looks remarkably well – I am so delighted Mittie you thought of sending that beautiful little present to Julia – It is just enough - Quite simple and yet handsome. I know it will delight her. I have made for her a

[missing page]

Philadelphia! our house and yard are ~~inexpreble~~ inexpressibly lovely this spring – Riding last week brother and I found another new ride on the river, the other side of hendersons hill, you get a view of two miles up and down the river [Chattahoochee]– It is some seven or eight miles to go there and back but with their good horses we accomplished it in no time – we would have had a profusion of strawberries but for the last cold change and great draught. Today we are to have our first mess, the Kings have had them some time. I do not wish to be long from home so I will not go to Julias until Mr Pratt goes to marry her. And then will only remain a day or two afterwards – I hear Jules wedding dress is a brocade silk high in the neck with long flowing sleeves – tight front buttoned up to the throat. It came from New York – I will write you what I think of it when I see her things – I do not think I have even written to you that Mrs Rosie[?] was enfamile! and had gone on to Philadelphia for her accouchment [accouchement - confinement of childbirth]. Is it not too strange! Mittie I do wish you could have seen Clara's head dresses <u>this</u> <u>week</u> – You have no way of judging them by the modest style they were last winter – "Coming events only cast a very faint shadow before" then. Clara invited me to spend two or three weeks with her but I chose the liberty of declining. Since I came home I have written to Sarah Green and had a long pretty letter from her on yesterday – She says she longs to hear from you and that I "know not how deeply she loves Mittie and Anna." I believe she really does and I have invited her to come over to see us They are just expecting Jane [Sarah's sister Jane Eliza] back from Florida and she can not now leave home – Carrie wrote me a long letter some time ago and begged me to tell her every thing I could about the darling little Mittie – "She says ~~that~~ she can not realize ~~is~~ that Mittie is a wife a real married woman." She says she knows you would dance a "the {m____ine}" just the way

[missing page]

same now if you are with us. Do Mittie give my very best love to Thee I would like so much to see Conie – You must kiss my dear {Mrs ____} right in the corners of her sweet mouth for me – I know exactly how it looks and the very spot I used to kiss – Mother sends you more love than I have time or space for. Sudie [Susan Elliott West] too with Irvine and both the gentlemen [Hilborne and Daniel Elliott] – Mother is really much better. The Dunwodys always send love to you and Thee Do give my love to dear brother Jimmie when you see him I would

[missing page]

Saturday morning

Good morning sweet little daughter – We had prayer meeting here last night. Mr Pratt prayed earnestly, and affectionately, for the absent member of our family – That

God would bless and be with, and never lose nor forsake
her – Darling Mittie with heartfelt conviction I could join
in that prayer – Tomorrow will be our communion sabbath
– I wish you were with us darling, and would go forward
and profess your faith in, and love to Christ – But I must
say Goodbye – The breakfast bell rings – After breakfast
– Anna is writing, so I thought I would slip in this half
sheet. The tidings better from Sav, but the yellow fever is in
Augusta – All quite well in Roswell – Darling I long to see,
and embrace you – Irvine sends much love, Peggy begs to be
remembered also. I wrote you by the last mail. Marion and
Tilly and Ellen and your aunt Jane send love to you Ruth
is in Roswell. She is to summer with Mrs Camp until her
confinement which is daily expected – God bless you my
precious child

> your own affectionate Mother
> M Bulloch

Mittie sent a wedding gift for Julia Hand and several
other items including "gray hound heads." These could have
been Staffordshire figurines, drinking cups, or jewelry. These
apparently went straight to Mrs. Bond in Savannah. Anna
then mentioned several friends including Sarah Green and
Carrie Shakelford. Martha's little note made dating this letter
fairly easy, as Ruth Ann Atwood Dunwoody delivered her
fourth child on 25 May 1854, a boy, named John Alfred.
Ruth's sister was Jane Camp of Roswell's Primrose Cottage.
Ruth and her husband, Dr. William Elliott Dunwoody, lived
in Marietta where he practiced homeopathic medicine.

Martha sent love from many of the Dunwoody wives
including Jane Marion, twice a widow; Matilda, wife of
Henry; Ellen, Charles' wife, and her own sister-in-law Jane
Bulloch Dunwoody. Throughout the letters from Roswell,

Dunwoody Family Tree
by 1860
relevent persons only

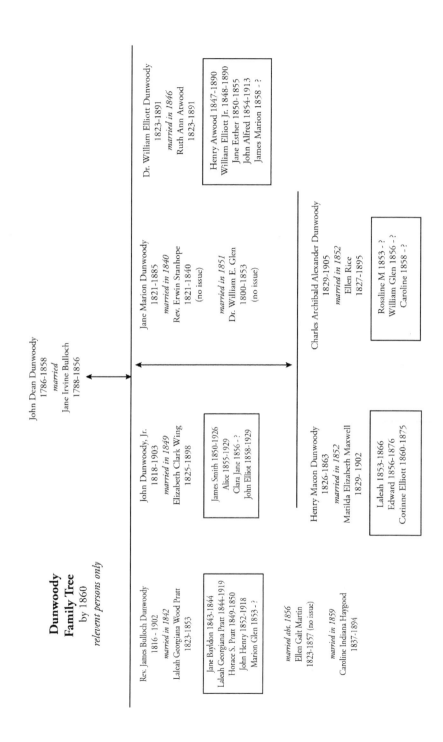

John Dean Dunwoody
1786-1858
married
Jane Irvine Bulloch
1788-1856

Rev. James Bulloch Dunwoody
1816 - 1902
married in 1842
Laleah Georgiana Wood Pratt
1823-1853

Jane Bayldon 1843-1844
Laleah Georgiana Pratt 1844-1919
Horace S. Pratt 1849-1850
John Henry 1852-1918
Marion Glen 1853 - ?

married abt. 1856
Ellen Galt Martin
1823-1857 (no issue)

married in 1859
Caroline Indiana Haygood
1837-1894

John Dunwoody, Jr.
1818-1903
married in 1849
Elizabeth Clark Wing
1825-1898

James Smith 1850-1926
Alice 1855-1929
Clara Jane 1856 - ?
John Elliot 1858-1929

Jane Marion Dunwoody
1821-1885
married in 1840
Rev. Erwin Stanhope
1821-1840
(no issue)

married in 1851
Dr. William E. Glen
1800-1853
(no issue)

Dr. William Elliott Dunwoody
1823-1891
married in 1846
Ruth Ann Atwood
1823-1891

Henry Atwood 1847-1890
William Elliott Jr. 1848-1890
Jane Esther 1850-1855
John Alfred 1854-1913
James Marion 1858 - ?

Henry Macon Dunwoody
1826-1863
married in 1852
Matilda Elizabeth Maxwell
1829- 1902

Laleah 1853-1866
Edward 1856-1876
Corinne Elliott 1860-1875

Charles Archibald Alexander Dunwoody
1829-1905
married in 1852
Ellen Rice
1827-1895

Rosaline M 1853 - ?
William Glen 1856 - ?
Caroline 1858 - ?

both Martha and Anna would write of greetings from the family slaves. In this letter Peggy, Anna's personal maid, sent her wishes.

Roswell June 10th

My dear Thee

I must really thank you for your affectionate interesting letter - It would have been replied to long before this, but I have been so completely dispirited by a prolonged attack of the mumps. I had it severly for two weeks on one side and then more slightly on the other side. We were all very much interested by the news of Mr Corniels engagement. Yours synopsis of Miss Porters character, is I think just what would suit him and I hope make him happy. The books Mr King was kind enough ~~enough~~ to bring are a most delightful treat. Daisy Burns I had read before, but will never the less find much pleasure in reading it out aloud to Mother. The heir of Redclyffe I have just finished I was exceedingly interested and thrilled by it. I declare Thee Guy's death scene is inimitable! Why I wept inconsolably! Now dont laugh for if Mittie has read it I have no doubt she is quitly of the very same weakness. I really felt as if I had lost my last friends. Your letter dear Thee quite churned me up, I was so afraid Mittie was not well, and you gave me such good accounts of her that last night or rather this morning (which made me late to prayers, and sunk me utterly in the Protectors estimation) after Sarah had waked me several times I went, to sleep again, and had the most vivid dream I have ever had of Mittie since her marriage. Thee looked in perfect health and I thought I said to her you look just as Thee described you so much more robust. Brother [Daniel Elliott] and several of the young men have just returned from an excersion down the Chattahoochee to the railroad bridge near Atlanta, they had quite a time of it, did not reach the bridge until eleven at night of course

21

the primitive inhabitants had sought repose, and were so unaccommodating as to repose them night loding [lodging]. - So the party of marooners contented them selves with the ground. A log of wood was brothers pillow and a narrow board two feet long his covering. Mr Tom King cut down some pine tops, and smoked them over a light wood fire to dry the dew off of them, and they were all in all to him. Mr Baird a person taller than brother and stout in proportion slept on a small black trunk - I don't know how. You would scarcely believe it they came home, had, had a delightful time. You draw such delightfully exciting castles for the fall! Mothers recipe for strawberry is "Wash the berries and drain them, then weigh them and to each pound of fruit put one pound of sugar. Let the berries be put, a lair of fruit and one of sugar, and remain a short time so - Then boil them very gently until the syrup becomes ropy and the berries some what transparent." Does it sound like an enigma to you Thee! Well just remember there is not a time that could not have been syimplyfied but for the variety of house-keepers, their delight is to mystify an unoffending young lady who is requested to copy me of their unfallible dogmas. How will Mittie keep house, I do not think however she will find it very hard. Judging from my own experience, two or three times this summer when I have had to take charge for Mother. There is nothing like a certain degree of assumption, it humbling the servants completely and at last even secures your own opinion of your abilities - for you you to take the trouble. The whole family of Dunwoodys always send love, but you know when all the others letters have been sent to the office and Peggy waits desemsolably by saying "da letter be too late missy" why of course I have only time to write rapidly

Your affectionate Sister

Annie -

Thee's brother, often called *Corneil*, Cornelius Van Schaak, Jr. (1827-1887) had recently announced his engagement to Laura H. Porter (1833-1900). The wedding took place on 6 July in Lockport, New York, Laura's hometown.

As in many of the letters written in 1853, Anna acknowledged a book Thee had sent with one of the King family men for her to read. *Daisy Burns: a Tale* written by Julia Kavanagh (1827-1877) became a popular success despite literary criticism at the time of publication. It is the story of a young orphaned child's life told in first person narrative. Julia Kavanagh authored 17 books and was widely read during the period. Her second book, *The Heir of Redclyffe* by Charlotte Mary Yonge (1823-1901), became the most popular book of the mid-1800s, even more popular than works by Dickens. It is a story of Guy Morville, his honorable Christian values, and his turmoil in life. Louisa May Alcott mentioned one of her sisters crying over the book in *Little Women*.

Tom King and Daniel Elliott's wild trip down the Chattahoochee River with other young men of the village turned into quite an adventure. When traveling during the antebellum period, travelers expected to be welcomed into homes along their journey and provided with food and lodging, if they arrived in a timely manner. No doubt, being awakened by a group of rowdy young men, the villagers near the railroad bridge turned them away, leaving them to camp out. The location mentioned as *downstream from Roswell on the Chattahoochee at the Western & Atlantic railroad bridge* placed the men on the Cobb/Fulton county border, south of Marietta and just north of Atlanta. This railroad from Atlanta, previously called Terminus, to Tennessee was completed in 1851.

Just half a year after their marriage, Mittie and Thee actively considered *keeping house*, a term denoting their desire to live in a house of their own rather than with family. During this period, young couples often resided with one or the other's parents until the arrival of their first child. In Roswell, Barrington Hall, the King family residence, was often filled with extended family. In additon to Barrington and Catherine King, the residence often housed one or more of their married children with spouse, unmarried children, and even employees of the Roswell Manufacturing Company such as George Camp and his wife. After their marriage, Susan and Hilborne West lived with Martha at Bulloch Hall for several years.

Roswell July 1, 1854

My dearest Mittie

You can not think how dreadfully I envied Mr. West [Hilborne] when he left us, I knew he would so soon see you my precious darling. Your last letter to Mother I tried to read out aloud to Mother and sister and it overcame me so I could not articulate any better than Uncle John can when he reads a <u>good</u> <u>sermon,</u> and applies it to the young men. Mother continues quite well and now it is more than wonderful how complete her cure must be. For we have the most intense heat to endure known here for four years. The Kings have kept a register and they say four years ago we had one such spell of heat. Sudie [Susan Elliott West] is better I think than I have known her for years - Of course her complaint is I suppose the same, but her general health is as good as I could wish it to be. Her spirits are perfect, she can at times walk without the slightest difficulty, sits up at intervals with much greater ease. While Mr. West is away I sleep with her. Mother told you of my having insulted Sally in a fit of utter hopelessness for my cold. Oh! It was such a remediless mistake. You know I could not bear to hurt her feelings after voluntarily calling her in. The first night she stood by my bedside grim and tall, the warmest night I ever felt, with a cup of "life {a_bu_lasting}" tea. Made me drink it so hot I thought it would ruin my teeth, then she tucked all of the covering in around my shoulders, all the time saying, "if you was good like Miss Mittie been, and would let me give you eggpop it would a done heep more good," but you see, Mittie when she had in the morning when I first consulted her, proposed the egg part of it I just cried out loud and said I could not taste. The next morning my cough was quite as bad as it had been previously and Sally told me in a kind confidential way "tonight little Missy I will give you some corn-cobb ashes tea - tomorrow you won't know yourself." What could I say! I just turned pale and when she went out of the parlor I told Mother from my heart I was so sorry I had called in Sally - I got Mother to tell her for me she thought "corn cobb ashes tea," might not be good for me, and then in an innocent way as if I did not know what Mother had told her, I gave her a very pretty crossband cambric apron, which she has made right up to wear tomorrow to church as it is "ordinance sunday." Sudie was to write a note to put in with my letter but she had to write to Mr West first, and will not have time. Tilly Rees [Matilda Rees] is not at all well she is so much more delicate than ever before that almost whenever she comes here we send the buggy for her. She begged me to give you her love most particularly the very first time I wrote again. Mittie you can not think how hysterical I am about you, if anyone mentions you rather suddenly I feel like screaming. I do try not to feel so darling, but we were so happy together and it is all passed. No darling I do not mean that, it is not all gone for when we meet our joy will be so much the more the heartfelt after this trying separation. You have not told me anything about your dear health lately so I hope you have felt quite well. I am going to make a little silk quilt for you, not wide, and about the length of a sofa, just to throw over you when you lie down in the daytime instead of a shawl. I think it is so lady like and convenient - I could finish it at once but I am so very busy now, making up underclothes, you know the necessity of this step for <u>me</u>, just at present. - I can not get anyone at all to help me, so I just concluded I must do it all at once myself So I cut out four beautiful summer night gowns. I have already finished two, just like some of yours. I have learned to make what Sudie and Mother call beautiful button holes! Don't you remember I used to make them, but then, they were round Darling [her mother] wanted to do that part for me and I let her make one or two for me and I saw how it tried her dear gentle eyes and I could not bear it. At last I got Charlotte to take one of the gowns, I would of course work the collar and sleeves she

[Missing section of the letter]

calamity, only this summer Mother is more abrupt than ever. All of your friends send love. You will enjoy Mr West so much - Mittie I love Mr West more now than I ever did in my life before. You can not think how quiet and considerate he is of me all the time. He is devoted to you and me - Love to Thee I feel always so happy when I think what kind, safe hands you are in I know all of Thee's goodness. He does not know how I much love him and appreciate him. I do not want you my darling to write me. I am so afraid it tires you

Your own sister
Anna

George Hull Camp also reported the heat wave of 1854 in his letter of July 8 to Walter Hull Camp. George stated, "We have been the past Ten days under a tremendous pressure of caloric pushing Thermometer up to 96 every afternoon and

I am in my office, coat off, wet as a rat with perspiration, a shower bath every day, and cool pleasant nights for refreshing sleep makes me vigorous, notwithstanding the heat."[12]

Anna wrote of her health and her many sewing projects, including gifts of same to two family slaves. She gave Sally a cambric apron which Sally wore to "ordinance sunday" when the church ordained new deacons and elders. Cambric is a lightweight, closely woven white linen or cotton fabric. She gave *Maum* Charlotte one of the nightgowns she had been sewing.

Anna's details about Susan's health provided the first historical indication that Susan Elliott had some type of protracted condition that left her weak. Anna also revealed the family's knowledge of Mittie's pregnancy when she expresses her worry about Mittie's health.

Roswell July 8th, 1854

My dearest Mittie
            I received on yesterday your last long letter and am only too glad this is saturday that I may answer it. This is your birthday darling, Mother and I have been all the time talking about it. Many, many, more may you pass, in comfort and peace, and on the next I do hope we will not be so painfully distant - I long to tell you what I can never write fully, how inexpressibly dear you are to me. You do not know what a good influence you always held on my character before I try to have it so still by thinking of what you would do if you were but you constantly being lively kept me from being so variable and I could not feel so grave and dull that actually to smile was an effort when you were telling either Sally some "tail", or mystifying Irvine I know we were exceedingly childish, but then we were so happy - I

27

am so delighted Mittie that Thee is with you every other day. You must not forget to let me know the state of feeling on the part of Cornelius, when the emerald is accepted. His want of good feeling and delicacy on this occasion is not all more glaring than it has always been to me on all family occurrences On yesterday afternoon Mittie, Mother called me to go out to drive with her when in the buggy I found she and Henry were going in search of a cow as, one of ours has just died from "hollow horn and tail". When this poor creature was found to be very ill, what do you think the numerous doctors, Mr Kings and our Henry, Sally and all the others determined to do for her! First to bore the horn then put turpentine and tar etc, etc into it, next to split the end of her tail and put salt and pepper into that and then tie it up - The physicians are doing well but the cow died - We drove some distance off into the Alabama road and then turned right into the woods where Henry stopped at a low log hut and asked if Miss Tallbuts (so pronounced I dont know how it is spelled) lived there, a miserably sallow sick woman with a red bluff of a baby in her arms came to the door and said well sir, she do live here, wont you light! They reposed but at once commenced about the cow, while it was hunted for and driven up Mother and I conversed with her, Mother about the cow and I about the baby - She said it had jest had the "bone hives" and hit wouldnt ha lived if Miss boue hadent a scairified it again hits heart." By this time the cow came up the most faint forelorn fragile looking spectre cow, I have ever seen, and you know what cows can be seen up here in the winter. Mother told her she might see her again about it - I think it will die in the mean time. Sudie says I must give her love and ask you to tell Mr West she has received her letter from Phil, but did not write this mail for she thought he would not get it at once - and she did not know where to direct it. Mother is quite well - The

28

sick little baby seems much better. Cousin Mammie sends love always to you. She speaks constantly of you both. Tilly Rees is better than when I wrote last - she stayed with Sister last night - Isa says I must ask you what she can call you she does not think she ought to say Mittie now that you are Mrs Roosevelt - I will write very soon again as this letter is so short and hurried - more love to you my darling from Mother than any one could possibly write -

your own sister
Anna

Martha's sick cow, probably with a digestive ailment, was diagnosed with "hollow horn and tail disease." This ailment, however, was only an "old wives tale" or superstition, as cows horns are always hollow and their tails are not after a certain point from the tip. Cows with fevers have hot horns and this may have led to the common misunderstanding. It was a common "complaint" of the times and mentioned in several farming books and journals of the period. Hollow horn was treated by cutting off the horns and filling the wounds with turpentine, which caused inflammation and usually a fatal abscess in the sinuses. Hollow tail was treated just as Martha's slave did, by cutting open the tail and packing it with salt and pepper or rock salt and sewing it closed. This treatment usually resulted in an infection in the tail, or failed to cure an already infected tail. Farming journals of the period such as *Western Farmer & Gardener*[13] often addressed these two ailments, with most attributing the problems to poor upkeep and feed of the animal. However, their cures all involved the same cutting of the horns and tail.

In January 1903, *The Southern Planter* still answered questions about hollow horn and tail.

I wish to know how to treat unhealthy cattle. I have a lot of young cattle which do not thrive, although they run in a good grass pasture every day and are penned in stalls at night. The person who attends to the stock thinks the cattle are afflicted with what he calls the "hollow tail." Now, if there really is any such disease I would be pleased to know what to do for it. Clifton Ward. Sampson county, N. C.

It is impossible for us to tell you what to give your cattle without something more definite as to the nature of the disease from which they are suffering. It is absolutely certain that they are not suffering from "hollow tail," for there is no such disease. Neither 'hollow tail" nor "hollow horn" ever make cattle sick or are known to any veterinarian as diseases affecting stock. They exist only in the imagination of ignorant people, who have no knowledge of the anatomy of a cow or of the diseases affecting stock.[14]

The result of the treatment was, of course, the death of the cow. Anna's description of their attempt to purchase a new cow gives us a look into the role Henry played in the household and at how Anna viewed the impoverished of their community. Early stories from Mittie to her children told of the young slave Henry cleaning the floors of Bulloch Hall by tying corn shucks to his feet. Anna's letter described a more mature Henry driving Martha's buggy.

Roswell July 15th

My darling Sister

    I had promised myself a long letter this morning as I have so much to tell you. I rose very early this morning on purpose that I might have a long time but I wrote to Mr. West <u>first</u> as I was only going to write a <u>note</u> to him and now it is nearly nine, and I only send this note to let you see I have not forgotten it is Saturday. I will send my regular letter on Tuesday. On yesterday Mother received your last letter. She was dreadfully sorry to hear about your cold, just think mine is not entirely well yet. Sally says she always knew Miss Mittie would have taken the "egg pop," and that I must tell you that last night at ten oclock both "poor old Sal and pretty Johnny came in to big old Miss for some stale dry bread cause they was both so hungry." Sister and I have tried several times to find any shadow lingering, of the very most remote {_____t} but can not. I thought it best to give it in exactly her own words as I most certainly could not give the <u>sense</u> of it. Uncle John is surrounded by little grand children that do nothing all day these, warm days too, but eat little pieces of dry, crumby bread and lean all over him. He converses with them about "why de lamp is daughter" - "Lee de map" - "Look a de door" (r not sounded) - "Ah Bacchus come, din e dink a waty." Now can you really think a <u>grown man</u> is actually interested in this. I of course have only given you his part of the usual dialogues. The replies can not well be written as they consist principally in spasmodic movements of little girls and boys (my relatives I am always scrupulously polite to them) around with precisly heat, to see the different things he points to without leaving their own ground some part of him. All are well Mother will not wait for this one minute longer.

Yours truly,

Anna -

My dearest Mittie

On yesterday we did not get our usual weekly letter from you - I hope though darling you are quite well. Sister heard from Mr. West the day he reached New York - He had then only seen Mr Jim Roosevelt, and heard from him that you had a slight attack of neuralgia [Intense, typically intermittent pain along the course of a nerve, especially in the head or face]. I do hope dearest you are very careful about your self. Oh how I long to see you my own precious sister. I some times think I am really wicked about the way I feel when I think of our separation. I feel almost a sullen despair. I know you are not <u>mine</u> and <u>I</u> can not have you. Besides Mittie this trial (one of the very greatest I have ever experienced) has in many ways done me good I only pray that I may always feel as resigned to the will of God as I now do. If I do not entirely deceive myself I will never doubt again but will always hope through him to subdue myself. It is my daily prayer Oh Mittie, that if we are separated here we may meet in that better world never again to part never again to sorrow or weep.

You can not think darling how well our blessed Mother is - She can eat with impunity almost anything she cares about - of course Tudie [Susan] and I watch her (more from habit than anything else) when she takes two or three pieces of green corn with other things formerly regarded as poison - She takes her regular little sleep in the afternoons and is pretty fresh at night. Devotes herself to the new cow. Mittie you would think the cow had more reason to regret being under the care of Sally as her physician than I had ever. Mother gives it most religiously whatever Sally suggests soot mixed in its food, or copperas - Irvine is more amusing than ever, he is improving too quite rapidly - He has lately commenced Virgil - Irvine told us last night that the other day Mr Elias asked Daddy Brister if he knew what day the fourth of July was, after considering a little time he said, "I think e de 31st" Irvine still knows the latest news from the Jew clerks - Mr. Pratt has rather an unfortunate set of boys this summer. A few days ago one of them got over Jimmie Kings fence and stole one of his watermelons and took it to the bowling alley where his companions shared it with him. They were finished, of course, and could have been arrested by the Marshal but Mr. Pratt used his influence to prevent this. The Dunwodys send much love. Mother will of course write on Tuesday. I hope a time is soon coming when I will have ~~less~~ ^{more} time to write and less work to do. We all love you more and more tenderly every moment. Love to Thee I hope he will not be persecuted by chills it is so trying I know to him - Remember us all to Mrs Roosevelt. Why did you say to the little girl that renders herself so very unpleasant to all around her, "go farther _dear_." You can not have already forgotten its lasting effect even with that perservering [?] cousin of ours Rosa Bacon. You ought to have some respect for your own character and keep down intolerence. You remember my lovely traits of character.

Your own sister
Anna

Anna's tales of Roswell seemed like those from any small town of the age. The boys from Rev. Nathaniel Pratt's Academy would have included her brother Irvine, who is not mentioned in the stealing of a watermelon from James _Jimmy_ King. Jimmy married Elizabeth Frances _Fanny_ Hillhouse Prince in 1851 and continued to reside in Roswell.

Roswell Aug 5th

My dearest Mittie

On yesterday I received your dear letter - I always feel after one of your letters a degree of impatience to see you impossible to control - I can see dear good Thee making you your arrow-root, so you still retain your old fondness for It - does Thee make it as nicely as Bess used to? Tudie seems more and more charmed with her rigalette. She says to me "My maid just think how comfortable ears will be, in the cool sniffly days in the fall." Mine darling anticipate because it is to be like yours. You can not want to dress like me more <u>now</u> than I do. Any thing that brings one's {?} past lives back to me is irresistibly precious to me. The boots look like delightful walking boots I know I will feel like an English girl in them. They are entirely too large for me, but Mrs West [Hilborne's mother] says I can easily get them exchanged at the North. The Bridal party has not yet visited me. They left on last morning for the Athens commencement, and will I rather think visit Madison Springs before Roswell when ever they come how ever you shall hear all about it. Eva King's other visitor has not yet arrived. Miss Clemens is still here. She is very small not fairy like at all almost an elf - now do dont think I am jealous of Toms lost affection - It is still positively reported that they are really engaged but that is all I know about it. Mrs James King has her cousin Miss Po of Macon visiting her now ("Why washy Po" of Macon dont you know him!") well his sister. Your present to me of the two bands and little sleeves has saved me much work. I will finish today the sleeves and band of the last chimese - I have scolloped six, these with your two compose a nice set of eight linens - I was too much appalled by...
[missing page]
when we first put his waistcoat on it hid two of the studs! well by some ingenuity of mine I pried out one to view,

34

with out hurting him seriously, by the straining his pants so low down on the hips, that the vest looked well open two or three buttons lower - The last stud I told him might get lost - as the button hole mother had put it in, was below the <u>waist</u> <u>of</u> his <u>pantaloons</u> - He immediately removed the treasure and left it with me to guard just until he could get back to it! As he walked off from us thought what a sleepless night would follow for Cliff King - But fortunately for his peace of mind he was not at the party - Rosina and Maj Minton have gone up to pay a visit to Mrs Oswald Smith, Mary Dean was left at home to keep house for the boys. She was taken quite sick and as her parents were away she was regarded by the community at large as their peculiar charge. She is a complacent spot (for she is smaller than ever) upon which large mustard plasters, all down her spine on the soles of her feet on her chest, on the back of her neck, and on her temples are put. These are varied from time to time by placing in their stead cloths soaked with chloroform, calomel, opium, morphine, lavender, and rat trap known by her as veratrum virde are taken internally. I heard this morning that Dr King was doing well but I did not hear if Mary was alive - I forgot to mention a warm bath which they thought exhausted her very much. She had a severe cold but much severer treatment. Irvine says he loves his little wife more than ever. He is an affectionnate loveable boy very tall and quite slender, and erect. He really dresses well - will not go to ride with me in the same suit he wears to school no matter how clean and neat. He puts on light nankeen pantaloons with a blue, loos fitting, jacket and a becoming cravat tied to perfection in the boys opinions (I think a trifle too stiff as the ends are sometimes even pinned down to his shirt) his straw hat with a narrow rim put on it so very carefully as not to rumple his hair - which is sometimes cut a little in notches in the back, as I am his barber, but he dont know this - I do not think for me it is quite as economical since he moved upstairs, he borrows a great many pins etc, hair grease too fades away before him - By the way how perfect that is Mrs Robert Roosevelt [Lizzie Ellis Roosevelt] gave Mr West. I am delighted to know how to make it too. Do you think I will succeed, I mean to try, but some how I always find out that "I dont know nothing about nothing." Mother is perfectly well and in such spirits! So different from last summer that I know strangers would take me for the parent and her for the daughter - She is so tender about you that when she and I get talking to each other we both cry water you would think we had lost our last friend - Do thank Thee for my beautiful riding whip I am afraid Mittie you will think I am a real jockey when you see me again my love for horses has developed so {_p___ly} this summer - send more love than I have time or paper to write it in I will write you soon at the subject of the first pages of your letter - I understand you exactly - you know I am stupid but by a kind of intention I know how things are. Good bye my dear darling yours always lovingly Anna

Madison Springs Hotel, Madison Springs, Georgia

Anna began her letter by telling Mittie how much Susan liked her "Rigalette." Anna often misspelled words, and here she meant a *rigoletle* which was a woman's light scarf-like head covering, usually knitted or crocheted. She then talks of a local wedding party and their attendance at commencement for the University of Georgia (established in 1785). Anna believed the party would visit Madison Springs on their journey home. Madison Springs, Madison County, Georgia, was a hot springs discovered by a man named Vineyard and known for its healing properties. In 1854, Athens' *The Southern Banner* ran the following advertisement.

Madison Springs, Madison County, Georgia. For the liberal patronage extended to my Springs, and feeling my entire incapacity for their management alone, I have arranged with Aaron Gage, Esq., of Mobile, Alabama, popular host of the Eutaw House, to take an interest in them. The hotel will be under his management during the approaching season. Mr. Gage's high reputation as a hotel keeper, connected with the fact that he intends making Georgia his future home, is a sure guarantee that nothing will be wanting under his management to give entire satisfaction. The reputation of Madison Springs for health, climate, variety and the efficacy of the water; comfort and beauty of its environment, the fine rides, agreeable walks and the distant mountain views, make Madison Springs popular during the summer months and always insures fine society. The table will be second to none in the country. The fine German band from Charleston is engaged for the dancing; one member will give dancing lessons and one will teach music. The Springs are twenty miles from Athens, where two lines of stage coaches are always ready to convey passengers.[15]

Eva King, Catherine Evelyn (1837-1923), was the only daughter of Barrington and Catherine King, and granddaughter of Roswell King (Roswell's founder). Visitors to the King household included Mary (Marie) Read Clemens of Huntsville, Alabama, who was engaged to Tom King. They married on 30 November 1854. Fanny Prince King's cousin would have been either Frances Poe (1831-1857) or Mary Prince Poe (1836-1909), both of whom were daughters of Congressman Washington Poe of Macon, Georgia. Washington Poe served as guardian for Fanny Prince and her sister Sarah Virginia Prince, whose parents had died in the wreck of the Steam Packet *Home* in 1837.[16] Major John Minton (1797-1871) had been a planter in Liberty County before he relocated to Roswell sometime before 1850. He was married to Rosina Ladson Fabian (1799-1874).[17]

Anna wrote Mittie a very detailed description of Irvine's dress and character and how details of dress could be modified to meet the occasion and circumstances. She also insinuated that Irvine would monopolize the time of Clifford King, making himself quite a nuisance. Clifford was the same age as Irvine, and the boys attended Reverend Pratt's Academy together.

Arrowroot is a starch obtained from the rhizomes (rootstock) of several tropical plants, and believed to draw out poison. Rat trap or ratbane is false hellebore (Veratrum viride). Although highly toxic, causing nausea and vomiting, it was used in the past against high blood pressure and rapid heartbeat. Dr. William King used several plant based medicines to treat Mary Dean. Dr. King studied at the New

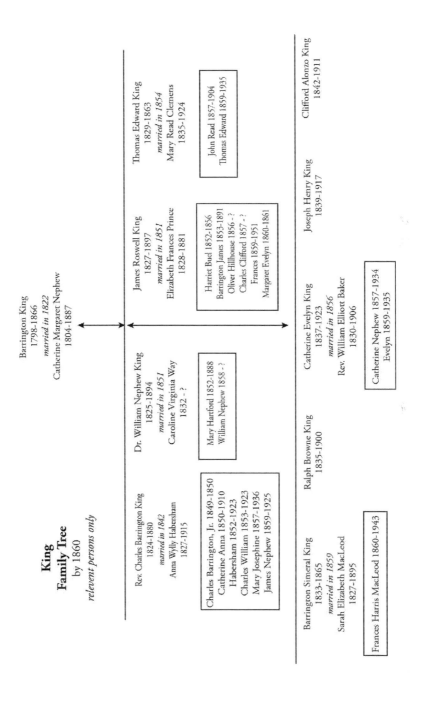

**King
Family Tree**
by 1860
relevant persons only

Barrington King
1798-1866
married in 1822
Catherine Margaret Nephew
1804-1887

Dr. William Nephew King
1825-1894
married in 1851
Caroline Virginia Way
1832 - ?

James Roswell King
1827-1897
married in 1851
Elizabeth Frances Prince
1828-1881

Thomas Edward King
1829-1863
married in 1854
Mary Read Clemens
1835-1924

Rev. Charles Barrington King
1824-1880
married in 1842
Anna Wylly Habersham
1827-1915

Charles Barrington, Jr. 1849-1850
Catherine Anna 1850-1910
Habersham 1852-1923
Charles William 1853-1923
Mary Josephine 1857-1936
James Nephew 1859-1925

Mary Hartford 1852-1888
William Nephew 1858 - ?

Harriet Buel 1852-1856
Barrington James 1853-1891
Oliver Hillhouse 1856 - ?
Charles Clifford 1857 - ?
Frances 1859-1951
Margaret Evelyn 1860-1861

John Read 1857-1904
Thomas Edward 1859-1935

Ralph Browne King
1835-1900

Catherine Evelyn King
1837-1923
married in 1856
Rev. William Elliott Baker
1830-1906

Joseph Henry King
1839-1917

Clifford Alonzo King
1842-1911

Barrington Simeral King
1833-1865
married in 1859
Sarah Elizabeth MacLeod
1827-1895

Frances Harris MacLeod 1860-1943

Catherine Nephew 1857-1934
Evelyn 1859-1935

39

York College of Physicians and Surgeons before studying surgery for three years in Paris.

Mary Dean Minton (1833-1905) did indeed survive Dr. King's treatment of her illness. Mary was the only daughter of John and Rosina Minton. She had five brothers; Stephen, John, and James were older than Mary; however, Charles and Axson were younger.

Roswell, Sep 9th 1854

My dear Mittie

I write this morning only to get to my own regular day for writing to you - On yesterday Mother received your letter. I am so intensely excited about your going to house keeping I know how very handsome and plain[?] everything will look - I don't know anyone else who has such perfect taste in all such matters as you, even where they have the [?] same measure, it fails in certain points, I know how exciting and romantic your dining room will look with the carpet of green with the oak leaves - Also Mittie dear, if you have added light and happiness to your family there in the same measure it has gone from us with you, they are too much blessed not to feel grateful for it - Your marriage my darling sister is to me in all respects perfectly satisfactory, You know how I love Thee himself and how we all adore and trust in him, and how strong our feeling of love and confidence are in the whole family, but still it is only when I think that you are happy and therefore I ought to be, that I can feel in any degree reconciled to our inevitable separation - But these are only my musings, when I feel too sorrowful to view outward circumstances through any other median than my own selfish heart which has not yet learned to love you at a distance - The idea never entered my mind that either of us

40

could ever leave the other, that we could ever be anything but Anna and Mittie, inseparable, always serving, reading, walking, riding and talking incessantly together. We never confided in each other because there never was anything to confide, each always knew all about the other.

But when I try to feel happy, and yet at the same time realize that this is all gone, I do not find that I have the slightest power over myself, no control what ever - It will tinge my thoughts, words, and everything, with a bad kind of temper that must be very disagreeable to all about me, and Sister is so perfect, so lovely, that the contrast only makes me {___} out in more bold relief - Sudie and Mother are too good to live, My veneration for Mother would amount to awe if it was not for the perfect love and trust, her gentleness and quiet sympathy inspires - Mittie, darling I read your letters over together and talk of you incessantly - And you cant think how easy it is for us to cry - I will write you a very different letter next time. I am collecting some ridiculous notes to amuse you with about up country matters and things in general - I did not feel at all like that kind of thing this morning so I would not attempt it - I want to describe Sarah Green to you at a dance given to me at the Marietta Hotel by some gentlemen - It was quite a pleasant nice little party in many respects for refreshments we had ice cream and Ice water! She wore a light blue grenadine flounced up to the waist low in the neck fitting exquisitively a light blue headdress made of ribbon done like your zephyr [a fine cotton gingham], coming in a Marie Stuart [of Scotland and France] to her forehead and falling on the side down below her shoulders, the point in front was confined to the hair by a delicate little gold cross - (not a big eagle) - The effect of the whole dress was lovely. She looked more sweetly than I ever saw her - Her manner though was as grave and devoted as the Holy {Fornia or Forena?} or any

41

other seriously conquered devotee could possibly have been and this you know was neither in keeping with her dress nor the occasion – You remember her gravity in the courtesy {quottim} that was a mere circumstance to this nights demeanor. I suppose the idea that it was at the Hotel she had condescended to appear that oppressed her. You must not think I am a reprobate to have received such a tribute to one as a dance at an upcountry tavern - These gentlemen engaged a large private parlor and had determined music employed and only invited our associates as in Marietta to meet me as I was going to leave and it was a kind of last meeting together of our party after traveling for three weeks in each others society, it was kindly meant{?} that I received it was right {?} The young men say they {?} all regard me as an enchanted Princess locked up in all kinds of castles when I get to Roswell they all feel that only some good Fairy can ever reveal to [them] the possibility of ever seeing me again I don't care you know, and they will all get over it and so it is always - you will and part will and part, wont it is not worth remembering who you have met and who not, unless you forget to know sometime when you meet again and all that. Irvine has actually injured his walk by the incessant use of stilts - Brother and Mr West are well both send love - Sudie of course - And now darling care of yourself for oh Mittie I believe it would kill me if anything should happen to you - Love to Thee - The Dunwoodys send love - Goodbye darling

Yours always,
Anna -

Anna expressed her delight in Mittie deciding to begin "housekeeping." Mittie and Thee must have occupied their new home about this time. This would be a big step for Mittie who would now have to direct servants, keep the household accounts, and be accountable for the daily events of the house. At some point, in the early autumn, probably September, Martha wrote to Mittie.

Martha Stewart Elliott Bulloch, age unknown.
Courtesy of the Theodore Roosevelt Collection.

Roswell N Sept 9ᵗʰ

My very dear daughter,

Your sweet little letter of 24 of August I received yesterday and am glad you have thus far escaped chill and fever – What a pity that your confidence will be shaken in that very beautiful place – I do not think you will have chill and fever darling – as you have been careful of yourself I am inclined to think from what Mr West tells me that the little boys Corneil & Hilly played too much in the water – I am sorry poor little Connie contracted it and will be liable to have it occasionally all winter. It is terribly tenacious of its hold. The past has been a melancholy summer in most places – Cholera and yellow fever have slain their thousands – But darling we have cause for much gratitude. None of our precious circle are missing – Roswell has been one of the most healthy spots in the United States – It has been warm and dry but perfectly healthy – There has not been a single case of illness in any of our families, or amongst our servants – One man, an acquaintance of Mr McLeans came up from Sav with yellow fever and died, which has been the only death in our immediate vicinity – We are very glad to have Anna back – She is writing you a few lines, at this time – Susy is well as usual – Stuart quite well again – All well at uncle John's – The two babies – Rosa and Cila can walk – This of course gives much pleasure to the respective Fathers and Mothers – Stuart was over there a few afternoons since and they were showing their babies. He told Baccus to cover over and bring his. Baccus came over and {c____} his flute I think he ought to have carried pussy Johnny. this said pussy Johnnie is a black cat with green eyes & white whiskers. He is a nipper also, but is a gentle {____} and Stuart pets him very much – Mittie darling I am so glad you are going to keep house. I think it is much best that you should do so. You must be a, also a smart little house keeper. Do not leave things too much to the discretion of servants and not be <u>afraid</u> [double underline] that I shall think your <u>taste</u> <u>too</u> <u>plain</u>. I approve highly of it – In choosing furniture while I would be careful that it should be the very best I could afford, I would also be careful to avoid ostentation. The great fault of the present day is the excessive extravaganza and fondness for show – Darling if Mrs Roosevelt has already chosen your bed & table linen. I wish you to hand her a check which I shall send you in a few days. It will be three hundred dollars. If that is not sufficient let me know. I was just a few days since, thinking what I should furnish toward your house, and these articles are just what I should like to get. I should send the draft at once, but you know in Roswell such things cannot be done in a minute - I wish, my precious child I could do all for you that my heart dictates, but I hope that you will make so good a wife that Thee will never have cause to regret his having married a girl without a fortune. It is important for your own happiness darling, and the happiness of your husband that you should be industrious, practical, and moderate in your desires – without these qualities you would not be contented if you possessed millions – with them you happy with what you and Anna call paltry stipends –

I must close or the mail will lose my letter – I will write again shortly

Your affectionate mother
M Bulloch

Martha wrote of Corneil and Hilly being ill. These were the children of Silas and Mary Roosevelt, Cornelius born in 1847 and Hilborne in 1850. Little *Connie* was Cornelia, the daughter of James and Lizzie Roosevelt, also born in 1850. The news from Roswell included two Dunwoody infants, who were now walking. One would be Rosaline, daughter of Charles and Ellen. However, the second, *Cila*, has not been identified, nor have her parents.

Mittie's taking up housekeeping remained a topic of conversation and from Martha's letter we know Mittie had discussed her purchase of furniture and furniture styles. Martha sent Mittie $300, about $6000 in 2015 values.[18]

Roswell September 15th 1854

My dearest Mittie

When you first see this great ruled sheet please dont think I have taken a clerks place under Mr Proudfoot, I only demand a sheet from Mother as I did not feel like going upstairs to get mine as it is dark – My cold has at last reached such a climax that Mother looks intensely melancholy and says after each of my coughing spells "just such summer colds as you have end in consumption." Her expression corresponds so well with her words that I always laugh and this only awakes my cough more – Tonight all have gone to the prayer meeting at Mr Kings – Mother would not hear to my going out so I find it much pleasanter to write to you when I have some time to think of what I am saying and do not have to scuffle all the time to save the last little negro in the yard from going off without my letter. Often Mother sends Peggy off with <u>her</u> letters directly after breakfast, which is about half past seven the mail closes at nine! Tudies and Mr Wests are taken a few seconds before nine rapidly by Henry or Sarah, and then <u>five</u> <u>minutes</u> <u>past</u> <u>nine</u> I beg Lawrence to rush with mine and to tell me if it gets in time – All the time he is gone little Jane cries - and Lawrence stays so that I used at first to think he did not know what the post office was and that he might stay away until he could find you to give you the letter him self - The fever is still making deeper ravages

46

in Savannah - and the poor victims who now fly from the deserted city seem only to go away to die! William Taylor has just sent over from Marietta for Dr King, Trudy is so ill - They have only lately left Savannah - I do not think I mentioned to you that Burien Burrough and Lee were both extremely ill with the yellow fever, that Burien died on the day one year after his marriage, and that when he died it was thought his wife could not survive him more than a few hours, and would leave an infant only six weeks old - But mysterious providence, she has actually recovered and knows what suffering she is called to bear - The Marietta party has not yet dawned upon Roswell. Carrie was taken sick so they had to put it of [off?] again - I have no idea now what day they will be ours. They have disappointed me by changing their plans so often! that I don't care now, much if they don't come at all - You dont like a commonplace thing that gets you worried and all that, you would rather give it up at once - Brother is not here or you should have his exact height at once he has spent this week since Monday in Marietta - On Monday early after breakfast I was just quietly reading the most pathetic part of a novel brother had recommended, and could have cried over it, when Peggy in her most excited manner perfectly regardless of my nerves rushed into my room saying "Oh! Missey do come down a new young man down stairs in de parlor came to see you he say so himself." I put down my book severely and asked her in my most dignified and indifferent manner "<u>who</u> <u>did</u> <u>he</u> say he <u>was</u> Peggy?" "Dr Norton ma'am." Well I just knew my doom was sealed - I calmly walked down into the parlor and there found Dr Lawton!! Of course common politeness made brother and even me ask him to let his servants drive away from the door and remain to dinner - He staid, all day - it was offensively warm, but we went over to the Alley and had sent for Susan Winston, and played several

47

refreshing games - I played two at once, a game of the pins, and a running accompaniment of coughs - Dr Lawton is fortunately a perfect gentleman so that he is quite pleasant and always entertains more than he expects to be entertained - Brother became so fascinated with him (it does not run in the family to be so) but he drove back to Marietta with him and has been there ever since - I am now in hourly subjective to incursions from him - Brother invited him to come back with him to spend some time and he has invited Brother, to visit him, in the winter on his plantation in southwestern Georgia! a love-letter came through this office a few days ago addressed in the quisical style the cracker's letters are usually and then the impatient swain added in the line just below the ladies name *jump, ride and get thar quick* all ornamental in that chaste manner - Imagine that young ladies feelings in receiving such a tribute of her loves fervor! How particularly devoted to her own heart, on the outside of the letter - This is my birth day - I actually had to dun the whole family just for <u>good</u> <u>wishes</u> of course I was too polite to allude to gifts etc! twenty one! so I will no longer have the poor pleasure, of excusing my follies, on the plea of youthful inconsiderations - Hum now a woman of age! I <u>must</u> <u>be</u> <u>discreet</u> or bear the consequences well, well, as I cant be the princess I must endure the latter - On the fourteenth Mary Eliza had another son I do not know its name - She was engaged to drive with cousin Marion and sent as her excuse the birth of her child - Mother and sister are quite well - The Reeses are going shortly to move to Macon. Mr Rees has a call to a church there - Do tell if you keep perfectly well - Good bye my own darling sister -

yours as ever
Anna Bulloch

Mittie dear the green stain on the page of this letter was made by a katadid hopping just where I was writing

Anna's twenty-first birthday in 1854 found her ill with a lingering cough, but well enough to go bowling with Brother Dan and Dr. Lawton. While Dr. Lawton has not been identified, Susan Winston who joined the party for bowling was the 24-year-old great niece of Catherine King, and an orphan. Susan lived with the King family at Barrington Hall.

Anna mentions several individuals in this letter beginning with Mr. Proudfoot. Hugh W. Proudfoot (1795-1871) served as secretary of the Roswell Manufacturing Company (textile mill) for twenty years. William Taylor (1829-1861) and his wife Drusilla Way Taylor (1832-1879) fled the yellow fever epidemic in Savannah for Marietta. Drusilla's sister Caroline Virginia Way had married Dr. William Nephew King of Roswell.

The yellow fever epidemic of 1854 began in August and lasted until late November. No fewer than 1,041 persons died. During the epidemic's outbreak, many of the dead were recent Irish immigrants. In the nineteenth century, Irish and German immigrants suffered more deaths from the fever than any other ethnic groups. Unfortunately, many residents saw this as encouragement or a guarantee that their cities would not be overrun by "foreigners" as had the large cities in the North. Savannah doctor Phineas Kollock said at the time:

> ...the extremely hot weather...has at length developed yellow fever among our Irish population. The disease is mostly confined to the Eastern part of the city. I do not feel apprehensive of its extending its ravages very much, although it is probable that we shall have cases occurring until frost.[19]

Only one week later, Kollock's view of the epidemic had changed and he "determined therefore to send my family to Habersham [County] immediately." Recent studies show that approximately 80 percent of those infected with yellow fever in the 1854 epidemic recovered.[20]

Tim Lockley's study of deaths recorded in the newspaper and other sources show that black mortality was very low compared to white mortality. Slaves and *free Negroes* constituted over half of Savannah's population at the time, but only 14% of deaths occurred among this population. This prompted one Savannah doctor "to remark that the blacks formed the 'privileged class' among the inhabitants of the city." As the epidemic spread, Savannah doctor Richard Arnold noted at the end of September 1854: "There has been a great deal of sickness amongst the negroes within the last three or four weeks, fortunately not nearly so fatal as amongst the whites."[21]

Among the white deaths was Reverend Benjamin Berrien MacPherson Burroughs (born 1829), a friend of the Bulloch family and distant relative by marriage. Berrien had married Althea Stark Law at Clarksville, Habersham County, Georgia, just one year earlier on 23 August 1853. He died of yellow fever on 25 August 1854, just six weeks after the birth of his son. Berrien's father followed him in death on 9 September, probably of yellow fever.[22] Anna's mention of *Lee* in association with Berrien has not been identified.

A bit of good news reached the family quickly by telegraph, which had reached the area in 1851.[23] Mary Eliza, wife of Dr. William Gaston Bulloch, delivered little Robert Hutchison Bulloch on the fourteenth of the month, only one day before Anna wrote the letter.[24] Naming the child after family friend Robert Hutchison demonstrated how admired he was by the entire Bulloch family. Unfortunately, little Robert Hutchison Bulloch did not live to maturity.

Stepping aside from the letters, family developments occurred as reported in other historical sources. On 3 October 1854, Mittie's half brother, Captain James Dunwoody Bulloch, on leave from the Navy and captain of the Steamship *Black Warrior,* returned to his home port of New York from his first run to New Orleans to find a letter waiting. He had been recalled to active duty on the U.S.S. *John Adams* in Boston. The letter, dated 12 September, left him with little option and technically absent without leave. James then resigned from the U.S. Navy for "reasons of a purely private nature" and continued to captain the *Black Warrior* until his reassignment to a new ship, the SS *Cahawba,* in December of that year.[25]

Roswell Sep 30th 1854

My dear Mittie

Your last letter to Mother has actually made me so imbecile that I can hardly entertain the girls - Your house keeping is a delightful dream - Your nice ladylike rules, and everything will be so pleasant - Oh Mittie darling how can I tell you how delighted and grateful I am that I will in time be an important relation - Oh darling it is too sacred for me to think of mentioning it to anyone. You must not feel unhappy about what makes me, makes us all, <u>so</u> <u>happy</u> and <u>grateful</u> No matter darling <u>how</u> <u>dark</u> it is now it will all end in so much happiness and then you will wonder how you could have felt so unwilling and depressed I have my heart - full to write you yet but must not write too much now or I will not have time to tell you how we have been passing our time. On last saturday brother returned from Marietta and [missing page] written. Mr Butler left yesterday afternoon - we are all sorry to part with him - I lent him the Heir of Redclyffe to read, because he reminds me of Guy in character. The Dunwodys are in {____} over Mr Davidson who is still with Cousin Charlie - Uncle John thinks him equal to Mr John Wells - I do not think I ever mentioned to you the death of Dr Wells - of yellow fever in Savannah - Aunt William Bulloch has had the yellow fever but not very violently - while she was ill with it Cousin William had a severe attack of the broken bone fever and then the roof of the house was blown off in the gale while they were ill - Just think of the two poor old ladies Aunt Read and Aunt Bulloch - they must have been more surprised than when Hall McAllister kissed them - Brother has a dog of William Taylors, training now in the sporting season - Her name is Fannie a good pointer. The young men have taken particular pleasure in training her as they call her "Fannie dear" come here," whenever Fannie Bryan is near "High on Fannie darling." Mother says it is five minutes past nine and I must not read this over - so good bye my own precious one - Oh Mittie dear I love and cry for you every day - Fannie sends her love with Carrie and Clara - yours lovingly Anna

Oh, Anna, she did write such flowing letters full of gossip and fun! However, at the end of September she still had news of yellow fever victims in Savannah. John Wells (1823-1867) was the younger brother of Dr. Charlton Henry Wells (1822-1854) who died of yellow fever on 12 September. The *Savannah Daily News* reported on 11 November 1854 that yellow fever had taken ten physicians and three medical students along with three clergy. Anna's letter tells that Dr. William Gaston Bulloch had suffered from fever after a broken bone. Aunt William Bulloch had suffered a mild case of yellow fever. Anna no doubt identified her in this manner to make sure Mittie knew of whom among their many Bulloch aunts she wrote. This would have been Mary Young Bulloch (1782-1860), widow of the late William Bellinger Bulloch (1776-1852), their grandfather's brother. Mary was William's second wife. His first wife Harriet DeVeaux bore his only child to live to maturity. Mary lost four children in infancy or as young children.

The so called Great Carolina Hurricane of 1854 came ashore at St. Catherines Island on 7 September and from there swept up the east coast. At Retreat Plantation on St. Simons Island, Anna Matilda Page King wrote in her journal "This is in truth a stormy day - high wind - some rain and a very high tide." Later that evening she added, "The wind is so high & so jerks the house I find it hard to write."[26] Near Darien in Liberty County, Hugh Grant at Elizafield Plantation wrote that day, "Blowing a gale from N.E. tides very high but no damage yet - look for trouble this night." On the following day Hugh wrote, "Dredful Gale. Everything underwater. Breaks in dikes 16, 18, 22....Every rice stack in the field blown and washed away. Lost 110 acres and 6,000 bushels."[27]

The Reverend Dr. Charles C. Jones, owner of a 700-acre cotton plantation at the mouth of the Maybank River, on the mainland facing St. Catherines Island, wrote:

> About eleven o'clock the northeast wind which had commenced blowing lightly on Tuesday began to come in with scuds of rain and thunder and heavy puffs of wind - a sure evidence of an approaching gale. Rice could not be taken in. Towards evening looked heavy towards northeast. Squally: heavy dashes of

rain. Had the horses put to the carriage and left after sundown; arrived at Maybank a little before ten. Every appearance of a gale. Moon just past the full. Made windows and doors all tight. Wind increased to a gale during the night. When we rose in the morning we were in the midst of it. Not a spear of marsh to be seen. A clear rolling sea all around us and reaching away to Bryan, Sunbury, and Palmyra, the whitecaps keeping it in a foam and the driving spray and mist shutting the distant shores from the sight.[28]

On 9 September, the *Savannah Republican*, printed:

It is impossible to leave our office, so terrific is the storm...which now shakes the building in which we write...and is unroofing the town, prostrating trees and chimneys and destroying vast amounts of property...slate, tin...shutters and sign boards whirl through the air, rendering it a perilous undertaking to venture out of doors...

Later reports confirmed the damage in Savannah, with the Trinity Methodist Church, the Exchange Building, the Medical College of Savannah, the theater, and every commercial building on River Street having lost their roofs. Every Savannah house, without exception, having a tin or copper roof was unroofed. The structural damage to Savannah and the surrounding area was severe. However, the loss of every cotton and rice crop from St. Simons Island, Georgia, north to Georgetown, South Carolina, created an economic depression that would not end before the Panic of 1857.[29]

While Anna gave us no more clues about Aunt Read, we do know she and Aunt Bulloch were kissed by Hall McAllister (1826-1888). This must have been one of those great family stories repeated many times over the years.

A typewritten page in the Theodore Roosevelt Collection at Harvard, probably prepared by Corinne Roosevelt Robinson for her book *My Brother Theodore Roosevelt* includes the following:

> "Extract from lines written in some album by Rev. N. A. Pratt, minister who officiated at marriage of Martha Bulloch and Theodore Roosevelt, Sr.
> " . . .hope that when her first-born shall follow her to the spirit world, another sparkling gem will adorn that Diadem of Beauty.
> "Be thou a follower of her thro' faith & patience inherit the promise.
> "With best wishes & prayers of your friend.
> "Roswell, 2 October 1854
> N.A.P."

While unable to locate the album, we can only speculate on its purpose. However, Mittie had saved the Reverend Pratt's sentiments. That he officiated at their marriage was a widely held family and Roswell story; however, Mittie and Thee were joined in marriage by the Rev. James Bulloch Dunwoody, her cousin.[30]

Roswell October 6th 1854 -

My dearest Mittie

It is very cold this morning and I have gotten up quite early, and came down to the sitting room and taken the little stand out from the corner where it usually stands and put it in the front of the fire and now I am already for a nice long talk with you unless Mr West comes out too soon to have prayers - Unless I redeem time in this way I might as well just give up trying to write to you my darling. For as soon as we finish the cups after breakfast the gentlemen propose either the alley [bowling] or walks and Carrie and Fannie, are readdy for anything, (Clara Green left us on Tuesday) we are never back again before twelve or one - We then read aloud to each other until dinner then after dinner in this lovely fall weather, you know how soon it is necessary to get readdy for riding. Fannie is as delighted with the two horses as I am. Oh Mittie how constantly we all wish for you darling - Brother the other day told Fannie if she knew you "it would kill her" - Tonight we are to have all of the Dunwodys over to tea with us - Annie and cousin Jack have arrived at last - Cousin John Dunwody too is here - He has come up to take Lilly to her Grandmother Mrs Horace Pratt. She is to have Lilly to educate and live with them until she is sixteen - Cousin Jimmie [James Bulloch Dunwoody] asked most particularly about Thee and yourself - He sends a great deal of love - And says you must not be too surprised if when you get completely "at home in your own neat and delightful house he runs in to pay you a little visit." In a month he will be back from Alabama and will then after a visit here take Cousin Marion and the other two children down {?} for the winter - Cousin Marion is so much more cheerful and is very pleasant what a life of self sacrifice hers is to the poor little sick baby - she thought little Marion is better she is still a great sufferer and often keeps her awake all night - Uncle John is more unsophisticated however now. Fannie told him the other day that her teeth were false and that she wore a wig he asked Carrie in the most earnest manner <u>does</u> <u>she</u> <u>Caroline</u>!

56

"Of course not Uncle" "I, you can't deceive me Miss Francis I know that you would try to <u>conceal</u> it if they were <u>really so fake</u>." Lilly stayed with us last night - She sends much love and hopes to hear from you very soon - We have had no letter from you darling at all this whole week I had a word from Thee - Do thank him for sending it I have not seen Hardtimes until now. Now dearest Mittie how can I tell you how lovingly Mother and I talk of you incessantly and when we speak of Mittie's house a flush passes over Mothers face and she says "I mean to go down into the kitchen and learn of our own house and have southern dishes to make up for her when I get there - I never knew Mother to anticipate anything so earnestly as she does seeing you. Oh darling that one darling thought I think of it every moment in the day - I know you think me romantic and foolish but I can not help feeling so grateful and happy about it - I could not realize that any thing so good and delightful could happen - do give my best love to Thee I will write to him very soon - Love to all who would love me - You have never said how you liked my likeness, I hope it pleased you - No one here thought it good - but I thought I might recall me to you a little - Now dearest you must excuse this hurried note -

Goodbye yours aff-

Anna

Roswell's prominent residents knew Sarah Green and her family quite well. Benjamin Green served as principal of the Kennesaw Female Seminary from 1850 to 1858. His wife Martha E. Marvin Green and an older daughter Jane Eliza were close friends of the Bulloch girls. Clara Green may be a cousin Clara Glenda Green, born in Georgia in 1834.

Having the Dunwoodys over for tea would be a major undertaking for the Bulloch household. Jane and John

Dunwoody had six children, all of whom were married by this time and five of whom had children. While Annie and Jack Dunwoody have not been identified, Cousin John, who married Mittie and Thee, was taking his daughter Laleah "Lilly" to her Pratt grandmother's home. Lilly's mother, also named Laleah, had died in October of 1853 just after the birth of her fifth child in only 11 years (only 3 survived until 1854). Mrs. Horace Pratt was Jane Farley Wood Pratt, wife of Horace Southworth Pratt of St. Marys, Georgia. Horace and Roswell's Rev. Nathaniel Pratt were brothers. Laleah's last baby, Marion Glen, would have been the child being cared for by his aunt and namesake Jane Marion Dunwoody Glen. *Cousin Marion,* as Anna called her, had been widowed twice by this time. She had first married the Reverend Erwin Stanhope in 1840; he died only a few months after the wedding. Her second marriage to Dr. William E. Glen, in 1851, ended with his death in 1853. Marion bore no children by either marriage.

John Elliott Dunwoody briefly attended the United States Military Academy at West Point before resigning to serve in the Georgia Militia as chief of staff for General Walter Echols. John served in this capacity for eight years, from 1838-1846. He then served in the Mexican War from 1846-1848. By 1850, John, his wife Elizabeth, and one child were living in Roswell where John ran a tannery near the Lebanon community.

While more letters must have passed between Georgia, New York, and Pennsylvania during the later part of this year, they were not saved by the family members. The yellow fever epidemic in Savannah ended soon after the first frost of the autumn on 15 November. In Roswell, the residents enjoyed good health and sent $250 to "the sufferers in Savannah."[31]

Chapter III
The First Half of 1855

The World in 1855

In the United States, the first bridge across the Mississippi River opened on 23 January at what is now Minneapolis, Minnesota. Early in the year, legal actions in several states again brought the Fugitive Slave Act into the forefront of the nation's consciousness. This controversial portion of the 1850 Compromise between Southern slave-holding interests and Northern Free-Soilers had increased Northern fears of a "slave power conspiracy." The act or law required that all escaped slaves upon capture were to be returned to their masters and that officials and citizens of free states had to enforce in this law. The return of runaway slaves continued to be a lucrative business for many unethical men.

World events centered on the Crimean, War, which continued until 8 September when British and French troops captured Sevastopol from the Russians. As the war raged, Florence Nightingale began her fight for hygiene as a defense against infection. On 17 November explorer David Livingstone became the first European to see Victoria Falls in what is now Zambia and Zimbabwe.

In the artistic world, Walt Whitman published his first volume of poetry, *Leaves of Grass*, on 4 July. Henry David Thoreau published his essay, *Slavery in Massachusetts*, based on a speech he had presented the previous year on 4 July in

59

Framingham, Massachusetts. On 18 October, Franz Liszt's *Prometheus* premiered.

The 1855 Letters

The first saved letter from a person other than Anna appeared late in 1854. That letter from Martha to Mittie must have been one of many during their first year of separation, especially considering Mittie's pregnancy. In mid-December, Martha and Anna along with Susan and Hilborne West traveled north. While Susan and Hilborne traveled on to Philadelphia, Martha stayed in New York to be with Mittie during her confinement.[32] On 15 February of the new year, Martha wrote to Susan, who had just returned to Philadelphia from New York, after the birth of Anna Roosevelt on 7 January. While Mittie and Thee settled in with their new daughter, Martha remained in New York to help out.

New York Feb 15- 1855

My very dear daughter

I received your sweet little note a few days since, and hope before this time you are much better of your cold, and that Hill is quite well. Mittie is much stronger than when you left, and the baby has grown very much. The little cheeks are more puffy than ever - (The peppers). I am quite well darling and walk every day when the weather permits - Yesterday it rained so much that we could not get out, and it threatens again today - I was pleased with Irvine's letter which you sent me and have one from him of a later date. I received a note from Marion [Dunwoody] yesterday Mr & Mrs Dunwody [John and Jane] were with them at McPhersonville - She says her little baby can walk. Does it

60

not seem strange? Nothing from Mr Blodget yet - Mittie received the trunk the day before yesterday. She is delighted with the chock olate, but says you need not get any more until you hear from her again. She thinks she can obtain it here. She wished you to get her stockings exactly like Annas; only by the size of her own stocking which you have - If you have not already purchased mine, you need not do so until I go to Philadelphia. Mittie wishes you to get her a gause [gauze] ball and send with the stockings. Mittie begins to swell a little, but I suppose the Dr can control that. What a relief it is darling that she is so much better - I think if the weather becomes fine we will take her downstairs in the dining room next week, and in a few days afterwards perhaps to drive out. I do not think she will get strong until she breathes the fresh air. Give our love to Mr & Mrs West, and much to dear Hill Goodbye for the present darling

Your affectionate mother
M Bulloch

Mittie says I must thank you very much for the chocolate & crackers -

Widowed twice, Cousin Marion Dunwoody lived with her widowed brother James in the mid-1850s. She cared for his two remaining sons, John Henry, about 3 years of age, and Marion Glen, about 16 months old. They lived in McPhersonville, South Carolina, near Pocotaligo where James served as pastor from 1845 to 1855.

Another source from February 1855 gives us more news of the family. Hilborne West wrote to George Hull Camp of Roswell on the 14th of that month about some grass seed he had purchased for him. At the end of his letter he reported:

> Mittie is much better. Day before yesterday she walked across the room. Her little daughter is also quite well. Anna has returned from her trip to New Orleans in good condition. Mrs. Bulloch is well.[33]

Anna's trip to New Orleans had been aboard her half brother Captain James D. Bulloch's steamship, the *Black Warrior*. Captain James escorted Anna aboard on 9 January, just two days after little Anna's birth. Brave Anna embarked on a winter cruise and nine days later arrived in New Orleans, where she and James took rooms in the St. Louis Hotel for the next five days. Their return trip included a stop in Havana, Cuba, and a north Atlantic gale.

James Dunwoody Bulloch, age unknown

Once the ship was back in New York, former passengers of Captain Bulloch's during the *Black Warrior* Affair hosted a dinner in his honor and presented him with a coin silver speaking horn to honor his bravery and conduct during the *Black Warrior* Affair of 1854. Perhaps Anna graced her brother's arm for the event.[34]

The horn's inscription reads: *Presented to Capt. James D. Bulloch of the Steam Ship Black Warrior as a Testimonial of the high Regard and Esteem of his friends the Passengers January 1st 1855.*

Speaking horn presented to
Captain James Dunwoody Bulloch

SS *Black Warrior* as engraved on Captain Bulloch's
silver speaking horn.

Sometime early that year Anna King of Roswell wrote
to Martha the following:

Dear Mrs Bullock [35]
Mother has told me of the trouble you are in, in
regard to Mittie's baby - as I have a very excellent reciept
for preparing food for infants, I thought I <u>wd</u> send it over
as you might like to try it. I send the reciept <u>wh</u> Mr King
copied for me, as you may find it necessary to be particular
in preparing the food - as I use it for my children when
they are much older, usually about 6 months. I take a more
simple method of preparing it. It is as follows - Put as much
gelatine as you can take up with your fingers to soak in water
for a few minutes - then put in the milk to boil - & as it boils
up once, stir in a dessert spoon-ful of arrow root - dissolved
in a little milk. - then dissolve the gelatine upon the fire, in
a little water, & stir into the milk - add a puliverized sugar,

& boil - about 20 minutes <u>stirring</u> all the time - Use a little more than ½ pint of milk & nearly as much water -
                    Yrs very truly
                    Anna W. King.

Anna King was the wife of the Rev. Charles Barrington King and sister-in-law of Dr. William Nephew King. By this time, Anna had borne four children, three of which survived. Receipt (Anna misspelled the word) is an old-fashioned term for recipe. Arrowroot, as mentioned before, is a starch obtained from the rhizomes (rootstock) of several tropical plants. It was often used as a thickening agent, much as cornstarch is used today.

                    Roswell April 14

My dearest Mittie
        Here I am at home again, in my same room I had the wedding time - Oh how I hurry by our dear old room - Sometimes I can almost see you - I have just come up to go to bed, but must write just this note to send by the mail in the morning - I did not intend writing you again until I could have time to send a nice long letter telling you how delightful every thing and every body at home was. But how I miss you all the time my dearest one. Since I came home I found a letter here from Julia Hand waiting for me asking me to be one of her brides maids on the twenty fifth of May - I left Savannah without the slightest idea of going to anything in the way of evening amusements but on friday evening night prayer meetings, so of course have neither white kids [gloves] nor party dress - except my blue & grenadine! At the store I found one of the very thinest and finest muslins I have ever seen so I got that and will

have to trouble you to get the edge and gloves and send them in an envelop as soon as possible. The silk the shade of the ribbon is to line my dark straw traveling bonnet - one more commission I must trouble you with. I owe a little philopoena present to Joe Bond which I really feel obliged to pay he was so very kind and attentive to me when I went from Darien to Savannah under his care. I would like some little thing ornamental that he could wear not gold sleeve buttons, (he has them) but some such thing if very fashionable studs might be pretty however I leave it to your taste entirely - This money may not be quite enough do let me know - I send it separate from the five for my personal commitment. I would like this too just sent by the mail as Thee sent me my beautiful little coral earrings while I was in Savannah. Please dont wait to write me back anything till your own task you know just what I want and from habit I still rely more upon your taste and judgement than my own - I would not have troubled you about this but I could not get anything in Savannah and Mr Bond has such exquisite taste - Mittie the dress you sent me is perfectly beautiful - I have not seen anything in Savannah half so lovely. thank you darling do tell me how I might make it up - Much love to Thee and all I will write very soon again.

Good night it is quite late Sarah who sleeps in my room is sewing at the table while I write she says do give my love to the others - I will Sister Protector.

Good bye
Always affectionately
Your own sister
Anna

After her trip to New Orleans, Anna returned to the South and visited family and friends in Darien and Savannah over the next few months. She arrived at her Roswell home to find a note from Julia Hand, the younger daughter of Eliza Barrington King Hand Bayard and the late Bayard Hand. Julia was a granddaughter of Roswell King. Julia married Dr. Henry Mortimer Anderson in July of 1854. The Hand family had moved from Roswell to Rome, Georgia, by 1853, after Julia's mother married Nicholas James Bayard.

Anna owed Joe Bond a gift as forfeit in a game of philopena. Philopena was a popular parlor game in which a man and woman who have shared the twin kernels of a nut each try to claim a gift from the other as a forfeit at their next meeting by fulfilling certain conditions, such as being the first to exclaim "philopena." Joseph Bryan Bond (1832-1908) of Darien was unmarried at the time and may have been *interested* in the quite lovely Anna.

As revealed in so many letters before this date, Anna shopped while in Savannah and requested certain items from Mittie that could be found in New York but not in Roswell or Savannah. While Savannah, a port city, imported the latest goods, Roswell was a small, inland village with limited resources. Even nearby Marietta, located on the rail line, did not offer the same quality and variety of goods available in Savannah or New York. Anna wrote of her blue & *grenadine*, probably referring to a deep red color. However, grenadine was also a fabric weave characterized by its light, open, gauze-like feel.

Toward the end of April, Mittie, Thee, Martha Bulloch, Nora (nursemaid), and baby Anna traveled south to Savannah, then by train to Marietta, then on to Roswell, where Thee left the ladies and his infant daughter Anna, called *Bamie*. These two newspaper notices document their travel arrangements. The *New York Times* reported on 23 April that:

Theodore Roosevelt, lady and infant, Mrs. Bullock, … Miss Bullock dep enr Savannah on SS *Augusta*.

The portion that was illegible most likely referred to the nursemaid for the baby. Who *Miss Bullock* could have been remains a mystery, but she may have been any one of Mittie's many Bulloch cousins. Anna had returned to Roswell earlier in April, so it was not she. Thee, in a later letter, mentioned traveling with three ladies, meaning Mittie, her mother, and another person of their social standing. The nursemaid Nora would not have been listed as a lady. On 26 April, the *Augusta Chronicle* confirmed their arrival in Savannah on the 24th. Steamship travel remained quite expensive at $20 for a cabin from New York to Savannah.[36]

The train from Savannah north traveled first to Macon, then north to Decatur, and finally on to Marietta, just 12 miles southwest of Roswell. The ladies and Thee finished their trip to Roswell by wagon or carriage, another three or four hours of travel.

Thee wrote his first letter to Mittie even before he reached their New York City home. That the letter arrived from Washington, D.C. tells us little of his return travel except for this stop in our nation's capital. A previous letter, missing from the collection but referred to by Mittie, tells of a stop in Charleston, indicating that Thee had traveled to that city on his way home. Perhaps he took a train to Atlanta then east to Charleston. From Charleston, Thee could have traveled directly home by steamship. However, his early morning arrival in Washington, D.C. leads the reader to believe he may have traveled home by train. The phrase "continual day & night travel" indicates they had no comfortable overnight

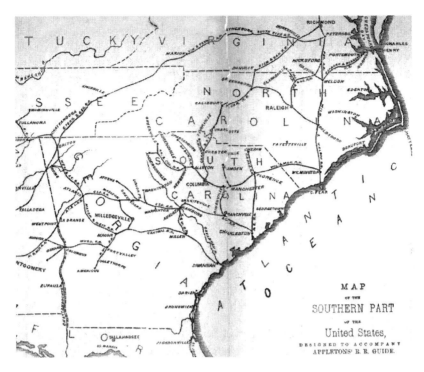

Portion of 1856 railroad map of the southern U.S.
Courtesy of the Library of Congress.

accommodations such as would have been available on a steamship.

Washington April 29. 55

Dearest Mittie

    We neither of us thought of my wanting any writing materials before reaching home and this is written on my two "bottoms" standing behind the desk of Willard's hotel office. I am afraid it will scarce reach you as soon as I had hoped but my calculations proved one day ahead of time. This morning I arrived at four took three hours sleep a bath and now feel as though my touch would not be contamination even to Mittie's soft skin which it certainly would have been before as I had not undressed myself before since leaving Savannah. I got along as you knew I would; the first day it was "north & south" diversified by our glass of ice cream and an all pervading sensation of having lost eleven trunks three ladies child and more, indeed, this lost feeling I have found it difficult to break myself of up to date. I tried to analyze in myown mind whether I was most happy with or without all these luxuries and do you know I really believe take them all in all I missed them; something that a couple of years ago I would not have dreamt that I could acknowledge even to myself.

My second day was a duplicate of the first with the exception of poorer eating and more acquaintances no ice cream and a dreadfully dirty look to everybody. I had made the acquaintance of a Dr. Emmett and he then introduced me to his wife a catholic from Montgomery with large bright eyes a scar across her forehead, complexion glazed deeper than Mittie's was before that last delightful wash. Dr. Emmett reminds me very much of George Morris with whom he has a slight acquaintance; he is staying here at Willard's with me, his wife a good deal used up from continual day & night travel but she was in good spirits to the last. I have had plenty of time to do a great - deal of thinking coming on here and while a majority of it was devoted to you I expended a little on your mother, Annie more especially as concerns their moving from Roswell, but church goes in in a few minutes, and I will reserve my thoughts until I reach New York when I will have full time to express them and to think still more maturely over something which has two such very different sides to look upon it from. I really have not yet made up my own mind which would be best even in a merely utilitarian point of view. What troubles me most is the utter impossibility of your mother resupplying herself with a home containing half the comforts of her Roswell one at double the price should this plan of living in Philadelphia prove not satisfactory or be given up.

I must go to church; how I would love you to be here to go to church with me as we went together once before from this very hotel. Everything here reminds me of you, but it will be still worse at home where I will see your image reflected everywhere, remember your promise about writing. Don't forget Mrs. Sanderson.

Yours ever
Theo. Roosevelt

Thee wrote to Mittie from Willard Hotel. Opened in 1847, Henry Willard combined six small rowhouses on the corner of Pennsylvania Avenue to make one large hotel of 150 rooms, elegant gentlemen's and ladies' dining rooms, parlors and three large "meeting rooms" or halls in the front. For many years, the Willard served as the capital district's only hotel. Thee stayed here only two years after this 1853 engraving of the Willard Hotel on the day of President Franklin Pierce's inauguration.[37]

The family's recent trips illustrate the difficulties encountered while traveling during this period. Thee and companions had traveled south from New York City by steam packet, a sidewheeler fueled by coal. By the 1850s, steam packets ran reliable scheduled trips between the major east coast harbors. On their trip, Thee and family most likely occupied several "staterooms." Staterooms consisted of tiny rooms with a platform bed and mattress, linens, washbasin, and some drawers for storage. Ventilated doors from each room opened on to the saloon where travelers spent most of their day. This common room for eating and socializing served as the parlor or lobby. By the 1850s, most steamships used coal for fuel. Smoke from the boilers filtered

1853 engraving of Williard Hotel on the day of
President Franklin Pierce's inaugurartion,
from *The London Illustrated News.*

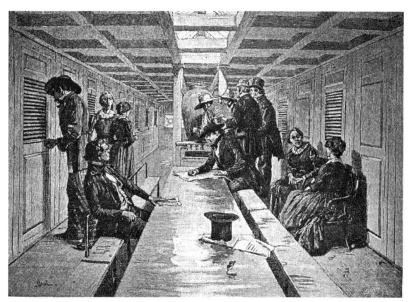

Engraving of a steamship's saloon, from
Some famous sailing ships and their builder, Donald McKay
engraving by Richard C. McKay, 1928.

with an oily back film. Most travelers left their ship much "darker" than when they boarded due to the lack of bathing facilities, hence Thee's description of his wife's complexion as they disembarked in Savannah.

Thee's return trip by steam locomotive proved equally as dirty as coal-powered engines on trains contributed just as much silt and smoke into the surrounding environment as did those on steamships. Train passengers often lowered windows to allow fresh air to relieve the stuffiness and smell of many passengers packed into a crowded railcar, allowing more smoke to enter the passenger cars. Thee had most likely "sat up" the entire trip as Pullman dining and sleeping cars would not come into use for another ten years.

Mittie shared the news of Roswell and her many visits to see friends and relatives in a series of letters from Roswell to Thee, who had returned to New York.

Roswell May 1st

My own dearest Thee

I wrote Mama [Mrs. Margaret Roosevelt] by the last mail as I said I would and felt too tired afterwards to write another letter. I had not sufficiently recovered from the journey. Darling it would be impossible to tell you how I have missed you I feel so a part of you I can not do with out you - it was so dreadful to be with out you - and when you left me standing in Mother's room - do you remember the letter I wrote you after you left me when we were engaged - that letter expresses just my feelings you valued it once would you now? As soon as I could after you left I busied myself unpacking, but could not divert my thoughts from you I have imagined every night and day where you were - and yesterday tho I could hardly expect a letter, I did, and got none. I am expecting one tomorrow <u>certainly</u>. I am going to think of you as in New York tomorrow, Ellen [Mrs. Charles Dunwoody] and Mrs John Dunwody [Elizabeth Clark Wing] came over on the evening we arrived Cousin Charlie was unable to on account of sickness. Old Aunty and Uncle [Dunwoody] came to see us the next afternoon and brought us flowers - they spoke of you in the most exalted terms. Aunty thinks so much of your having brought me here once more. Evelyn King and Dr. King [William Nephew] came on that same afternoon and since almost every one had come, all expressed their greatest surprise at your speedy departure. Mr and Mrs Barrington King called while we were out - but saw the baby. When they found we were over at Aunt Janes, they came over to see us - and Mr King very earnestly asked for the baby's <u>scab</u>! you know Dr Bulloch [William Gaston] was promised this lovely article and since I have been asked once or twice for it. Dr King [William Nephew] says he intends to come over and steal it. On sunday Mother and I walked to church together and were joined by Barrington [Barrington Simeral King] and Mr Adams [Theodore Dwight] {____} most intensely. Barrington has sent Anna a beautiful bouquet accompanied with a scented and embossed card. Yesterday afternoon we went to return some of our visits and I intended writing you in the evening when to my despair Barrington and Nat Pratt called. I could not leave of course and they staid so dreadfully late I was fit for nothing but bed - so I got up very early this morning and had just commenced when one of Mr King's little negroes came in and handed me a beautiful bouquet - fresh with the morning dew and a card written "To Miss Anna Roosevelt with Uncle Billys love" from Dr King - yesterday by request I sent Bam to see them - had her all dressed and she made quite an impression Every morning she gets up quite early and goes in the piazza and yard before breakfast. Nora picks

74

flowers and puts them all around in her little sunbonnet. Bam has gotten so accustomed to being out of doors. that she will fuss to get out. Nora appears perfectly charmed - she told me the other day that she did enjoy herself. She has a good appetite and Mother always has for her at night a good bowl of gruel this I make her drink. Maum Sylvia came in and took the baby one day. Nora in telling me about it said "when that <u>lady</u> took the baby - you remember her reception of Maum Charlotte - Anna and I have promised to go and spend the morning with Aunt Jane - we are going to take our work over. Yesterday afternoon when we were walking Mother said, I do wish Thee could see you now ~~Bam~~ he would be perfectly delighted with your improvement - my face is getting so full and I have such a color

Darling I know you would be glad to see me, and I do not know what I would not give to be in your arms, petted and loved. I love you inexpressibly dearly - when you write tell me if you love me and how you love me. I want to talk to you. I want to see you. I cannot live without you. I do contemplate seeing you my own darling one. I hope you will be comfortable - please tell me how you get along and how you enjoy Brother Jimmie's [James D. Bulloch] being with you and what you do in the evenings - tell me if you would like to have me with you, but I know you would however I want you to write me if you would. Remember your promise to write me <u>constantly</u>. I will be dreadfully disappointed if I do not hear from you on every mail day. I can not write any more I am afraid my letter will not be in time. Dearest I miss you at night when I wake up I almost expect to turn into your arms but you are far away. I hope you are quite well no more chills. My hair drops more than ever, tis so thin I can scarcely fix it at all. I am trying the castor oil but I wish so much I had it regularly prepared. I can not disguise the perfume - Write me everything about yourself and how you love me - Good bye my own dearest one

Your own wife Mittie Roosevelt

Anna and Mother send their love to Brother Jimmie and yourself.

Mittie's letter indicated that Anna quite often received male visitors including Barrington Simeral King (1833-1865) and Nat (Nathaniel) Pratt (1833-1906). Etiquette of the period dictated that Anna have a chaperone present during these visits. Although two years younger, Mittie, now a married lady, could fulfill this responsibility.

New York May 1ˢᵗ 55

Dearest Mittie

I arrived here this morning at half past five, was received by Ann in rather questionable costume and tried to feel myself at home. It is of no use; everything is in apple pie order but there is a kind of dreariness reigning everywhere, the one pillow on this bed positively gave me a shiver. I even handled the crib which I used to regard as rather an encumbrance to our room, with a kind of reverence.

I took breakfast with Jim [James Alfred Roosevelt] after a perfectly delightful bath at our house I had quite a little business talk with Jim as I had made the most of yesterday in Washington & Baltimore and accomplished fully as much as I could have hoped.

My next visit to mother's, on the way to the store, gave me a general insight into family matters which remain very much as when we left. Laura [Roosevelt] has one of her head - aches.

At the store where I write this Rob [Robert Roosevelt]

made his appearance and gave me an accurate account of Lizzie's [Rob's wife] unprecedented success with the fair. Their table cleared two hundred & sixty dolls [dollars], the whole fair made eight hundred dolls. My boxes sold for three dolls apiece, Lizzie must be in good spirits.

Everyone seems glad to see me Mary Ann furnished me with a string for my drawers and seemed quite overcome to hear that the baby was well; I was afraid that she would fall weeping in my arms and put me in Pickwick's position. She restrained her feelings.

Ann offers to cook ham and anything else I may want.

Rob enquired whether I had yet received a letter of recall from you, and I will say that from the remarks of several members of the family they do seem to give you credit for having more love for me than I had supposed they did.

I have thought over the sale of the house and can't bring my mind up to thinking it advisable. It seems to me that as the interest on the sum realized say $4500 would be but about $300 it would be better to keep it for one year and one servant to take care of it while the plan of living at the north is tried.

If your mother has made any positive arrangements or could get more nearly its value don't read her this; indeed whether or no you must do as you think best about it. If you think Hilborne [West] would regard this as interference on my part be particularly careful.

I have a quantity of things to do to day Mittie darling and have had to compress this into very much of a business shape but I know you would like to hear from me immediately on my arrival; was I mistaken?

Yours Ever
Theodore

Just as Mittie told Thee of her days in Roswell, Thee told Mittie all of the family news. Thee names several of the family servants in his letter, just as Mittie gave names to some of the Bulloch family slaves. As told previously in one of Anna's letters, Martha continued to be interested in selling Bulloch Hall and moving north. Apparently, she had approached Thee with the idea and requested his input. Thee apprised Mittie of his thoughts, but was wary of offending Hilborne West, who by this time handled all of Martha's business and legal matters. It seems Martha was willing to sell the home for only $4500, far less than its value. Her named price equals approximately $90,000 in today's currency.[38] Thee's concerns about Martha's resources seemed to center on her ability to set up her own home in the North, where costs greatly exceeded those of the rural South. In addition to a house and furnishings, Martha would have needed to employ servants as she could not bring any of their slaves North with her.

Roswell May 2nd

<u>Thee dearest</u> how disappointed I was to day. Company was in the parlor when Peggy returned and as she passed the door I saw a letter of course I thought it was for me as you had said I would hear from you in five days - and it had been six since your left me. Theede when you left me before I heard from you from Charleston only <u>two</u> days after your departure! now it will be nine even if I got it by the next mail and perhaps I will not get any then. Darling why have you neglected it has made me so sad all day - I had hoped that this afternoon I would be answering your letter it would have been such a comfort to me to have had something from you

Thee there were many minutes you could have found but I will say as you once said in a note to me when you thought I had neglected you "do not write dearest unless it is a pleasure". Darling I long to hear you say once again that you love me. I know you do but still I would like to have a fresh avowal. You must love me for one could not love another as much as I do you without its being returned. You have proved that you love me in a thousand different ways but still I long to hear it again do you understand "this raphsody" 'twill be a joyful day when we meet again will it not Thee. I feel as tho I would never wish to leave your side again. You know how much I enjoy being with Mother and Anna Mother all the time says she wants me to improve for you to be surprised, constantly they plan things for "when Thee comes" but still darling you can not imagine what a <u>wanting</u> feeling I have the <u>month</u> you are with me will be the happiest of my stay. Thee I want you to tell me exactly when you will come I want to know <u>the exact time</u> - tell me in the very letter in answer to this. After writing these three pages full of my love for you I can not tell you half I feel I would like to fly to you -

Do you remember when I left Philadelphia after we were engaged you gave me a little copy of Grays poems - because you had used it. when I was married I left it here the day after you left me me I took possession of it again and look at and read in it every day. I hope I will hear from you on every mail day t'will be such a pleasure. I want to hear all that you did in both Washington and <u>Baltimore</u> and all about your arrival in New York. What you do morning noon and night. Darling remember me in every thing and do not do anything you think I would not like to have you do remember how dearly I love you and how every action of yours affects me - don't read this lightly - I love to think in doing anything of you connected with it - if we were only together but 'tis useless to wish Blessed one I love you devotedly truly.

The letter to day was from Brother [Daniel Stuart Elliott] to Mother - he will be here on next Tuesday - he says in his letter that he does not know but that he may have to escort Mrs John Lewis, forty trunks and a mocking bird. (This is the same lady who thought of coming with us) up the country, - Mrs John Lewis in the mean time has arrived on last Friday - the day after we did - is it not like Brother not to know? Last night Mr Pratt [Reverend Nathaniel Pratt] had an exhibition of his boys - Some were to speak for a prize (a Port-folio & knife) Uncle John [Dunwoody], Mr Camp [George Hull Camp], and a Mr Baker were to be the judges there was a tie between one of the boys and Irvine- - but the Judges decided against Irvine as he was a Roswell boy (the first prize had been already given to Joe King and the second was tied between Irvine and this boy from Savannah) All the Audience were in favor of Irvine and a great many said to him - "Well Irvine you have gotten the honor if you have not gotten the prize" the poor little fellow bore it remarkably well. after the spelling Mr. Pratt invited them to a "Treat of lemonade and cake". This is the day you were to arrive in New York and Brother Jimmie will be in I suppose by this time. I want to hear how you have arranged everything - How I slept on my darling that night from Macon and he held me close in his arms Mother says as 'tho I had been a baby -

May 3 I had to stop yesterday evening as it was growing so late and now 'tis before breakfast - Mother is out in the entry talking to one of the crackers about a little rain that came up last night. I heard him say I hope we will have more as the almanac says rain from the first to the eighth and I suppose it will but one day - While I was dressing Mother brought in a sweet rose and I have it in my breast pin. I have picked one of the leaves off just this moment and send it to you, Thee the roses are out in a beautiful profusion how I wish you could see them. Anna and I are going to take a walk this morning the first we have been able to take on account of the extreme dust - I keep the baby a great deal in the open air almost the whole afternoon she seems perfectly charmed with every thing out of doors and perfectly quiet when there. I want you to ask Lizzie Ellis if she will execute a commission for me - Aunt Jane is delighted with our India silks. and asked me if by any means I could get her one. I told her I would ask one of my sisters and I had no doubt but that they would do it for me. Please ask her. Good bye my own darling Thee.

your wife
Mittie Roosevelt

Mittie's first letter to Thee from Roswell was a love letter in every sense. While she gave Thee some news of the week, her first few pages described her longing for her now departed husband. Mittie reunited with a book Thee had given her during their engagement, probably *The Poems of Thomas Gray* published in 1768. Gray is considered by many to be the second most important poet of the eighteenth century but the most widely read. His most famous work was entitled *Elegy Written in a Country Churchyard*.

Brother Dan had written that he would most likely escort Mrs. John Lewis to Roswell upon his return. John Lewis (1782-1866) was the father of Robert Adams Lewis who built the house now known as Holly Hill, very near Bulloch Hall. A successful Savannah merchant, he held a partnership with a Mr. Stone and they sold "every kind of merchandise." He retired to Roswell sometime before 1850 along with his second wife Margaret Adams (King) Lewis in a home once located somewhere near the Minton House.[39]

The Mr. Baker who served as the Academy's judge may have been the Reverend William Elliott Baker who married Catherine Evelyn *Eva* King in 1856. The couple was mentioned in an 1855 letter from Ruth Ann Atwood Dunwody to Jane Atwood Camp. Mittie would have been unfamiliar with William Baker.

New York May 6th 55

Would that my own little Mittie could accompany me to church this afternoon. I have put on her chain and wondered how she would like me in my spring clothes, knowing that she thinks a good deal about my exterior.

My long expected letter came yesterday just after myown had gone, it was a real luxury and I have read it over half a dozen times since. I wont answer the questions about how much I love you as they are already answered in my previous letters, besides you would know how sincerely I must love you by the way in which I miss you. When brother Jimmie goes it will be still more desolate, in fact I don't know what I will do. I invite all my friends to call on me as often as possible and offer them every inducement in my power. I will pay some visits too. But I cant make up for the absence of one who I love more than anyone else, particularly when my doubt is expressed about the possibility of yellow fever.

There seems strong probability of our spending the summer in town and I would love you to think more favorably of a cottage in the country. Father talks of building four, two near to each other; all near Orange [New Jersey] and I would like you to approve of the plan. It seems to promise me more the pleasure of being with ^{you} than any other plan. Indeed then I could be always out in time to take a drive with you in the afternoon and as Rob's stable and mine would be combined we would require but one man to take charge of our horses. Do think over it all, it does seem the only feasible plan for our enjoying the ^{next} summer. All seem to think it would tax mother's health too severely for her to take charge of the whole family again. It would be pleasant too to see this plan gradually improving and allow us an opportunity of seeing whether we could ever enjoy living in the country altogether which used to be one of our little fancy sketches you know. - - -

Do continue trying the caster-oil and I will bring you (not carry) down some prepared here when I come. The more I think of it the more repugnant I feel to your having your hair cut; wait at all events till I come down.

This morning Dr. Dewitt preached a very good sermon. Brother Jimmie went with me.

Saturday evening went off as usual all were there (but <u>one</u>) and they seemed to enjoy themselves. Brother Jimmie dined and spent the evening there, coming up home between dinner & tea to see if a telegraph had reached the house announcing the arrival of the Alabama on which he thought Mr Hutchison [Robert] might be and knew of at least there would be some of his wine for him.

We both of us incontinently dropped asleep and never woke till time for coffee at mother's.

This I suppose was the affect of the late hours which I make it rather a point to keep. Indeed bed does not offer me the same inducements ^{as of yore} and I rather regret when the time comes for me to retire all alone. We breakfast punctually at seven.

I have just killed a small insect which I enclose to ease your mind with regard to any risk to the carpets, or anything else in that line left out. I dined today with Rob, and Lizzie lectured me on not coming in to her house when I wanted company instead of knocking on the partition for Rob to come in to me.

83

This evening Rob took tea with ^{me} being very anxious to try a pate de fois gras which we discovered together the other day.

He was to have given us notice if some soft waffles turned out successful but not having heard from him I suppose they were not.

We discussed the cottage project of which Lizzie thinks very favorably, but as it cannot be put into execution till next year don't let it trouble you.

I was really touched this after noon by finding on a little paper in my port-folio in your hand writing "I wish I was perfectly happy," and written a little lower down "Theodore." It made ^{me think} whether you would ever be so with me Mittie and I half wondered whether you would have really as much reason to regret being detained in Roswell as I hope and believe you think you would. I wonder whether you ever think as seriously as I asked you to think of the future, do you remember me always at night in your prayers? I do both you and little Nina although I suppose from my rare mention of her you think she is forgotten. There is one regret I have to make again that you will try never to give way to the feeling of being "provoked" with anyone, which you know you told me you "could not help" when I last saw ^{you;} do try for my sake.

I am afraid you won't like the last sentence but you always want me to give you advice for your own ^{sake} when one word ever I think I can benefit you, and you ^{know} that my love is so true and heartfelt that ^{unless} it was really a kindness to you I would not say it.

Mittie darling when I repeat to you that I love you more than anybody else in the world and that every effort that I see you make to do what you acknowledge to be right rivets that love still more strongly. I know you will think it worth the effort. I don't believe that sentence I quoted would ever have been written had you never felt "provoked."

Now my darling one I must close having indulged I am afraid you will think in altogether too serious reflection to write a pleasant letter. Excuse its solomness by thinking I cannot always be lively while you are absent

Your Husband
Theodore

Love to Annie
Moth. Killed May 6th 55 and dedicated to the memory of his wife by Theo Roosevelt
Moth

Thee attended church at the Collegiate Reformed Protestant Dutch Church where Dr. Thomas Dewitt presided. The Roosevelt family worshiped at this church regularly. James Dunwoody Bulloch, Mittie's half brother, stayed with Thee during Mittie's absence.

Robert Hutchison, a family friend from Savannah, often traveled to New York and Europe. He had been married to Corinne Elliott, Martha Bulloch's stepdaughter by her first marriage to John Elliott. However, Corinne and their two small daughters died in June of 1838 in the explosion and sinking of the Steamship *Pulaski*. Robert married again in 1848 the sister of James Dunwoody Bulloch's wife Lizzie, Mary Edmonia Caskie (1822-1852); however, like her sister, Mary died of tuberculous. Robert married again in 1857, Ellen Laura Caskie (1836-1858), also from Richmond and first cousin of his second wife.[40]

By 1855, Mittie and Thee occupied 33 East 20th Street, next door to Robert and Lizzie Roosevelt. The structures shared a common wall, and from this letter we learn of a pass through between the two homes. Cornelius Roosevelt, Sr. purchased the home, built in 1848, for his son in 1854. According to some envelopes, letters often arrived at the Roosevelt business address, 94 Maiden Lane, New York.

New York May 7th

Dear Mittie

   I received your letter giving me an account of your journey safe arrival etc but as I had received Thee previously, you may depend I was well informed on all these subjects, I had plied him with questions so effectually that I believe I had left nothing unasked. We are pretty much as you left us, nothing decided for the summer, Corneil Laura and I went to Peakskill on Friday to look at another place for them, it would not do, and we returned fatigued, and Corneil very low in the mind. Our Saturday passed off very pleasantly, your brother [James Dunwoody Bulloch] joined our party, we did not leave the dining room at all, and each one seemed in a good talking humour, the boys smoked and <u>talked</u>; the girls sewed and <u>talked</u>. Lizzie Ellis has been very much elated with her success at the fair, her table made about 260 dollars, altogether I think they made 800. Lizzie was much less absorbed in consequence of having got through with this important affair, she says she feels confident of one thing now, that she could get her living at any time. I took all the children to the fair and bought for them whatever they selected, and as Mittie itte baby could not come, I bought her a little pink sack, which I will try to keep the moths from devouring. It still continues cool here, I feel this probably a little more sensibly from having a little rheumatism in my right shoulder, it makes my hand unsteady. I do not know

33 East 20th Street, New York City,
Birthplace of Theodore Roosevelt
from *Harper's Encyclopedia of United States History*[41]

whether you can read my writing. The time for the departure of our friends next door is drawing very near, Mr John Carow arrived on Friday, he has tried very hard to persuade Father and I to accompany them abroad, but you know this is quite out of the question. We have been dreadfully horrified with in a few days by a disturbing accident occurring in our neighborhood, an episcopal clergyman of whom we had some knowledge, falling from the window of the Everet House, on the opposite side of the park, and being instantly killed; his wife was out visiting, and did not return for some hours after his death. Thee is comforting himself in your absence by being hospitable, and entertaining his friends, he had a little meeting of brother and a <u>few</u> friends ^{on Friday} and it was so agreeable, that Corneil did not return until one oclock, poor Laura so unaccustomed to his absence, became nervous, and was unable to sleep, thinking someone was trying to get into the window etc she looked as if she had been the carouser next morning. Laura desires much love to you and Anna. Remember me most kindly to your dear Mother, I can see her taking her comfort in that pet baby, how did Erwin [Irvine Bulloch] like it, he must be glad to have something to look at beside the goats - Father sends his love, remember us both to your Aunt and Uncle [Dunwoody] and believe me

your truly affectionate

Mama - [Margaret Rooosevelt]

New York May 8th 55

Dearest Mittie

I received your much prized letter yesterday; while I regretted your disappointment in not hearing from me as you expected I was glad that long ere this you were convinced by my first letter that it was no forgetfulness or neglect that prevented your receiving it sooner.

Brother Jimmie dined out to day & I reopened your letter and looked again at the rose leaf (imagining just where the breast-pin was round which you had entwined the rose) while I took my solitary meal. I know there was just a little white piece of neck showing near it, and what would I not have given to have just kissed it once. I remember so well the place where you wore my violets before we were even engaged.

I asked Lizzie Ellis to get the india silk which she was perfectly willing to do but would like to know if you have any preference as to colour. Is it for Aunt Jane herself? would you prefer the plaids large or small? How many yards?

I bought the prepared Castor Oil for your hair, an enormous quart bottle, it looks as if it ought to be beneficial.

I also carried your bands down to have them mended but it seems rather questionable whether I will succeed or not as they are very badly bent almost at the centre. I have not given it up yet however.

I called on the Misses Morris last night they received me very pleasantly and have promised to introduce me to George's lady-love either going with me or inviting us both there.

Josephine certainly did look to me very handsome, although I had almost given up thinking of her as so.

Mr. Hutchison has written me mentioning the day of his arrival and requesting me to send our porter down for your demijohn of wine lest it should get broken. He shipped brother Jimmie's in the last steamer had it put in a stateroom locked up and made the Captain promise to carry the key in his pocket until he should deliver it to brother Jimmie personally.

I will call on him of course when he arrives and if possible have him to spend an evening at our house although this last will be very much like drawing teeth. Just think of what a doleful evening I will have, all alone with him.

Here Rob has arrived and wants me to take soft waffles at his house immediately. Good by dearest.

It is one o'clock in the morning, The Captain and myself having been discussing your mother's different prospects and both seem to agree entirely as to our views.

He is writing at the same moment to you, I should say your mother. We get along very pleasantly together and I discovered tonight for the first time have very much the same opinion of Dan.

Do remember your letters to me and think how very much I prize them, think Mittie darling that the principal event of the day is always receiving your letter and that the day I do not receive one I always read over the one of day before, I will not say how often.

Rob's waffle party went off very soberly or rather there was so much time between each supply of waffles that the conversation flagged a little until it became a regular joke. They were certainly very good and Lizzie has promised to teach you how to do them.

I have bought a little tea-pot with a spirit lamp under neath which will keep water delightfully hot. It is bronzed and I hope will meet your approbation. You can have no idea of how cozy it looks. And now good-night darling one.

I must once more try my lonely couch remaining ever yours and always thinking of you.

May 9th.   I bid good bye to Brother Jimmie this morning he said he would feel really homesick when he first went to sea this time, my house had seemed like a home to him. I will miss him very much too.

I hope to be with you once more on friday the first day of June unless unexpectedly delayed, unless you would prefer not coming home as early as we intended, but I know you would not, so there is no use of opening an old discussion. You do not feel now darling as if you would have me absent from you any longer do you? Tell me candidly.

Weir dropped in to pay a farewell visit to the Captain last night and after visiting Rob's with us staid at my house until one o'clock when I recommenced my letter to you, he has been very polite to the Captain, indeed all have.

Now dearest I must close remaining ever

Your Loving Husband

Theodore

I will write Annie in a few days, remember me to all.
Write long letters darling, and take plenty of regular exercise.

Thee wrote to Mittie much as she did to him during this separation. They both took time to make intimate expressions of love and longing before moving on to their daily affairs and social life. Lizzie Ellis Roosevelt procured the desired India silk, a popular plaid used for all types of dresses and shawls. Mr. Habersham delivered Mittie's demijohn of wine as he had done for Captain Bulloch. A demijohn is a bulbous narrow-necked bottle holding from 3 to 10 gallons of liquid. The elusive Dr. George Morris had a new lady love according to his sisters, Josephine and Fanny.

More important conversations took place between Thee and James Dunwoody Bulloch about Martha's living arrangements and her moving the family north to Philadelphia. Thee indicated that he and the Captain were in accord and shared those views with Hilborne West. They also discussed brother Daniel Stuart Elliott and agreed as to their assessment of him. Unfortunately, if either shared this information with Mittie or others, the letter is now lost.

On 29 April while traveling home, Thee wrote to Mittie from Washington, D.C. His letter arrived in Roswell on 7 May and Mittie in the following letter responded to Thee's descriptions of his trip.

Roswell May 8th

My own dearest Thee
      I was delighted yesterday to get your letter from Washington and counted how many times you were affectionate I know being at Willards must make you think of me - for every thing to me there is associated with you - I am so glad you found a pleasant acquaintance in the cars - you seem to rather admire Mrs Emmet than otherwise. Darling I long to get a letter from you not written hurriedly. I felt all the time in reading my letter yesterday that you would stop - you must find time to write me a long letter. Aunt Jane sent over a little carriage for (<u>Anna</u> ^{Nina}) to ride in while she remains in Roswell the baby luxuriates in it yesterday Nora took her almost to the other side of Roswell - She laying back in lazy indulgence - and went to sleep returning - it has been so cool for a few days past I have been obliged to abolish her sun bonnets and have had to let her wear my <u>blue worsted hood</u> with fear and trembling of an accident of the worst character - it is early in the morning and Nora has just taken her over to see Aunty - I send in this letter the commission ^{I spoke} of in my last letter to Lizzie Ellis - they wanted to send the money but I could not possibly remember the price so I just told her you would get them and bring the bill with you. Was this right? Explain to Lizzie why I trouble her - Anna has been drawing the Flower pot and just brought them in - you would think

them beautiful I have been helping Mother fix her drinks and I always fix the the salt cellars every morning - Thee tis all a perfect falsehood about Sarah she was not married at all - nor had she been in the least bad {?} was entirely a slander of her lovely and affectionate sister Peggy - but we think Sarah is in love with a Marietta negro boy. Daddy Luke came over sunday to see us all dressed up in his new suit of clothes as formal as he could be - said he had three Masters even if his own Master was dead - he sent "heap of thanks" for the knife. Darling would you please have as much of a care of things as possible I mean just to let them see you are observing - you see my glass about is at their mercy - Thee I am reading Hyperion in one of Annas copys of Longfellow we are anticipating you reading to us when you come - Darling I would have been so glad to have you near me that I would not have thought it contamination to have been so near you <u>before</u> your bath I would not care how soiled you were - Thee I want you to wear your <u>gloves</u> when you travel back - tis so exciting to think when I will meet you - tell me the exact time write me all the time it is my greatest pleasure I have - you cannot imagine how receiving a letter from you made me think of when I was engaged - it seemed exactly as tho it was {?} then - oh dearest let us have our first love be always the same - good bye my own dearest

yours only
Mittie Roosevelt

my darling does not like Anna

Henry Wadsworth Longfellow published *Hyperion* in 1839. This romantic story, based on his own failed marriage proposal, tells the story of a young American, Paul Flemming, traveling in Germany.

Mittie mentioned three family slaves in this letter. Sarah served as Anna's personal maid. Peggy was Sarah's sister. Peggy's duties are unknown. *Daddy* Luke Moumar (or Mounar) had been the dedicated assistant to James Stephens Bulloch before his death. He remained attached to the family, and their love for him continued to be shown in letters and documents for years to come. It seems Mittie and Thee must have brought *Daddy* Luke a new set of clothes and a knife, perhaps from New York.

New York May 9th 55

Darling Mittie

I received another letter from you this morning. It contained, besides a great deal of affection which I of course class first, the very information about the silk that I asked you for in my last. I had half expected it I know you were unusually so particular, and the previous request to "ask Lizzie to buy me an India Silk" was so very indeffinite.

I mentioned casually Uncle John's [Dunwoody] loan of a wagon for the baby to mother this evening when she suddenly drew up before me a picture of the number of casualties that had occurred to babies of her acquaintance riding in wagons that was certainly startling. My thoughts of Peggy occasionally as horse did not lessen the risk. Will you give Norah my respects with the request not let "Bambino" fall out. I like her to ride.

Did I describe to you my dinner & tea service? it strikes me forcibly as it is just being laid at present, Ann having presumed I would not be home to dinner to day and given me time to write this while waiting for it. First as being the largest article on the table comes an enormous blue China coffee pot with an oblong half of the spout broken off. Then my plates spoons, Table and tea the latter decidedly blacked, the effort apparently of egg upon poor plate; next come my three prong steel forks with ivory handles combining table and tea fork in one, then last and least my bone salt spoons which are decidedly neat and convenient but not very strong.

I stopped at mother's coming up today and she discovered what I had appreciated all day that I was desperately cold. The day has been one continued chilly rain. Mother immediately thought I was on the point of a chill, gave me some bitters & wormwood and insisted upon it that in case I had one I must send for her immediately.

The bitters, a warm fire, and mother's affection soon warmed me up however and I now feel that if however well I now feel, that if there were any symptoms they are passed.

A fire is crackling in our little grate, my old shade, (which I am not afraid of {___}) covers the drop-light, the big table is covered with a white table cloth and my dinner while I am writing at my little table drawn up near it, (no side table being required), but I must close for the present and eat my dinner. Would I could help you to some.

May 10th.   Another evening is here. Ann is feeling too proud of her accomplishments which feeling I had to give a blow to today. Garry the other day showed her how to make lobster salad and so she determined instead of cooking two eggs and letting me make it as ordered, she would surprise me with some of her own manufacture; that I was obliged to discard. She is dreadfully crest fallen. It had no consistency and an inordinate quantity of mustard indeed. I think of the latter she took the same quantity that Garry used for the whole party.

We have been very busy today at the store, but I am sorry to say that business generally has not improved and we will have to put all our own good resolutions in practice on your return, with regard to expenditures.

Mittie darling you cannot think of how speaking of this makes me feel towards you, I remember so well the time when you would have considered it the greatest hardship in the world to be obliged to think of money. Now I feel that our interests are so entirely united that I speak of it without reserve and this unity of feeling must continue to bind us more and more closely together. On all subjects we must learn to feel for and confide in each other. O mittie many and many a time have I recalled those conversations when you showed a determination to feel interested in the pursuits which necessarily must occupy a large portion of my time and thoughts. You will be a companion to me will you not dearest in all my hopes and thoughts? Do think darling now while we have so much time for thought what our duties are toward each other and a higher power, and so always point out to me any way in which I do not fulfill them.

I must now say good-bye to myown little one as I have to dress myself for a visit to Mrs Kermit which I ought to pay before her departure. This is thursday morning and Rob has some friends there too.

Your Own Husband
Theodore

Thee commented on the downturn in the family business, probably a result of a recession which began in 1853 and continued until December of 1854 when the economy began to recover. During the recession, interest rates rose, fewer people invested in the railroads, and security prices fell. The economy stabilized in 1855, however, it never quite recovered by the time of the Panic of 1857.

Roswell May 9th

My own dearest Thee

I got your dear letter to day and was very much entertained with every thing - you do write so interestingly and tell me any little thing just as I like to hear. I am afraid however that you are enjoying yourself too much with out me. You know I am glad you are happy but Thee darling I would like you to miss me very much. I can not bear the idea of every body thinking that you enjoy yourself as well if not better with out me, and cannot endure the thought of you your self being as contented without me Dearest think constantly of how we need to be together. why darling when I waked up at night my impulse was to turn immediately to find you and it was so delightful to fall asleep in your arms - I don't want your love diminished in the least for me has it

I was glad to hear about Julia Mickler I always ~~think~~ like to hear about her was it not like Julia to have the excitement about her engagement ring - in New York she was always fearing lest she should loose it - when she would wash her hands she would often leave it on the marble of the croton basin[42], Mr & Mrs Butterfield have not returned - have they? I wonder how Mary was persuaded {___} to go over on board. I know Brother Jimmie has enjoyed his visit to you - we were all so amused at his sleeping through Weirs call 'twas so like Weir to wait and not wake him up. Mrs Parsons is a person I have always thought disagreeable in repose, on a "Spree" she must be dreadful - I hope it will be her last visit over the piazza or through the door - I cannot conceive how you came to ask her in such a familiar way - when you your self told me of how little respect you had for her. I would rather not have had ~~had~~ any of them if it obliged you to invite her Dearest darling I don't mean anything but it made me feel really sad to think you could find pleasure in her society - not only to have staid until eleven in her company but to have invited her in such a social manner over the very same evening - I should have thought one hour enough for any of them much less her self. my own dear Thee you understand what I mean? I cant bear Brother Jimmie to think her a specimen of your acquaintances - does Lizzie still have that wretchedly unrefined set every Thursday - I cannot account for such taste in her selection - Theede it was so sweet to have you say you really did feel as tho you needed my care and would ^{be} most happy to be under it again - my darling I would be only too happy to be under your dear care and to have you say how much you loved me. I wish you had gotten a letter from me to read over on Sunday judging from myself it would have been so pleasant. I read yours over and over and generally keep the last one about my person it is the next pleasure to being with you - I hope you have commenced getting letters by this time I write by every mail and could write you oftener. I hope I will hear regularly from you it will be an intense disappointment if I do not. Darling it is not possible you could leave me here the whole summer without you my <u>first love</u> in every particular I hope we will be spared such a trial - Oh Darling one I pine to see you what will you do when we first meet remember you are to tell me the exact day on which to expect you. I love so to think of one particularly loving look you used to give me when you would call me your "own little darling" I will expect the greatest love from you and the dearest kind of looks.

Thee Nora like a foolish Irisher left off her flannel (the nights are still cool) and took a severe cold which fell upon her breast causing a large boil on her bosom which was very painful - we were very uneasy at first, fearing lest it should rise but Mother watched it very carefully and soon tis nearly well - for two nights I have had a good deal to do with the baby once she woke at about half past three and did not go to sleep till five in the morning - it is so hard to be lively under such circumstances expected to laugh when you would so much rather sleep, the reason was I was so afraid of Nora getting strained whereas if she did not exert herself, she would be well so much sooner, she would not tell us for the first day till she got alarmed but it has proved to be only superficial The baby is very well and Mother and Anna enjoy her. Do tell Mama that Irvine is devoted and some times rocks her to sleep. Nora asked me the other day when I got a letter if you had asked after the baby - unfortunately you had not. If you were only here my blessed darling I could be so happy I feel sometimes perfectly impatient to have a glimpse of your face - which is so darling to me. I will finish in the morning - you can see from my writing that I am a little tired. I have been marking linen during the morning.

May 10th I determined this morning to write my letter over because I had enlarged unnecessarily upon a disagreeable subject - it is exactly what I should say were I with you but from a distance it might seem as 'tho I were angry or rather annoyed whereas I was filled to overflowing with tenderness to you my own Thee - but I find if I copy it over I cannot send my letter by this mail and I know you would rather get even this letter than none. Thee I can say any thing and every thing to you - and I don't want you to have company in the house when I am away that you would not have when I was there. Darling you must be sure and call upon the Misses Morris [sisters of Dr. George Morris]. I wish I were home so we could pay them some united attention. You know last fall I was too sick to kind of mention it incidentally

I will write to Mama without waiting for a reply. I had intended to before you told me now I will take double pleasure in doing so - be sure and give my love to her. I am so sorry she does not look well - Give my love to Sister Lizzie. Thee Mr Hutchison has just sent up to George

Ladson one hundred dollars - it happened just at the time that George's friends were in a worried state as he had not sufficient funds to defray his expenses. Every year he has promised to furnish two hundred till George comes in for his salary George was here yesterday afternoon to find out Mr Hutchison's address as we did not know it we told him he might direct to your care -

Theede I wanted to tell you that if I were you I would not try to hire Tom Kings horse. I am under the impression that he intends using it & I am afraid he will only offer it - perhaps you had best hire in Marietta - besides darling I do not think the horse has very pleasant gates. I saw Jimmie King riding him and it looked very hard. Anna says they have injured him. Irvine has just measured and found that the nearest point of the house to the nearest negro house is fifty seven feet. Mother will have lightning rods put up as soon as she is able - you have to depend upon any one who happens to be passing through - if there were any person in Marietta she would send for them, but there is no one. Good bye my dearest Thee I love you tenderly devotedly - and you must love me - tell me if you do

Yours and yours only
Mittie Roosevelt

oh for one petting and to sit in your lap I think one birth will have to hold us when we return.

George Whitefield Ladson's father died two months before his birth in 1830 in Liberty County, Georgia. George lost his mother at age four and was adopted into the family of John Dunwoody, a kinsman. George studied at the Academy under the Rev. Nathaniel Pratt before attending Oglethorpe

University. George would have been a student there in 1855.[43] Mittie indicated that Robert Hutchison had taken George under his wing and was paying for his school expenses.

Irvine measured the distance from the main house to the nearest slave cabin and found it was only 57 feet away. This revelation provided Bulloch Hall's archaeologist with a new course of study in 2013. The mention of purchasing lightening rods to be placed, presumably on Bulloch Hall, led the staff to wonder if a slave cabin had recently burned near a home, possibly even Bulloch Hall. Based on this historical documentation, Bulloch's staff discussed archaeological methods to locate this third slave cabin, most likely located some 57 feet north of the main house toward the current slave yard and reconstructed structures.

After discussion with Dr. Terry Powis, Kennesaw State University, and Connie Huddleston, Historic Preservation/ Archaeologist Consultant for Bulloch Hall, the consensus of opinion was to begin the investigations with a non-invasive metal detector study. This suggestion came from Dr. Powis based on recent technological improvements in metal detectors and their current use on archaeological sites. This approach also allowed Bulloch Hall to place interpretive signage at the site of the third cabin and to preserve the site in situ.

On 10 August 2013, Dr. Powis, Patrick Severts, and Connie Huddleston conducted a metal detector survey of the area in question. An artifact *cloud* became apparent immediately. Due to Bulloch Hall's desire to preserve the site in place, artifacts uncovered were dealt with in a "catch and release" manner. All, with the exceptions of the modern dimes, one iron nail, a Civil War era military button, and a stoneware fragment, were reburied just as uncovered.

This brief and relatively non-invasive archaeological study indicated the historic presence of an heretofore unknown slave cabin. It is possible this cabin housed the household cook as she would have needed to be in the house early and would have been required to be nearby throughout the day. Bulloch Hall installed an interpretive marker at the site in 2014.[44]

New York May 11th 55

I have been visiting this evening and feel just in the mood for talking over anything with myown little one before going to bed.

I had Ann up at dinner time to show her how to make the salad and fortunately was very successful, although I did it with fear and trembling. Then just as I was in the midst of dinner mother dropped in to see how I looked, she found me as she expressed it very comfortable but not looking quite as happy as when with a little more company. Her visit quite brightened me up for I had been feeling as you know I sometimes do a little out of spirits, she only staid a moment. I don't believe there is one member of my family but yourself who ever think that I am out of spirits. Lizzie Ellis quite lectured me for apparently enjoying myself so during your absence. I make it a point to have something to do if possible every evening, from the very reason that I feel so lonely otherwise.

Tonight was appointed by Miss Morris at my request to call upon Miss Kelsey but that young lady had an engagement so that after staying a few moments at the Morris I took my departure to see Nelly, or rather more particularly Mrs. Lathrop who is staying there. All Madison has suddenly become infected with the "chills" and Mr. & Mrs. Lathrop among the number. It has diminished her natural flow of spirits a little but that is the only change. The light was not very bright but in it Nelly did not seem to me to have changed much. Mrs. Lathrop had her dog and Mr. & Mrs. Hopkins one between them, both ^{dogs} inhabited the sofa with me. The rooms were more showyly furnished than ours but I would not exchange for a good deal.

Coming home I stopped again at mothers and we had a long talk together, a large part of it about you. I almost always see her once or twice a day, indeed all the petting I get now is from her, owing to the desertion of the one who understands best how, and has the best right to pet me. Do think of me often darling, I love you as ever

Theodore

Roswell May 11th

Your letter written on last sunday my own dearest Theeade gave me unspeakable pleasure you need not think I would not like to indulge in serious reflections - believe me tis of more value to me than any letter I have ever received from you in my life, these last pages brought the tears rushing to my eyes - their every line spoke of such tender love for me. I had regretted sending my last letter, but when I read yours to me this morning I would have liked to have recalled it. I can not bear having said any thing which would ever make you feel uncomfortably - for I know my own darling one would never do any thing he thought I would not like him to - and Thee dearest I dont believe you ever did any thing but for the purest motives think it was all from my love to you at any rate for I would not have cared if it had been any one else than you my own darling husband (I feel such a feeling of protection when I use that word I love to be under your care) - Darling you cannot think it would be better for me to be detained at Roswell without you - I know in your heart you do not think so - without you Thee I feel as tho life would loose its charm - you know I love my Mother and Anna but I could not be happy or contented away from you it seems to me as those my very thought and feeling had some mysterious connection with you - I can not enjoy any thing with out the feeling of its being so much more pleasant were it only shared with you the simple fact of seeing the flowers create an involuntary wish that you were by my side - Darling I do try and think of the future - the thing I want most for both of us is an assured hope - the calm serenity commingled with doubts and fears would be to me a longed for rest and the purity of character it must require so delightful - Darling if my prayers can be of any avail you have them I <u>never forget you</u> - tis a sweet thought to me that you my darling that I most love pray for me and our little baby - Darling I will try for yours and my own sake not to be provoked but this is a hard thing I am very sensitive and impulsive you know what my temperament is - I do think it worth the effort - you know my own dearest one the very fact of its devoting your love more deeply for me would be a great inducement, but I ought to do it for a higher purpose - Thee it is a repetition I would never tire of to have you tell me that you love me more than any body else in the world - I will never forget my treasured letter - I love so to feel the confidence that I do know your "heartfelt" love and if it is any pleasure for you to know I love you you can be certain that I do most intensely - I love you always and all times but this afternoon I love you with so much tenderness I can not express half I feel - I wish I were near you I have been thinking constantly of how lonely you would feel when Brother Jimmie leaves you - I am so glad he went up to dine at Mamas - do you think they all seemed to like him - I hope they did - I am so glad we are in New York on brother Jimmies account - you know it

104

gives him so much pleasure to visit one place some thing like a home - a feeling he has had so little opportunity of enjoying - Thee you do not know what pleasure it has given me - the thought that you like brother Jimmie and he you - I was very much pleased with my dear Mamas letter - I will answer her soon, I write you so often I have hardly time to write any one else - I wish she and Father would have gone to Europe on account of Mamas health - altho we would have missed her most dreadfully - Darling I will try to think more favorably of the Cottage plans - the reason I objected so much I felt that I would like to feel free of care during the summer - it would be a great inducement to have you with me certainly every afternoon - I do hope we will not have to stay in town this summer - I would like to be with Mama.

While we were at tea last evening the door opened and in came Brother [Daniel Stuart Elliott] - he would have been here much sooner but fell asleep in the car and passed through Marietta without waking - thirty miles up the country - he seemed delighted to get home and see us - he brought for Anna and myself <u>five</u> <u>dollars</u> worth of Dickens fresh candy in a wooden box beautifully put up - only imagine the quantity we could almost set up a small store with it - he brought also in a cage the whole way from Savannah a mocking bird, it must have been an intense trouble - every morning Mother has to have cooked for it a potato and egg - which are mashed together in a ball - we had quite a time deciding where it would be hung - after breakfast we fixed it outside of the ~~Dining~~ parlor window - but a little while afterwards saw a cat watching it with a most designing look and she could have jumped easily upon the cage so it has to be removed and suspended from one of the upstairs windows. He said to day that he anticipated your coming - so my own dear Thee if he should be here when you are please try and make things pass as well as possible - he has many faults

105

and is very disagreeable at times but I still think Brother is very affectionate - and I think it is right to be as pleasant as possible. I know you will do it for my sake - May 12th This day two years ago we became engaged dearest Thee it seemed to me just as I wrote it - I only stopped in time yesterday to walk about the yard with Mother and Anna you can not imagine how perfectly beautiful every thing looked the hills back of our lot with the sun light upon them - how much I wish we could spend our summers here. It is very probable that Mr Baker will offer for the house and altho there are many many reasons why Mother would prefer living here and the place in summer would be an inestimable loss still she feels upon the whole perhaps it would be best to sort out while she is able. Darling do be sure to see about the carpets being left safely - Thee will you please bring me a pair of gauntlets - I want them for walking in my traveling ones are too much soiled, Darling will you please send me the size of your neck - I am going to have surprise for you - send it immediately - it is such a pleasure to get your letters you have no idea how I enjoy them. Anna sends love and says she is so anxious for the time for you to arrive - good bye my own dearest Theeade I write again tomorrow.

your own
Mittie Roosevelt

New York May 13th 55

My Own Little Darling

On a quiet bright sunday morning like the present you can't think how I do miss you. I feel that I would be with you all the day, and that we would enjoy such weather doubly together. Everything begins to look like spring but [it] is more the feeling of the atmosphere than anything else which makes me want some one to enjoy it with me. We have a little ^{glimpse} of the country over Mr. Goebel's wall and the sounds of his numerous birds remind me still more forcibly of the country. It is just such a day as would give you a pleasant impression of a New York spring but I suppose they are all like it in Roswell.

I am beginning to look forward myself to the time when I will be there I will leave tomorrow night two weeks, but as I may be detained by business one day in Washington don't make any accurate calculation upon my arrival I think I will reach there the day I appointed.

As I did not finish breakfast till ten this morning and this is written after that meal I must stop here and go to church -

I have just returned from the 29th St church, having walked down with mother father Lizzie Jim and his two juveniles to the on 14th St.

Lizzie sends you word that "there is <u>no</u> hope of a country place and she is in despair." Jim however adds as a postscript that the croton-water still runs in New York. This will be our only refreshment for the summer months. This morning which I was longing for you to be here to enjoy has turned as it approached midday positively sultry out of doors, although it still remains delightful within.

I passed last evening with Mr Hutchison and handed him your mother's letter as well as one from Brother Jimmie.

He sent up the description by a porter with one for fear of accidents and as I was spending saturday evening with mother it remained there till Chryster came. This brought the direction under the criticism of the family, it was addressed to "Mrs Mittie Roosevelt" I was sorry as you know they were not prejudiced favorably towards him, any more than myself. It certainly shows ignorance stupidity or bad manners. He said that while he appreciated the motives

107

that prompted me to grant your wish to visit the south he still considered it a very unadvisable step. He considers Dan a very singular fellow particularly on consequence of not spending his last evening in Savannah at his house. Brother Jimmie meets at present with his full approbation, indeed he is going to propose him as a member of the club while in town this time. I suggested a doubt with regard to the advisability of one who would probably marry and be a family man joining the club but he entirely over ruled this by a unavoidable argument, that he himself was a member. There was no getting over this, particularly as he agreed fully with regard to the grounds on which I based my objections.

I do not know that I mentioned it but Gordon Norris and his wife are here and about to sail for Europe in the same steamer with Mr Kermit and Laura Carow. I intend visiting Gordon's wife as soon as possible, he asked me yesterday for any information I could give him to help him in determining his route & I will try to get a few moments to look over my old papers tonight, and make him out a memorandum which he will probably never take from his trunk if he should honor it by a position there.

I rather look forward to glancing over my European trip on myown account if only to recall; what I think of with so much pleasure, to my memory.

Mittie darling do you know that after you come back I would like if it meets with your approval for us to read over together the notes I took when there and then I might write them out more plainly in one book. I think with the incidents I could add from memory you might find it interesting.

Tell Annie I will <u>carry</u> Pelham South with me and if I don't find the Last of the Barrons in my library buy it too, as I ought to have it, if I have not. Give a great deal of love to Annie and tell her that next to you I depend upon her more than anyone or anything else for my enjoyment while in Roswell.

Aunt Cornelia and Laura Fitch dropped in at mothers yesterday just after dinner. Little Freddy has been over run but fortunately but little hurt.

They ^{Aunt Cornelia and Laura} are both going out of town to take dinner at Mrs O'Connor's place today on Sunday. I think Aunt Cornelia made it a point to tell mother knowing how she would disapprove of it -

10 PM   Mimmie & Johny dropped in through the piazza window to see me after afternoon church and were very much pleased with my pictures, Johny became more sociable than I have ever seen him. I took my tea at the Norris' rather unexpectedly and upon Gordon's expressing a wish to make his plans for his European tour ^{with the assistance from us} at my house but not liking to leave his wife, I persuaded him to bring her and Mr & Mrs Moke tomorrow evening. They accepted, and now I would give anything to have myown little darling here. I have always wanted you to know the Norris but the fates seem to have been opposed. Mrs Moke says that next winter she hopes to see you oftener.

If I only had some silver I could give them some tea as they are coming at quarter past six. If you were only here we might have had an informal evening, now as soon as we have looked at the maps and everything they will go. Gordon's wife is a very pleasant bright kind of a girl, apparently very full of life & spirits, not pretty.

Now Mittie darling this letter has extended at intervals all through sunday, this afternoon there was communion and I was very forcibly reminded of the last time I saw it given when we sat side by side. Would that we felt prepared to sit side by side at the communion table! Darling do you think ever of serious things?

109

Do write me of your own health I do hope that our little baby is perfectly well again does it notice more than it did?

Write me every particular of what concerns yourself and remember me always as your loving husband

Theodore

Thee's third letter to Mittie from New York, like the first and second, continued to tell her the news of the family, his daily activities, and whom he visited. Thee attended church with his parents, brother Jim, his wife Lizzie, and two of their children. Jim and Lizzie had two girls by this date, Mary, born in 1848, and Cornelia, born in 1850.

The Roosevelts appeared to have not particularly liked Savannah resident Robert Hutchison. Hutchison, a Scotsman by birth, had made his own fortune in Georgia and was a good friend of the Bulloch family. His address of the letter to Mrs. Mittie Roosevelt instead of Mrs. Theodore Roosevelt was considered to be in very bad taste. Several period accounts of Robert's personality indicated that he often spoke his mind when not warranted and expressed his opinions freely. Although he had traveled with Daniel Elliott in Europe in 1852 and 1853, he was displeased with what he took as Daniel's recent snub. James Dunwoody Bulloch, "brother Jimmie," however, stayed in his good graces. James' late first wife and Robert's late second wife were sisters. Both had died of tuberculosis by this date.

Thee spoke of several individuals and couples in this letter who have not been identified. He was preparing a European itinerary for his friend Gordon Norris based on his own travels on the continent in the early 1850s. Thee mentions Aunt Cornelia; however, an exhaustive search of both the Barnhill and Roosevelt family trees has not identified any Cornelia. That "Mimmie and Johny" came in through the piazza window revealed them to be the children of Robert and Lizzie Roosevelt. Margaret, named for her grandmother and called Mimmie, was born in 1851 while Johny would have been only 2 years old. Rob and his family occupied the adjoining home which shared a piazza or porch with Mittie and Thee's home.

Thee promised to bring for Anna, two novels by the English author Edward Bulwer-Lytton. *The Last of the Barons,* first published in 1843, was an historical novel based on the power struggle between the English King Edward IV and his minister the Earl of Warwick. Bulwer-Lytton portrayed the king as weak and licentious while the Earl was a warrior, patriot, and good father. Science and romance play secondary themes. The book is still widely read today. The second book, *Pelham; Or, the Adventures of a Gentleman,* was Bulwer-Lytton's second novel, published in 1828, and told of a dandy named Henry Pelham and is a murder mystery, as well as a love story. Like many novels of the day, it focused on the manners and lifestyles of the English aristocrats.

New York May 14th 55

Dearest One

I have just been reading over your sweet letter, for it [is] sweet although there is a little bitterness mixed with it. I certainly fully coincide with regard to your opinion of "Lilly Parsons" and hope she will not have occasion ever to come again, although I don't think there was any great harm in the impromptu invitation, which they accepted as informally as given and were certainly much more quiet and demure as at our house than at Robs; still we agree fully with regard to the future. Miss Anna Willis invited me to meet the same set at her house this evening but I refused. There was a slight sprinkle this evening which prevented the ladies of Norris' family from coming to see me, but he came to make their apologies and we studied up his plans together. Fred Elliott also dropped in accidentally this evening, and we walked together, when he went away at eleven o'clock, down to the New York Hotel together to deliver Mr Hutchison's letter. You know darling I do not pass one moment more than I positively require in bed because it would be so dreary to be there awake <u>alone</u>.

Indeed darling you ought not to blame me for trying to enjoy myself to the uttermost you know while it is a pleasure trip to you it is by no means a pleasant stay-at-home to me even with every amusement I can find. Darling one do write me in your answer to this if you think under the same circumstances you would have gone if you had thought as much of it as you have now.

You know myown little one I do not blame you in the least, but I want you to answer this question cordially.

Mittie do not feel disappointed should I not arrive in Roswell until saturday the ²ⁿᵈ of June, I find it almost impossible to get accurate information about the route when going by land. Depend upon it dearest I am so anxious to hold you once more in my arms and pet you as you can be to be petted, and that I will not stop one moment more than necessary by the way. You know how I love you darling and what an intense pleasure it would be now to carry you up to bed in my arms and have you anxious not to let me strain myself.

Good Night.

May 15ᵗʰ   While at dinner party yesterday the front door bell rang and I heard a very loud clatter of voices of which

112

I could distinguish nothing; at last a little boy's voice asked for a drink and Mary Ann while leading him down stairs inquired "how is Miss Clara Franky"? "As cross an old thing as ever," was Franky's response, then came a stentorian "Hush, Mr Roosevelt is in there": and from this I was left to dream myown conclusions of who the party were. I asked no question indeed I have addressed but two remarks to Mary Ann since my return and these were relative to sewing on shirt buttons or draw strings. -

I exerted all my taste to please you in the selection of my summer cravats this afternoon. I do hope they will prove satisfactory but I regard these as the most dangerous of all my purchases. But I know you have learned to look deeper than the mere outside by this time and will prize my heart more than my dress and that, darling, you will find right in every particular. I do love my own little pet as much as she can desire, sometimes I think a little more. Mr Hutchison has been spending the evening with me, I called at his hotel and invited him to walk up with me and have a "quiet chat."

We had a long ^{talk} principally about family matters on which while we did not always agree our disagreements were always stated so formally and with such an unbounded display of politeness that neither party could take offense. I have been rather amused then otherwise with the evening's conferences and ^{am} happy to inform you that no open hostilities were declared, in fact, I have no doubt "his heart warmed" towards me when he departed about as much as ever.

Tomorrow night I spend my invitation at Yonkers with Ike Knox (a son of Dr Knox) who is going to have a few friends there. He wanted me to spend Sunday with him but I thought it was best not to and compromised for tomorrow evening. I will write you all about it in my next.

Mr Hutchison said this separation ^{between us} would increase and know your love for me. I hope there was not much room for increase but if there was do let it reach the highest point before I arrive at Roswell.

Farewell myown dearest one

Your ever loving Husband
Theodore

Roswell May 15th

Dear Thee

You can not think how constantly we think and speak of you coming. We have counted the days and can not realize that in about two weeks we will have you here. I wish that Mother and I could just take and lock you all up and keep you here all the summer. We are so anxious to hear how your evening with Mr Hutchison passes off. As soon as brother heard of it he said well I know Mr Hutchison will enjoy it exceedingly and be very much gratified by the compliment, for he admires Thee very much. Your letters are so interesting just as soon as Mittie has read them once to her self I make her read your letter all she will read out to a third party. The moment we think the Mail has arrived Mittie and I post off Peggy, and watch Anxiously for her return, you know how long a little negro can take to go an exceedingly short distance. Now while Nora is taking her breakfast there is no one to take care of the baby so Mittie has had two pillows brought into the parlor and put on the floor as a little bed for her and she is playing in there just as lively and happy, laughing out loud and crowing all to her self - Mother and Aunt Jane say constantly Oh that child has her Fathers lovely disposition Mittie and I think this so very personal, now why could she not have her <u>Aunt's</u> "lively disposition," How very pleasantly brother Jimmies

114

time seems to have passed I had a note from him by the mail of yesterday - I can not believe he actually wrote it himself. I have promised to let the baby add a short postscript

I love my Father I want to be him. {indecipherable}

She wrote this a little badly because the pen was not the kind she is accustomed to. Thee do when you see Laura give my love to her very particularly. Much love to your Mother. Mittie read her entertaining letter to me - I should so much like to have seen Lizzie at her table at the fair - Goodbye my dear Thee -

Your aff Sister
Anna

Roswell May 16th

My own dearest Thee

I got your two last letters to day. I wish you were not alone I cant bear the idea of your being all alone never mind my own darling one in a very short time you will be with me and if you are going to enjoy it as I expect to you have a great deal to anticipate. Theede how lovely 'twill be to look right up in your dear face and feel you warm against me. you beg me some times to think of you it needed no asking. I do it as a part of myself I will try dear Thee to spend as little as I can this year. I do hope we will only spend our income. I wish one business would look up tho. Theede I am going to be a companion to you in all your hopes and thoughts if you will only let me and trust me as your own dearest and nearest - one who above all others will sympathize with every feeling Darling you do not feel as 'tho it would have been better for you if you had never married me? tell me candidly - Dear Thee loving each other as we have told each other we

115

do it is our duty to make one interest - every thing should be sacrificed to it and oh my own dear husband my darling Thee if we <u>love</u> 'twill be no effort. I love to be your care and to be dependent upon you. You know I have always thought that 'tho the love should be just as strong on both sides still I love to see a man have a peculiar tenderness and care for his wife - Darling do you know that I have written you almost every day, sometimes I am only going to write one of these sheets for if I have written any other person it tires me to bend over too much - tis my pleasure to write you my own darling but I know tis just as you would have me do if you were here. You need not have any fear of little Bam being turned over Nora generally drags her when ever Peggy does she is very gentle in harness, and you may be sure I would have no risks run with her. I dont think tis well to be nervous about a child I think every care and precaution should be taken but there is more or less risk in almost every thing but they all are equally provided for and after you have acted as you think best even if an accident should happen I should not feel to blame. I mean this dear Thee I do not think we would be right to deprive her of any innocent enjoyment for fear of accident so when you think of it how almost everything could have {___} back. Darling dont you agree with me. I hope the dear little baby will be perserved. Thee you know Mother thinks that she is teething - Anna and I dressed to go over to Auntys [Dunwoody] and sat in the piazza waiting for Mother and Irvine. some chickens had just been bought and Mother was busy having them put away so we had to wait some little time, when we arrived all were ready for us and the drawing room lighted. Ellen [Dunwoody] has the box I gave her in the parlour with shells in it. Mother has some she is going to give me to put in my box (dont you know you always say that I want to have everything I hear anybody else has you used to scold me

116

darling did you not) old Aunty said she hoped when you come to have more of such tea meetings, Mrs John Dunwody poured and old Uncle had been over to his farm and had become completely tired out. This he mistook for a severe spell of sickness and was confined to his bed - when Mother went into see him, he told her he had a hot fever - she told him that his head was perfectly cool - we returned at about half past nine and found the baby wide awake in Noras lap - she trying to teach Sarah and Peggy their sunday school hymns but Bam was too fidgety. Nora appears charmed with the negroes I saw her examining Sarah on sunday to see if her ears were clean. Anna and I commenced yesterday to walk every morning immediately after breakfast. I dont go very far - May 17$^{\underline{th}}$ I wrote last night in the parlour with every body around Irvine was writing his debating speech and every now and then conversing about it so I am afraid I have made frequent mistakes - speaking of Irvine he has had a shanghai chicken setting when a few nights ago Mr Kings white hog (the little negroes call it so) broke in and eat up all the eggs, Irvine lost his appetite completely for his dinner and spent the afternoon in nailing the bars securely in and now old Mauma has to climb over to feed the chickens. Thee darling if you leave before any place has been decided on for the summer please leave the carpets safely - ask sister Lizzies - advice I do dislike the idea so of there being down the whole summer. be sure to bring gloves with you and have every thing quite nice. I would have liked to have seen my own darling one in his spring clothes and hair chain - I do think of his exterior but would rather have him love me than any thing else. Tomorrow two weeks you will be here I suppose by the time you did when we drove over together I will be all ready for you - but I must stop - love oceans of it for my own darling dearest Thee from his affectionate wife.

Mittie Roosevelt

117

Thee I hope you did not have a chill but I suspect it. please take care of yourself

---

New York May 17th 55

My Own Dearest Darling

I do not know how to commence this letter, I have been thinking for at least five minutes for some term to express my love for you. Your last letter made me think of you so very lovingly. Oh! <u>how</u> I would love to hear you repeat to me yourself just what that letter expresses. Do Darling try to cultivate those feelings, you cannot imagine my pleasure at receiving such an answer to a letter which I almost feared you might have misunderstood. I have just returned from the store having spent last night at Yonkers. This morning Ann did not know I was away and prepared breakfast for me, and then was too modest to look, for an indefinite length of time, in my room to find out.

There goes a ring at the bell and Charley has called to take me a drive. -

Ike Knox was very polite and his wife equally so. He had been pressing me over ever since he had lived at Yonkers to pay him a visit and was very glad to have me at last. When all the party had dispersed except one other gentleman and myself Ike enquired from his wife what had become of some oysters he brought up for supper. The servants had all retired and we determined to cook them for ourselves. Two of ^{us} set the table one went to the cellar for some butter and Mrs Knox did the principal part of the cooking. Of course under these circumstances we eat just twice as many as we otherwise would have.

This morning the first thing that met my eye was the

118

Hudson River. My window ^{opened} onto a beautiful view of it and the fresh country breeze as it blew into the room was perfectly delightful. As I went and came in the cars I was forcibly reminded of the time a little more than two years before that I had last gone over that same road to West Point with myown dearest-one.

I had much more opportunity of looking at the scenery this time than then. We must sometime go up in one of the steamboats, I feel as though going all day in one of those with you would be such a luxury. Only I would want to have a retired place where no one else could see me kissing ^{you}: Oh! For one kiss. What is it that makes me prize a kiss from you so much when I have no such longing with regard to anyone here?

It seems to me as though your breath would be all gone before I could separate myself from you were you only now by my side.

I have one piece of very astounding intelligence to give you. Miss Morris was going to introduce me to Miss Riley this evening, her first effort having failed, but upon my arrival at her house ^{she} announced to my utter astonishment that the engagement was broken off this morning. She would not consent to go South with George and of course he could not agree to remain a hanger - on to her family here which was proposed. She gave her sickness as a reason. Poor George I am really sorry because I think the effect will be so injurious on his future life. He had his faith in women severely tested by his first attachment and this seems to be a death blow. I am really sorry for him; not that I think his present feelings will be very dreadful for I rather suspect he takes it more cooly than the first but it is the influence afterwards.

I enclose the correct measure round my neck; that is not including collar or anything. The paper just fully meets round my neck. I am very curious about the surprise and would certainly not have bought a summer cravat had I heard of it the day before.

Our business seems to be worse and worse we are now fairly doing nothing and this should be our busy season, I hope it will not spring up again just as I go away.

I enquired from Ann whether she was very regular in opening the parlors and keeping the moths out, She answered in the affirmative. She seems to get along as well as ever, indeed if anything I think she rather improves. She markets for me.

I have just bought some patent tapers so that I no longer am so painfully reminded of Annie.

I have much more to say but must be coming to a conclusion. The more I see of those girls at Robs the more I congratulate myself that you are not like them; but I would never have loved you had you been, much less have centered my _whole_ love upon you. Do repeat to me in your answer what you have so often told me that you love me more than anybody else in the world. It may be the last letter I will receive from you; I don't want you to write after thursday or friday as it would not reach me. I will think of it during the tedious hours on the Rail Road, don't forget to write it and above all to _feel_ it. Remember how sincerely and devotedly yourown husband loves you.

Thee.

May 18. Tudie [Susan West] writes me that some things are coming by Express. What shall I take with me and what leave?   Yours Ever

Again, a tale of dear George Morris appeared in Thee's letter. This time George's sister told Thee of her brother's broken engagement to Miss Riley. As no further details of George or his sister were given, the family remains unidentified as does Miss Riley.

Roswell May 18th

My own dearest Thee

Yesterday's mail brought me two letters from you one your last written on the eighth the other dated May 1st and evidently the first letter you wrote me from New York - I thought it so strange you had never told me of your arrival and how you had succeeded in Washington and Baltimore. Anna got a letter from ^{of} Carrie, written on the first so the detention must have been some where here. Darling I was glad to get both of them you have no idea of how interesting your letters are and how I anticipate them and enjoy intensely reading them over and over, I have not yet forgotten the letter I wrote you about Mrs Parsons. Darling I love you dearly. Dearest one tis delightful to me the idea of being with you again and I would not put off that for anything. you know exactly how I feel {___} there is something scarcely that would give me more pleasure than to spend the summer here - but without you I would not do it for anything, I long to see you - you have no idea how Mother and Anna anticipate your coming. Brother [Daniel Elliott] is pleasanter than he has ever been he is so much more considerate of every one now Thee darling dont read this really {___ly} by. I am almost sorry ^{I wrote it to} you for you are prejudiced my own darling one. he leaves today to pay Miss Tyrel a visit, he will be back in a week. Darling I would have written you as usual yesterday but I did not feel at all well so Mother and Anna persuaded me to wait until this morning and Anna said she would write you a note as I would not have time to write as much. The baby was out this morning some time before breakfast, riding about the yard - she scarcely ever cries, Brother said the other day - well I never took an interest in a baby before but how strange one does feels to a connected baby. I was so amused at your fear of Mary Ann falling in your arms from emotion, when you told her the baby was well.

how dreadful 'twould have been to have had a pig in your arms instead of merely in the room with you. Darling I am glad you have brought the prepared ~~and the~~ castor oil. I hope it will do me some good - my hair has not stopped dropping in the least and is painfully thin but Anna thinks that she sees fine hair coming. I hope so but I am rather incredulous. You know the reason my hands were so dreadfully hurt I fell down stairs and knocked one on the banister. I am so glad brother Jimmie enjoyed his visit and that they were all so polite. Darling I do pity you with Mr Hutchison I do hope he will be engaged on that evening. I wish I could be with you to help entertain but I am glad we have gotten the wine - the idea of Brother Jimmies having a state-room to itself. I am so glad you have called upon the Misses Morris. I hope you can get the pattern of Georgia diamond {?} - not that they have the same however. Darling I have been so much amused at your "dear little bronze cozy tea {?} kettle" I think I will keep you in suspense as to whether I will let you keep it. I might darling you need not feel too uneasy about your little pot. Anna has just been making the baby write you - she made frequent plunges {?} with her head, but grasped the pen. I will write you about Mother in some other letter - you and Brother Jimmie make a mistake in thinking she is obliged to sell the house she is not in debt. if she stays here the repairs of this house would be much more than her furnishing the quantity of rooms she expects to. But darling let us talk it over when we meet.

We are all going to take tea with Aunty this evening. Theode I am so glad you love me so much tell me about in every letter I had rather hear that than anything else and oh how

122

much ᵗᵒʷ I do love you I am going to sit in your lap the moment you come. I must stop - good bye

Yours devotedly

Mittie Roosevelt

Don't say anything about Brother not even to Brother Jimmie - The baby has just come in with this little sweet briar in her hand.

Mittie reported that her half brother Daniel Elliott had gone to visit Miss Tyrel. Upon Daniel's return from an extended stay in Europe in 1853, he spent time in both Roswell and Savannah. Much of his time seems to have been taken up with courting various young ladies.

Once more, Mittie mentioned Martha Bulloch's desire to sell her Roswell home. Mittie made it clear that Martha was not in debt, but that she would have to make repairs on the house and furnish rooms for herself, Anna, and Irvine in the North as well.

Roswell May 19ᵗʰ

My own darling Thee.

I could have written you yesterday, but I did not feel well and knowing I would have time at any rate for a note before the mail I determined to wait until this morning. I have had quite a little sick turn. I was feeling so well and had such an appetite when I first came, but I am a great deal better and hope I shall recover entirely before you come. I am so sorry I should have been sick for every one was remarking how well I looked, my face was so full and I had such a color, It is just before breakfast. Anna is drawing the flower pots and has just placed on the table a glass with a lovely sprig of white rose buds and one pink. Mamma just before brought in a saucer of fresh churned butter which Mother said was for me to eat with my milk wafers. I have just finished breakfast. Nora brought in the baby sound asleep. she had been walking in the garden Bamie notices a good deal is perfectly devoted to her own little hands. sucks her fingers dreadfully. Then 'tis one of Nora's regular duties to bring the carriage in every evening, once she neglected to do so and I gave her quite an impressive little talk. The next evening after she had brought it in she was in the room with the baby when suddenly Anna and I who were seated in the parlor heard her walk rapidly by and say to Sarah - oh the carriage is in the yard and I believe it is broken up - she had dreamed a horse had kicked it over and believed it was really so. I was very glad for her to get the scare. Aunty and Uncle spent the day with us a few days ago she asked when you would be here and said she hoped you would be here on the seventh of June as they would on that day celebrate the forty-seventh anniversary of their wedding day. 'Tis a long time to have been married is it not dearest? Aunty says that the baby is a very blended likeness of you and I. Your eyes, my mouth. I wish I could see {?} your dear darling eyes oh how I love them. I will with the greatest pleasure look on your European trip with you. You know I have always been interested about it and constantly ask you to tell me some thing about when you were in Europe. I wish I could have been with you the evening Gordon Morris [Mittie meant Norris.] and his wife were at our house. tell me (but I know you will before this reaches you) how you found the time. Theede try and get here by the first day of June I have so put my heart upon it I would hate to be disappointed. I hope you will continue to write before you leave so I will get letters from you the week you are traveling, I have to wait now until Monday before I will hear from you again.

124

I love to get my letters they are very interesting to me. I hope you will enjoy your visit and I think you will my own darling. I could of course enjoy myself in turn the rest of the summer but I do hope some thing will turn up. have Lizzie and Rob thought of any country place. We have not heard from Brother [Daniel Elliott] since he left - I think it showed very bad taste in Mr Hutchison disregarding my views as he did. I think it would have been a great deal better if he had sent it in your name if he objected to that. Mrs Theodore Roosevelt should have been to say the least of it more ^{according to} etiquette. Brother and himself must have had some time of it this month. I don't think we will ever come to have him very near us darling - but I do wish he would give me his hand some set of china and his water colored beads!?

Anna says she will be very glad if you will <u>bring</u> Pelham with you I would get the "Last of the Barons", Thee you will be sure to look up your books before you leave. Theede Mother wants you to get another knife such as you got for Irvine - and I want you to get for me a small round fine sponge for the baby. Nora left hers in Savannah and she is now using Mothers. I hope my various commissions will not trouble my own sweet one - good bye dear darling your own little

Mittie -

I think of you constantly you must think of me all the time. Anna says the first two or three nights I slept with her I would throw my arms around her and call her darling but she knows I meant it for you do you think so?

New York May 19th [55]

My Own Dearest One,

I have received a letter in which you mention incidentally that you "did not feel at all well." Why did you not tell me what was the matter ^{with} you darling? I have in vain all day tried not to be uneasy about you. If I had only known exactly what it was it would have been so much better, and you promised to tell me every particular of your life. Be certain to tell me all about it in your answer to this so that will be I presume about the last letter you will write. It was particularly unfortunate as this being Saturday evening I wanted to have been in particularly good spirits. I suppose it might have been nothing, but it brought up to my mind the idea that you might be sick so far away from me and this seems insupportable. Do take regular exercise as you said you would, and try to gain as much strength as possible the first part of the summer, to prepare yourself for anything you may have to go through the latter part of it.

It gave me inexp^resible pleasure to have you say you "would not spend the summer South without me for anything", I always knew you loved me and hoped that you would feel so but now I am certain of it. I love to receive your letters I don't need you to miss writing me as up to the last moment. How I would love to have you by my side; I have just returned from mother's and am sitting in one of the covered arm chairs in the dining room with my little ^{table} drawn under the side gas lights, not feeling equal to the trouble of lighting the drop light. The pattering of the rain which is falling in torrents outside adds to my feeling of dreariness; I wish you were with me.

I was much obliged to the baby for its first little token of affection for me in the shape of the sweet briar, it reminded me of the spring-like look of Roswell.

Last night I answered Susan's letter informing ^{me} of having sent some things to me by express. I invited Hilborne to keep the last few days of my bachelorhood with me. Susan quotes from a letter from Irvine to her, as a comfort to me. "Mittie cried a great deal after brother Thee left, but she does not cry now."

I thanked her for her kindness in attending to your commissions and am waiting anxiously a letter from you telling me what to leave, if anything beside the baby's cloak. I have not yet opened the box and do not intend to until I am obliged to pack up. I must now go to bed and as I answer Annie's letter tomorrow may not have an opportunity of adding much.

Your Own Husband

May 20th Dearest one I must add a few words more I have just returned from hearing Dr. Dewitt preach one of his beautiful sermons. They always seem to be just what I require and no one elses ever have half so much influence over me. His subject was the ascension of Christ and he persuaded us to turn our thoughts above, where he now is. It was one of the Doctor's happiest efforts and I would have liked very much for you to have heard it. While I am very far as you know from wanting to force you inclinations I would like very much if you could think it would benefit you as much to attend this church as any other. It seems impossible to obtain a pew in Dr Alexander's at all events, and some how one sermon of Dr Dewitt's goes more to my soul than a dozen of Dr Alexander's; this may be in part however early association

Think it over Darling one we both of us want a settle place of worship and if you think it would be better for you to go anywhere else tell me candidly for you know I would regret for ever having influenced to your own injury, in this matter above all others. You need not write about this but we will talk over it when we meet. -

Yours and Yours Only Thee.

Roswell, May 21st

My own dearest Thee

I was up in Anna's room she had just finished rubbing my hair with castor-oil when Peggy came with letters one from Sister to Anna. and one from you my darling one 'tis such a pleasure to get your letters. I just devour them and then read them over and over and keep one about me. I am so glad you understand what I meant about Mrs Parsons perhaps I was too severe about her. darling I want you to enjoy yourself as much as you possibly can. I only can't fear the idea of other people kind of making you happy. Theede you tell me to tell you candidly to tell you if I would leave you again, now darling you cannot imagine what a pleasure my coming seems to have been to Mother and Anna and I feel if as 'tho I had done rightly to come - but my own dearest Thee I hope I shall never be separated from you again I do not half enjoy any thing without you and you have no idea of with what a thrill of pleasure I look forward to in seeing you. I will think of you then as coming on the second of June. I know you would not have put off even a day if you had not been obliged to, write me tho if there is a change in your plans, I would like to know the exact time on which to expect you. Nora came in a little while ago to ask Anna and I to come and see how the baby was playing with Mauma - when we went Bamie was laughing and playing beautifully. Mauma smelt so delightfully that I asked her what she did put on herself she says she always puts roses

128

and shrubs in her clothes. Sister [Susan West] wrote that she had gotten the baby cloak for me, but tis so warm I will hardly need it out here - so please dear Thee give it to Marianne and tell her to put it up very carefully in linen towels and tie up camphor and put with it the other things she may send please dearest bring with you - I hope they will not trouble you. How much I would have liked to have you carry me up in your arms only darling I am always afraid of straining you. do you remember how I used to kiss you on the way up the stairs, you will find my love at its highest pitch to greet you when you come what a sweet idea that of being near you again is - indeed I love you most truly and tenderly. So Gordon Norris was able to leave his wife and pay you a visit. I am glad Fred Elliott was there too. you remember how nice he looked the day he told us good bye on board the Steamer. Mother says he was the most pleasing looking young man she had seen at all. I did not know that Ike Knox lived out at Yonkers. in fact I have always only associated the Morris' there. I will finish in the morning.

May 22nd   Good morning my dearest darling what would I not give to see you this morning instead of this poor writing. I feel better this morning and I think I am going to be quite well again I have dieted very strictly. Yesterday afternoon we walked all about the yard instead of taking a regular walk - went down to the garden the baby and Nora accompanying us. I wished so much that you could be with us. I know so well that you would have enjoyed it so much. Henry Pratt called upon us yesterday morning. he has just come home to pay a visit as he will leave in the fall for South America, he has been appointed as Missionary to Bogota he says he does not know when he will come home as the trip there is so very expensive. it seemed sad to think of his being obliged to be separated from all his family for such an indefinite period.

Anna has been devoted to me my dear Thee. she has rubbed me with camphor every night since I have been unwell. oh Thee I do hope Mr. Baker will purchase this house. when you are here you will be able to fully appreciate how lonely Mother and Anna will be when ~~they~~ we leave and tho it will be very sad to give up this old place what is that as Mother says in comparison to leaving your children, neither party can be travelling all the time, but when you come we will talk it all over. We have not heard from Brother yet. I hope he is enjoying himself. Every one has been quite curious to know where he has gone. Mrs King was here the other day and told us that they suposed he had gone to the Convention at Augusta [Democratic State Convention]. Theede brother says that he amused Mr Hutchison very much just before he left. he had been to the Club and there saw "old Fipps" playing whist with girls a sum of money by him so he told Mr H. that he was acting the part of the prodigal son and the fatted calf at the same time. I congratulate you that you have survived the evening at home to Mr. Hutchison. I am glad you were polite to him. Did he make brother Jimmie one of the Club? Yesterday afternoon Mrs Camp sent her little baby here to see Nina. she was looking very mildly at times when the baby suddenly leaned over and made a plunge at her siezing her by one ear on one side and by a lock of her hair on the other. Bamie puckered up her mouth and cried out. Nora seems very much hurt by this conduct on the part of the visitor. Darling I will write you by the next mail and that will be my last letter. you will get it on the day of your departure you must write me to the last. Theede I have enjoyed our married correspondence very much. I have told you 'tho before how much I valued your letters. give my love to Mama - Anna and Mother send theirs to you. I must stop. good bye then my own dearest one ever your own wife.

Mittie Roosevelt.

The Mr. Baker whom Mittie mentioned in relation to buying the house could be one of two people. The Rev. John Fabian Baker (1827-1885) married Francis Lorinda Pratt (1835-1857) in November of 1855. He was a Presbyterian clergyman.[45] However, the Rev. William Elliott Baker, who would later marry Catherine Evelyn King in July of 1856, could have planned to take up housekeeping in Roswell. However, this young couple departed for Sacramento, California immediately after their marriage the following year.[46] It seems more likely the Rev. John Baker had expressed in interest in the home.

Henry Barrington Pratt (1832-1912), son of the Reverend Nathaniel Pratt, had graduated from Oglethorpe University, which was at that time located in Midway, Georgia. In 1855, he graduated from the Princeton Theological Seminary before being ordained as a Presbyterian minister. He became a missionary in South America.[47]

Mrs. George Camp, whom attended Mittie's wedding, brought little Walter over to see the Roosevelt baby. Jane Atwood Camp had borne two boys by 1855, George, now four years old, and Walter not quite two. The Camps lived in Primrose Cottage, near the Presbyterian Church, and George was employed by the Roswell Manufacturing Company.[48]

Roswell May 23th

My own dearest Thee I am just as great a loss as ever more to find any time to express my love when I read the beginning of your letter it seemed like my own feelngs for you expressed - each of your letters makes me think more lovingly of you expressed if this could be possible. I do not like to be writing my last letter to you altho the reason why I do not write again is so sweet, thus you will be on your way to me before it could reach you. Darling I love you most truly and purely more than any other person. I feel that you are every thing to me - that there is some thing in me connected with my husband oh dearest one I hope we will be with each other a long time. My Theede I hope I will not be separated from you again. We ought to be truly grateful if we are allowed to meet again it seems to me as 'tho you were doubly endowed to me - I so often read your words and looks they have ever been so gentle and loving to me - I love to think that I am the one most loved and that I am constantly in your thoughts - I cannot bear the idea of your having to travel all alone I would give anything to be with you - think all the time how I am counting every hour as one less of separation - and this my heart is beating at the idea of your coming I could fill pages of telling you how I love you - we must have long talks together I feel as 'tho it were full time to be with you. Darling I love to remember how sincerely and devotedly my own husband loves me. When I expected you before I was married 'tho I was excited by it and I know I must have loved you - it was not with this deep tenderness and from that I expected you now. Thee I wonder if you feel as I do - but I want our interests to become more and more the same. I do not want the last shadow of reserve to be between us - You will get this on the day which you leave New York I hope it will reach you in the five days - but I expect letters in the week that I expect you - Thee it is very warm now. I have taken off my flannel which you may remember I did on the day which you left me but it was so cold I had to put it on again by Mothers and Aunt Janes advice I have taken off the babys flannel skirt tho not her little under shirt. Thee she reminds me of you. (You know how you respire the baby is exactly like you - she always leaves the print of her head on the pillow she is evidently teething - I think you will see quite a change in her - but darling I am not looking as well as I did the first week or two of my stay. I only tell you this for fear of your being disappointed - and my hair is very thin - I expect you will think I am taking rather low views of things - but then I ought to tell you every thing about myself when you come we will face a decission as to whether I should cut it off or not 'tis very poor

[missing page]

with so much interest. When we come back we found tea on the table - they had been waiting for us neither Irvine nor Nora had had any - Aunty says she is going to make me some grape jelly as soon as the grapes come in that's good darling - Mother is going to preserve some for us also - other kinds. Mother got a letter from Mr West to day that I want you to read when you come. I like it very much there are two sides to every question but it seems very unreasonable in her to wish him to leave {?} his business - particularly when they would go North every summer Yesterday evening Mother Anna and I walked over to Auntys - the old people were seated in the piazza they made us stay to tea we had quite a pleasant time - Cousin Charlie drove up just before tea he had not been at home since breakfast very busily engaged in completing some improvement It proved to be a failure - he was going back to undo everything and go back to the old plan - I felt so sorry for him for it must have been so discouraging but he seemed quite cheerful. I do hope he will succeed - Thee the old people enquire of you always

24th Last night all of the Kings including Mr Adams called on us but I was so tired that Mother persuaded me to go to bed and excuse myself. I slept soundly till Anna came to bed which she did taking with her a large palmento fan you have no idea how ludicrous it looks to see her in bed gravely fanning herself in the middle of

[missing page]

Theede I am afraid it will be very warm when you are

travelling you must take good care and not fatigue. I will be almost glad for you to stay the day in Washington 'tho the most tiresome part of the journey is to come after. I will have plenty of cold water in readiness for you and be so glad to see you. Anna seems to anticipate your coming - but Darling I do not think any one could long for another as I do for you - If you see Mama please give my warm love - I suppose you will - Thee the locusts this morning are making a continued buzzing noise, but they have not eaten everything as the papus. Any thing have they seem to take it out in noise, I am so very glad Ann Butler continues good - I hope she will continue good bye my own darling Thee my dearest husband - that you will reach me safely in my earnest hopes and prayers - You have my entire love your own devoted

Mittie

Charles Dunwoody arrived home while Mittie, Martha, Anna, and baby Anna took tea with their cousins. Charles Archibald Alexander Dunwoody (1828-1905), a graduate of Franklin College, now known as the University of Georgia, owned a shoe factory and was a successful merchant. He and his wife Ellen Rice had one daughter, named Rosaline, and probably continued to live with John and Jane Dunwoody who were both in ill health.

New York May [23] 55

Dearest Mittie

I have spent the last half hour trying to find out the exact moment when I will be with you but all in vain. It seems according to the guide book as though none of the Rail Roads connected for any other point than Charleston

(South Carolina) and I have at length closed it with a vague idea that you need not expect me till saturday.

I hope you will be quite well when we meet but am really beginning to doubt whether Roswell air agrees well with you. It would be too bad if what was meant to have done you so much good should prove detrimental. I will be very glad to have charge of you again although I consider you now in very good hands. I was delighted to hear you say you could enjoy yourself in town the rest of the summer but I hope as sincerely as you that we will not be obliged to stay here. Still it is so pleasant to think we are all in all to each other. I was very much struck with this the other evening when I heard Mrs Stebbins talk of going to Newport and having her husband come up on sunday. I could not help drawing a comparison between an absent one and herself which was by no means flattering to her.

George Morris is reported as quite sick and has gone to Saratoga with his sisters to see if it will improve his health. Mrs Stebbins told me that his sweet heart's treatment had worried him almost to death.

I have been visiting the different families tonight; Lizzie Ellis first to return a book containing dinners for each day for a "small economical family." Then to Jim's to know about the carpets; Lizzie advised under present circumstances decidedly having them left down, at least till we returned and had a fixed abode for the summer. next to father's to try to find a two dollar and a half gold piece which as missing out of some money he brought me up. Mrs Sampson was there with Mr Sampson, she giving numerous specimens of her strong mindedness.

I had not paid Mary one visit since your departure and devoted the last hour to her. She is in first rate spirits, but seems to increase visibly. I had a very pleasant talk with her. And now darling one it is twelve o'clock my usual bed hour, I always reserve the pleasure of writing you as much as possible to this time of the evening, it is the quietest and loneliest part of the twenty four hours. Good night dearest. May 24th I am gradually packing up, a more difficult operation than I had imagined. This you will not be astonished at when you see the immense amount of room an enormous great bottle of oil can take up enveloped in an box of double its size to prevent breaking. I devote the majority of my trunk to it. Then come two silks and and what Mary Anne said could be put anywhere, some white bundles for you. These with my unusually large outfit rather fill my trunk & valise; but I will have plenty of roof returning.

This is the last letter I intend writing as I hope to reach Roswell within a day at farthest of the next mail. I feel that I will quite miss it too, it has always seemed such a natural occupation to one since we have been separated. You have found it unnecessary to ask me to write constantly have you not darling?

I wonder in looking back at what I could have had so much to talk about but this ceases to be a wonder when I feel that now there seems to be more than when I penned my first line.

When we meet I wonder if we will talk much, I am almost afraid we will not have anything left unwritten, but then again I feel that I would not want to talk for a while because it would interrupt my kissing a sweet little face that will be laid up against myown. Whose face will that be?

In as much as I got Irvine two knives I hardly know which one to duplicate but have determined that all must be supplied with point knives by this time, and so will bring one as near like his four blade one as I can find. I hope it will prove right.

Your mother and the baby with but one sponge between them I should think must occasionally interfere in

136

their ablutions and I will try to remember getting another one. I bought myself the other day a love of a felt hat which was delightfully cosy to my head and of the finest material; when I reached mother's with it she advised ᵐᵉ to go immediately and buy a straw as she knew this would have to be discarded on my arrival in Roswell. If it must, it must but I will first hear your opinion of it. - now <u>dearest</u> one farewell until we meet. Oh! how I am longing for that meeting. myown dearest darling one good night

Your Own Husband

Theodore

Thee told of the news from New York amidst his expressions of longings for Mittie. His visits with family included Lizzie Ellis Roosevelt, his parents, and probably Mary, wife of Silas Weir. The term "increasing" referred to Mary being pregnant. By 1855, Silas and Mary had two sons, Cornelius in 1847 and Hilborne Lewis in 1850. Roosevelt family trees, however, do not show another birth until 1858.

Thee's purchase of a high quality felt hat would have cost him about $2.00 or about $40.00 in today's currency. Had he purchased a simple straw, the cost would have been greatly reduced to about $2.00 in today's currency.[49] Thee was a wealthy New Yorker and could afford the best the establishments had to offer; however, in previous letters he had discussed with Mittie the need for economy of purchases due to the lack of business for Roosevelt & Sons.

The next letter came from Margaret, Thee's mother, to him in Roswell. Thee had by this date, no doubt, reached Roswell to bring Mittie and Anna home.

New York June 10th 1855

Dear Thee

Two weeks tomorrow since you left, and not one word, I have been made realy uneasy by your silence I can imagine you sick of a fever, the baby ill (particularly as I heard incidently that Nora was failing) or that Mittie required care which you were unwilling to let me hear about, it is a great mistake not to tell me however, for I imagine every thing possible and impossible; we were talking it over last evening, saturday you know, and Mary suggested you might be getting ready to return, particularly as we heard you had written to Savanna for passages to be taken on the first of June, this is realy the case Thee, Mr Wood wrote this whether the mistake of the month is his or yours. I am rejoiced to be able to tell you we have found a refuge for the summer at last, you know I always said I did not despair, we have taken some rooms at the water cure establishment, I have selected one for Mittie, with a smaller for Nora next to her; it is a lovely looking place. Mr & Mrs Emlen visited it yesterday and returned delighted, but Mittie must prepare herself for plain fare, I expect we shall all return in perfect health. James and family, Corneil, Laura and little Maria, you and your Father and myself will complete the party, I think if the others have not engaged their places they would have gone with us. Corneil commences building immediately and as the water cure is only two miles off, it will only be a pleasant little ride over two or three times a day to superintend. We have had a great deal of fun over our prospects, if Mittie had been here she would have contributed her share of wit I have no doubt, I should like to be present when you tell her and to hear her say to Thee how we {____} The girls call it nothing but the Lunatic asylum, and as it will be quite new to us, we expect to enjoy it much. The persons who keep it are very respectable pleasant looking persons. And it has quite a good reputation for comfort and cleanliness. James has visited Washington

138

since you left and heard of you Thee so we know you were safe so far. Father insists it is not time to receive a letter yet. We have not engaged our rooms for any specified time this summer, so that if there is any cause of dissatisfaction we can leave immediately. The children go on as usual, Mary Weir and Corneil have all had symptoms, as well as Lizzie and Leila, Lizzie, Ellie and myself, and servants too many to speak about. None have appeared yet at the water cure may be they are waiting our arrival. Kiss Mittie and the baby for me. Remember me affectionately to Mrs Bulloch and Anna, and please remember me kindly to Mr and Mrs Dunwoody. I regret so much to hear of his declining health. Mr & Mrs West [Hilborne and Susan] came over to see him off, but the poor fellow was dispossessed {?} of his berth, some mistake of the Captain. God bless you my darlings; keep you in safety, and return you to your

Mother

A typical mother, still checking in on her now grown children, Margaret Roosevelt was worried about Thee and Mittie. In this letter, after chiding him for not writing, she also brought him up to date on the family's vacation plans, who would be going, and where the family had taken rooms. James and Lizzie Roosevelt's presence was assured with their two children in tow, Mary and Cornelia. Corneil and Laura, the newlyweds, would also travel with the family, and it seems Corneil was building a home nearby their destination. The identity of little Maria is not known at this time. Mr. and Mrs. Emlen, parents of James' wife Lizzie, had endorsed the facilities following their visit.

Thee arrived in Roswell during the first week of June. He and Mittie returned north with baby Anna. Once again the Bulloch women lived in different homes separated by difficult travel.

Chapter IV
The Second Half
of 1855

Roswell June 29th 1855

My dearest Sister

Every day only makes me long more to be with you. My intense desire to see Bamie is perfectly inexpressible. I keep the little sleeves you cut off and one of her darling little socks all the time in my work basket. Whenever I take them up it gives me a perfectly desolate heartbroken feeling. I do not think this is morbid so I would try to overcome it, but I do not think any one could see and know Bamie and not love her. Mother heard this morning from Mr West. He writes that you are better and look more like your former-self than he has seen you for years. The baby still languid! I do long to hear that it is well. Tell my dear Thee I will write to him next. I am so much obliged to him for his letter to me - Hager has just gotten home and with her your letter written in Savannah - Mother is anxious to hear from Dr Bulloch what kept Hager so long in Savannah. We are exceedingly provoked with her for giving you so much annoyance - Mother says she regrets that she did not just call Hager in before she said any thing to her at all about going on with you and telling her that if your baby was not so sick she would not of course send Hager on but that she did not know - but its life might depend upon it - So she had concluded to take care of Irvine herself while Hager was gone and that she must get ready without any objections

<u>at</u> <u>all</u> and go on - If this course had been pursued nothing would have been thought wrong about it and Hager would have been back at least three days earlier. But you know what negroes are just give them the least liberty and they will be turned by any one from their duties - Of course Mam Jane ~~to as~~ was the sole cause of it all. We did not even hear whether Hager was in Savannah or on the road all this time, poor Henry has been feeling dreadfully all the time and the trial has been as great to him as if Hager had been really faithful. He is indeed a good house servant, and I do not know what Mother and I would do without him. Mother seems well but thinks most seriously of moving North in the fall even if she does not sell the house. It will of course be a great loss to her but what is that, compared to the delight of being near you and Tudie - I am sure, so little do I care for anybody or anything (even Money!!) in this world but my dearest ones that there is no sacrifice of feelings. Comforts, associations, or any thing in this world I would not make to be near you. I will finish my letter in the morning. Saturday morning. Mother and Irvine are out looking at the fig trees - They are perfectly covered with fruit. Barrington King has promised to come and teach me how to seal up some hermetically when they are ripe to send on to you! I will hope it will prove more successful than Mr Wests efforts. I will write you soon a long letter, I would not have put your letter off for the morning knowing how little time we have, but just when I would have written to you Mauma begged me to write to Nancy for her - Mother and Irvine send much love to you and Thee. Good bye my own darling sister how tenderly how intensely I love you and the baby.

Goodbye your sister
Anna Bulloch

Anna's letter gives a glimpse of the family's worry over their slave Hagar during her absence and Anna's feelings about "negroes" in general. Nothing more is known about Hagar, however, *Maum* Jane asked Anna to write to Nancy. This was probably Nancy Jackson who had accompanied Martha and James Stephens Bulloch north to Hartford, Connecticut, in 1832. Nancy had escaped slavery and remained in the north.[50]

Roswell July 20th

My dearest Mittie

On yesterday I returned home from Marietta where I had been to spend a few days - Eva King invited me to go over with them in their carriage and spend one or two days at the Hotel and attend the commencement of the Military institute - I was very glad to go only to hear an oration delivered before the graduating class by Henry Law - It was a most finished and eloquent address - What a regret you feel to see a man so tallented throw himself so completely away - Charlie Way took the first honor, delivered the valedictory - I had no idea he was so intelligent his farewell was really poetic - I did not like to go and leave Mother as I would be absent two nights but she urged me to do so as she had heard of Mrs Burrows (you met at the Sulphur Springs) being in Marietta and she said if I did not go with Eva when she invited me I would have no way of getting to Marietta and she was really anxious to have me call on her and invite them over to visit us. I called on Mrs. Burrows, she seemed quite pleased to see me - Her health is very bad she looks so faded - The little daughter kissed me when her Mother told her I was Miss Mitties sister - Mrs Burrows sent her love very warmly to you - Mrs John E Ward is spending the summer in Mr Jones's place I called on her too - She asked very affectionately after you and sent her love - She questioned me particularly about darling Bamie, and then took me into her room to see her little twins seven or eight months old - They are perfectly lovely, one a noble looking boy, the other a lovely, rather more delicate looking girl - I just kissed and played with them and only longed the more impatiently to see Bam - Mother has seen Tom King - He is to pay cash (six hundred) in the fall for the furniture and rent the House for the two hundred and fifty - Mother made the offer to him which Thee suggested - he did not accede to it but seemed to take it into consideration - He says he will take the best possible care of everything and will make such little improvements from time to time as he feels able to - Mrs Clemens is to spend next winter with Marie and as Senator Clemens never takes his wife to Washington with him and Marie is their only child I think Mrs. Clemens will most probably make this her usual winter home. So I think it more than probable Tom will in a few years be only too glad to take up Mothers offer for it is so tedious to undertake building in Roswell, and property in this vicinity every one thinks will soon be more valuable than it is now - This I believe will be owing to increase of manufactories - I try in vain to imagine dearest little Bamie in her short dresses and little slippers - how lovely she must look - Have you entirely recovered from your cold darling? I suppose dearest Sudie is with you now do kiss her for me - Mr. West has written lately of her having had an attack and refers to it as if we knew all about it - we knew nothing of it our last accounts of her were that she was not well and that the heat had debilitated her - We have had a most delightful summer as far as the climate and all that goes - I never knew it so cool and pleasant - Saturday Morning - Mother received your letter yesterday - I am so sorry dear Bam had a boil I suppose her ear was as carefully tended as when she had the little chafed places behind them. Bam does not like to feel pain at all, her old Aunt is so sorry for her she wishes she could have had it for her - You would be distressed to see Rosa <u>her</u> face is entirely covered with the most loathsome sores! I feel so sorry for her I can not bear to see her - Ellen still pets her and speaks to her in that finikier little way! Mother was delighted with your letter - We looked at your name on the fig leaf yesterday afternoon about sun-set - it has become quite indistinct, and the bush where the little thread is tied is weighed down by fruit - Prayer meeting was here last night and Miss Lizzie Rees and Isa stayed and spent the night with us - Tilly is going up on the first of August from Macon to Cave Springs with Mr and Mrs Rees to visit her friends. I do not know when she is coming to Roswell. I think she might have come when we have written so often and begged her to come, and it is our last summer at home, and when she knows how lonely we are - But I do not believe she would leave Mr. and Mrs. Rees for anything or anybody - Aunt Jane received your letter yesterday also - Poor little <u>Axon</u> is still lingering, although the disease has now reached his heart they fear - I have so much work to do, I sew incessantly from morning to night, and now that Axon is so low, I like to walk up there at least once a day to see how he is - so it really is impossible to call a moment my own - I will write to dear Sudie on tuesday - Mother finds writing so very trying to her eyes I would not let her write so much the last two weeks - I mean to try to write so often to you both that she will not write so much -

Love from all to all -

Good bye, Your own
Anna

Anna's exciting trip to Marietta with Eva King included attending graduation ceremonies for the Georgia Military Institute. Established in July of 1851, the 110 acre grounds included a parade ground, academic building, four student barracks, and a residence for the superintendent. Originally funded by private donations, the State chartered the school in 1852 and presented it with muskets, swords, and a battery of four cannons. The school's extremely strict discipline and academic standards resulted in 50 to 75% of students leaving each year. Union forces destroyed the Georgia Military Institute in 1864 during the Civil War. It never reopened.[51] Charles Way, with whom Anna and Mittie obviously were acquainted, was Charlton Hines Way (1834-1900) of Liberty County, Georgia.[52]

Georgia Military Institute
"The War in Georgia -The Military College, Marietta.
From a Sketch by Capt. D.T. Brown, 20th Conn."
from *Frank Leslie's Illustrated News*

Olivia Buckminster Sullivan (1819-1890) of Boston, Massachusetts, married John Elliott Ward (1814-1902), a young lawyer from Liberty County, Georgia in 1839. By 1856, Olivia had given birth to four sons, all had died before this date. One daughter, Olivia, born in 1849, survived. In 1854, they had twins, John Montfort and Anna Louisa. Their

146

year of birth and age upon Anna's visit helped date this letter to 1855.[53]

As in previous letters, Anna mentioned her half sister, Susan Elliott West's illness. Never, in any of the letters, does a family member specify from what Susan suffers. However, here and there letters provide clues such as her general weakness, inability to stand for long periods, and "attacks" which occurred periodically.

Anna also reveals the illness of *Axon*, a resident at the Dunwoody house next door. A glance at the Dunwoody family tree for the period provides no answer about whom Anna was speaking. Axon could have been a slave child. Ellen was the wife of Charles Dunwoody and their daughter was Rosaline. Visiting Roswell were Miss Lizzie Rees and Isa. Miss Elizabeth *Lizzie* Rees was a spinster whom Anna and Mittie knew from Liberty County, Savannah, and Roswell. As the Rees girls' parents were both deceased, the Mr. and Mrs. Rees Anna mentioned were most likely the Reverend Henry Kollock Rees (1822-1892) and his wife. They resided in Macon, Georgia. Isa was most likely Isabella Pratt (1828-1862), a cousin of the Roswell Pratt family.

Despite Anna's comment that Matilda *Tilly* Rees was unlikely to leave the Henry Rees family, she did marry before the end of 1855. Matilda married the Reverend Francis Robert Goulding (1810-1881). Goulding, a widower, had six children, some over 15 years of age. Goulding served as principal of a boys' school in Kingston, Georgia, at that time.[54] Kingston is located in Bartow County, north west of Roswell.

Martha wrote to Mittie in September about their departure for the north. Her letter provided some details as to their change of residence and travel plans. Anna had again been away from home and had probably been to Tallulah and/or Toccoa Falls, in Rabun County, Georgia. These north Georgia mountain attractions were quite popular as an outing destination.

Roswell Sept 20th

My own precious Mittie

I can just write you a few lines this morning for Sarah over slept herself and did not bring water until six oclock. I received your sweet letter of the 12. I frequently think of the long days you are without any companion except little Bam who although very sweet is not yet very companionable. Anna arrived last evening just before tea. The moon was shining beautifully and Irvine and I were sitting in the piazza when she drove up. I was so glad to see her. She was delighted, dear little thing! to get home again, and to get her letters and hear from you all - She was perfectly charmed with the falls but as she writes you on saturday I will say nothing about it. She was quite surprised to find to find every thing sent except what we will carry with us. I have done all of my troublesome packing now. I expect to be busy helping Susy to get Tillys wedding ready - She is to be married on the 18th of Oct at 5 oclock in the afternoon so as to reach the cars in time which go to Kingston where Mr Goulding resides that same night. Lizzy [Rees] and Miss Rice are both quite excited about it. Mr G has six children, but I suppose Tilly does not mind that. I am going to make a large iced cake, as a present for the wedding - We are all quite well dearest. I will write you again before long. Oh what a shocking accident was that on the Camden and Amboy rail Road! Darling don't travel on that road until they get a double track. Oh how grateful we ought to be that we have all been spared another summer.

How many thousands have been called into eternity while we are spared - Have you read the account of the pestilence in Norfolk, and Portsmouth? I send Anna's letter to me from Clarks ville [Georgia] to amuse you.
Good by darling. Love to Thee and James when you see him.

Your own mother
M Bulloch

The train accident to which Martha referred attracted nationwide attention in September of 1855. No doubt, all members of her family had used this train line on numerous occasions as it was the only one between New York and Philadelphia. The Camden and Amboy Railroad and Transportation Company served this part of the nation beginning in 1840. Their New Jersey State charter allowed them to have a monopoly for this area's rail travel. Although many customer complaints had been lodged against the company for excessive transit duties and track accidents, their term of charter was renewed in 1854 when the company agreed to build a double line of track. This had not been accomplished by 29 August 1855 when a tragic accident occurred.

At 10:00 o'clock on the morning of August 29, 1855, the regular train for New York left Philadelphia on schedule and less than an hour later was waiting at the Burlington station. Here the eight o'clock express from New York, traveling in an opposite direction on the same track, was expected to pass en route to Philadelphia. Learning that the express was behind schedule and still some twenty minutes distant, the conductor nevertheless held his train at Burlington only ten minutes beyond its usual time of departure, in accordance with company regulations, and then at 11:02 pushed on. Within three miles the New York train was sighted, and both halted at once. In order to clear the track for the latter, the Philadelphia train reversed and commenced backing in the direction from which it had come, the nearest turn-out being nearly two miles behind.

It was a moderately windy day and the dust, rising in clouds from the track bed, rendered proper observation by the brakemen and conductor difficult. As the moving train neared Burlington, suddenly a two-horse carriage was seen speeding toward the crossing directly in advance of the backing cars. In an instant the rear car, striking both horses, had been derailed, but the engineer, unaware of what had happened, continued backing his train. After rolling along the embankment for nearly three hundred yards, the lead car, followed by three others, swerved and plunged into the adjacent ditch. Crashing heavily one upon the other, the four wooden coaches were virtually demolished.[55]

Local residents, doctors from Philadelphia, and railroad personnel rushed to help the injured and trapped passengers. Twenty-four passengers lost their lives and between 65 to 100 were injured. Within hours of the crash, an investigative jury of 19 men had been called. Their finding released on 5 September blamed the driver of the carriage, an elderly doctor who survived unharmed.[56] The brakeman, the conductor, and the railroad, stated in part:

Accident on the Camden and Amboy Railroad (as seen in Sinclair 2012).

And the Jurors . . . do further say, that by the "Running Regulations," issued by the said Camden and Amboy Railroad and Transportation Company, the possibility and probability of collision between opposing trains on a single track is so great, as to prove that some efficient means should be adopted to prevent the recurrence of the cause which has called this Inquest together, and that the safety of the passengers in life and limb, is of more importance than the saving of a few minutes of time.[57]

The second tragedy of which Martha wrote struck closer to home. On 7 June 1855, the SS *Benjamin Franklin* arrived from the West Indies to outside the port of Portsmouth, Virginia. Within days, crew members discarded one body illegally and threw the mattress upon which the corpse had lain overboard. Soon afterward, two crewmen jumped overboard to escape what would have been sure death from yellow fever. Their arrival on shore doomed the people of the city, and soon thousands fled the pestilence. Upon the ship's arrival, the port's health officer had boarded the ship to speak with the captain. All in the city knew of outbreaks of yellow fever in the West Indies. The captain assured the officer that the only two deaths had been heat and heart related. Just in case, the port officer ordered the ship into quarantine down river near Craney Island. Eleven days later, the ship was allowed to sail into port for needed repairs.[58]

Within days of the ship's landing, Dr. John Trugien traveled to a house near the wharf. He found the three residents of the home suffering from yellow fever. Officials ordered the *Benjamin Franklin* back into quarantine. This measure proved to be too little and too late. Yellow fever spread

152

quickly through the wharf district of crowded, run-down tenements that housed mostly Irish laborers. Yellow fever is caused by a virus found in tropical and subtropical areas in South America and Africa and is transmitted to people by the bite of an infected mosquito. In 1853, yellow fever had killed more than 8,000 in New Orleans and infected Captain James Dunwoody Bulloch.[59] In 1854, more than 1,000 had died in Savannah from the disease.[60]

In 1855, most people believed the virus spread from person to person. A few doctors and biologists had begun to believe this to be untrue and suspected that filth somehow contributed to the spread of the disease. Attempts had been made in many southern cities, including Portsmouth and Norfolk, to reduce waste in streets and alleys. Within days, wealthy residents of these two cities fled to mountain resorts or further north. Those without means moved to the edges of town, often camping in local woods. New York officials declared the epidemic areas "infected" and barred vessels and persons from entering their city from either of these two ports. Other cities soon followed suit. The ferry between Norfolk and Portsmouth stopped running.[61]

The fever spread throughout the two cities infecting rich and poor alike. Entire families succumbed. Quarantines of the area prevented food, medicines, and any type of relief from entering the cities. Finally, the quarantine was lifted enough for supplies and willing doctors and nurses to enter. The nation's newspapers had reported the dire situation and drawn national sympathy and needed donations.[62]

In Norfolk and Portsmouth, the living buried the dead within hours. A slave John Jones drove a wagon about Norfolk and collected bodies, placed them in coffins, and drove them to the cemetery. A fund was discussed to buy John's freedom, "if he lived."[63]

By the end of August, over 10,000 had fled Norfolk. The few left suffered from shortages of food and fresh water. Civic leaders, doctors, nurses, the clergy, and volunteers worked tirelessly to ease suffering. Many of these also fell to the fever. On one September day, the fever took five doctors. Nearby cities sent coffins by the hundreds. Civic leaders considered moving all from the town to nearby camps in an attempt to thwart the spread of the pestilence.[64]

The few Norfolk city leaders still living by the end of September told the world that the fever was not dying out, it was just running out of victims. It is estimated that "Portsmouth's population was down to 2,200, 2,000 of whom were either battling the fever or recovering." Of the seven Protestant church leaders who had remained in the city, four died. By early October, 20 of the 87 visiting physicians and half of the cities' own doctors had also been taken, including Dr. John Trugien, who had first recognized the fever.[65]

In early October, Portsmouth and Norfolk residents began to return. On 14 October, residents awoke to find a heavy frost that killed off the disease-carrying mosquitoes. Fever deaths now numbered only five to ten per day. Period estimates of the dead listed more than 2,300 in Norfolk, however, that number did not include many hastily buried bodies, servants and slaves, or those who died after leaving town. Portsmouth officially buried over 900 individuals, accounting for one out of every three residents. John Jones, the slave, refused his freedom as he would have been forced to leave town and his enslaved family. Orphaned children by the hundreds needed care. Widowed women were forced into prostitution. Norfolk and Portsmouth became destitute cities for decades. One of the worst epidemics in American history attracted the attention of Martha Bulloch as it did so many Americans throughout the summer and fall of 1855.[66]

This last letter from Martha in Roswell to family in the north suggested their departure from Roswell occurred in the late fall or early December of 1855. Anna's previous letter provided more details about Bulloch Hall's rental by Tom King and his wife Marie. On 5 September, Tom King wrote to George Hull Camp from Roswell about his desire to "go to work housekeeping." This turn of phrase meant that Tom and his wife desired to move out of his parent's house and live independently. Tom rented Bulloch Hall from Martha sometime later that year. In his letter he stated:

> Mrs Bulloch is offered 2500$ or 2700$ credit for Henry and Family. Now I would be a flangy fool to sell my factory Stock and purchase such dead capital. No sir, at such figures I let them slide and will pick up the best I can.[67]

Henry was one of Martha's slaves. He had been with the family for a number of years and served in all sorts of capacities. Nothing is known of his family or what became of them. Tom King, however, realized that slavery would probably end and considered the purchase of slaves as "dead capital." His mention of *factory stock* indicates he held shares of the Roswell Manufacturing Company.

Phil[a] December 28th

My dearest Mittie

Ever since you left I have missed you so dreadfully, that I could not bear to write I felt so low-spirited. our Twilight hours were spent by Tudie, Mother, and me wishing for Bamie. This morning when Mother got your letter Tudie said Oh! I do wish the "tin toe, pinkie," would jump out of the envelop, how delighted the {__} aunties would be. I keep the chair her little clothes were put on at night just where it was when she was here and look at it the last thing at night and first thing in the morning. And I think how it would delight me to see the little shoes and stockings and brush and comb there again. Today Mother and I are going again to the meeting of the Dorcas, society I told you we thought of joining - we went on last friday for the first time and were very much interested. We met Miss <u>Brener</u> {?}, she asked Mother very particularly about you said she was away while you were here or she would have called. Tudie is delighted with brother Jimmie's presents she says she thinks she may find at Baileys now, something that will suit her. I saw there on yesterday a set of pearls handsomer than any I ever saw an entirely new style - Large strands of pearls plaited together in a most graceful form - If Mother gets the black silk (she is delighted with the sample) she will send on by me for you to get it for her. About my dress. I am so much obliged to brother Jimmie for it what made him think of having it made for me? It is so kind is it not? I wish it dark, either what you suggest, the color of yours trimmed as you say, or a cobalt blue trimmed the same way - Mother wishes it blue as it is very becoming to me, but the other might suit the blue in my bonnet best. However I will most frequently wear the maroon with the bonnet, that I now have - I send the length of my dress right in front and just behind. You can keep the dress and the basque of my green silk for me until I come. I long to see you. Mother and I sit in her room in the mornings and talk of Thee and you often and that darling baby - I think I will go on to see you at the same time Miss Lilly and Miss Smith [daughters of Roswell's Archibald Smith] visit New York so as to avail myself of this escort. I will let you know as soon as I hear when Miss Lilly is going. How delightful you have all made buddies [Irvine] visit - we have all missed him very much. I know it will be something for him to always look back upon with delight this <u>first</u> visit to you in <u>New York!</u> Last evening Joe Jones called upon us we found him very pleasant. He asked most particularly about you. I always liked him better than Charles - The Misses Dunlap received seventy!! christmas presents, and were obliged to return them all, to seventy particular friends - there not so <u>very</u> unfortunate to be friendless on such an occasion. Mother and Tudie and Mr West send love to you and Thee - Tell Thee I have commenced to study french in earnest. After I have paid my visit to you I will get a teacher Mr West Tudie and I learn it together and we are not at all sure of our pronunciation. Do kiss my dearest little one for her Auntie. Oh the little velvet feet - I could kiss them over and over again. Mother had a long letter from Uncle John [Dunwoody] - he sent love to you and Thee - Cousin James [Dunwoody] will visit New York very soon and then pass through this city - I am really anxious to see him -

Good bye -

yours dearest Mittie affectionately

Anna

Joseph Jones was the brother of the Reverend Charles Colcock Jones of Liberty County, Georgia. He was studying medicine in Philadelphia. The very lucky Misses Dunlap have yet to be identified.

Martha, Anna, and Susan joined Philadelphia's Dorcas Society, named for Tabitha Dorcas referenced in the Acts of the Apostles.[68] Established in 1816, the Philadelphia society's mission was to provide clothing to the poor; however, they also provided food and money. Dorcas societies reached their zenith of popularity in the 1800s. There are still many in existence today.[69]

Chapter V
1856

The World in 1856

    The start of 1856 began another year of political turmoil between the North and the South. With the disintegration of the Whig Party, two new parties vied for those votes. On 18 February, The American Party (Know-Nothings) convened in Philadelphia, Pennsylvania, and nominated its first presidential candidate, former President Millard Fillmore. On 17 July, the Republican Party opened its first national convention in that same city. This convention nominated Major General and former Senator John C. Frémont of California and former Senator William Dayton of New Jersey for President and Vice President, respectively. The Democratic Party refused to nominate sitting President Franklin Pierce and instead nominated James Buchanan, an experienced politician and the current Ambassador to the United Kingdom.

    The Know-Nothings ignored the issue of slavery and instead focused on anti-immigration and anti-Catholic policies. Frémont, for the Republican Party, opposed slavery and the Kansas-Nebraska Act. The Democratic Party pushed *popular sovereignty* as a method for each state to determine its own status as free or slave. The election went to James Buchanan.

    Advances during the year included the patent of the tin-type camera by Hamilton Smith of Gambier, Ohio.

This camera made photographic images affordable to the masses and created most of the images of the coming era. The Bullochs' home state of Georgia became the first state to regulate railroads. New advancements in fabric dyeing created new colors and processes. Gail Borden (1801-1874) invented and patented a commercial method of condensing milk to preserve it for longer periods of time.

On 30 March, Russia signed the Peace of Paris ending the Crimean War. While Europe enjoyed peace, violence erupted on the home front. On 21 May, Lawrence, Kansas, was captured and sacked by pro-slavery forces. The following day in the U.S. Senate, South Carolina Representative Preston Brooks caned Massachusetts Senator Charles Sumner, a devout abolitionist. Senator Sumner had delivered a two-day speech entitled *The Crime Against Kansas,* which blamed the South for violence occurring in that state. Only some of what he said was true and his specific target was Senator Andrew P. Butler of South Carolina, who was not present during Sumner's speech. He accused Butler of being the instigator of the Kansas situation describing him as the "squire of slavery, its very Sancho Panza, ready to do its humiliating offices." Sumner denounced the Kansas-Nebraska Act and all who had sponsored it. In the Senate, only the extreme abolitionists supported Sumner's ideas, and many moderates considered his speech to be un-American and inflammatory. Butler's nephew, Congressman Preston Brooks, attacked Sumner with a cane while he was seated at his desk in the Senate chamber. The severe beating left Sumner unconscious, and rendered him incapable of resuming his duties. Brooks, on the other hand, became a Southern hero. A pending resolution of censure in the House of Representatives caused him to resign; however, his home state of South Carolina unanimously re-elected him. Sumner, lauded as a near martyr, also received re-election; however, he was unable to resume his seat until late in 1859.

The 1856 Letters

As 1856 dawned, the letter writers continued old friendships and activities as new relationships developed. Significant changes occurred in the later part of 1855 when Martha moved with her remaining unmarried children to Philadelphia. It is doubtful she "took up housekeeping," but instead rented rooms for her family. Early 1856 found Anna and Irvine in Philadelphia either living with or near Susan and Hilborne West. Irvine attended school at Dr. Faire's Classical Institute (Philadelphia). Martha visited at this time in New York with Mittie and Thee.

April 29

My dearest Susy,

I received your little note last evening - darling I was glad to hear from you - I am quite well and go out every day for exercise Yesterday I got in an omnibus and went down to Stewarts to match some silk for Mittie, but I rode the most of the way back also, so did not fatigue myself - Mittie is, I hope, getting well She would be better but is at present suffering from a boil - I do not think she will be able to go to Phil[a] until the second or third week in May - I am very anxious to get home although unwilling to leave her, but she seems so averse to my leaving her, that I scarcely know what to do - You will perceive by the letter which I send you that Stuart [Brother Dan] expects to be back by the tenth of May, on his way to Europe. What a changeable creature! If he is here on the tenth and expects to spend a week with Mittie then it will be the seventeenth at least before she could leave - I cant tell yet how it will be arranged - She is very weak still - scarcely able to walk from the lounge to the bed - I long to see you all It was a great treat to see Hill. I could leave Mittie now, and return - but she is too weak to take Bamie [Anna Roosevelt about 14 months old] back in her room, and Bridget could not be trusted with her entirely at night - She sleeps in the room which opens into mine, so that I can have some supervision of her - The little thing is delicate & is now very restless cutting more teeth - Three have come out since I have been here and the fourth is nearly through - Then she will have to cut four jaw teeth which are now swollen - when those are through, she will have twelve teeth - I am quite uneasy about her back - there is something wrong there - She cannot stand more than a second on her feet then her countenance expresses pain, and she seems to crumble down - She eats butter and hominy very well - took a good saucer full nearly this morning - I am glad Anna likes the things - Tell dear Irvine I like him to play but that he must try to improve Perhaps after a while he will become more fond of reading - I am so glad you have got the book-case and that you are pleased with it - Do you go to the new Church? and has Mr. Bruce come? - Mittie sends much love I have been delighted lately reading The life and writings of McCheyne He was a lovely and warmhearted Christian - Oh what a delightful prospect to spend Eternity in such society - Darling I think I have enjoyed much peace of mind lately from the sweet hope (I dare not say assurance) that I am washed in the precious blood of Atonement - I pray continually that I may not deceive my self - I think I feel more than I ever did that my whole nature is {d-} and that if I ever am saved it will be because my Savior died to save me - The blessed plan of salvation seems to be more and more unfolded to me - and the more I see of it, the more I think I feel like taking my place in the dust - Love to my dear Anna Hill and my precious little boy - I have had some talk with dear James [Dunwoody Bulloch] about his soul - and I have loaned him your Keth on Prophecy James is a lovely young man - He only lacks religion to make him perfect -

Your affectionate mother
M Bulloch

At age 56, Martha continued to be a vibrant and worldly woman. She resided in New York City, had a variety of reading interests, was a loving and caring grandmother, and doted on her remaining children. Martha went to the very popular A.T. Stewart's Dry Goods Store to match Mittie's silk. Opened in 1846 by Irish immigrant A.T. Stewart, the store served New York's affluent residents, offering such luxuries as a lady's shawl for $2,000. Located at the corner of Broadway and Reade, Stewart's sat on the block where the most fashionable promenaded to be seen and to see the goods and luxuries New York's merchants had to offer. A. T. Stewart became the city's richest resident as his store profited nearly $2 million annually during the Civil War.[70]

Martha's reading choices included Robert Murray McCheyne (1813-1843), a Scotsman and minister, who dedicated his life to the Scottish church and its congregations. A renowned Hebrew scholar and missionary, he co-wrote several tomes including *Narrative of a Mission of Inquiry to the Jews* (with Dr. Andrew Bonar) and *The Eternal Inheritance: the Believer's Portion, and Vessels of Wrath fitted to Destruction, two Discourses*. The book on prophecy she loaned Brother Jimmie was probably Alexander Keith's *Evidence of the Truth of the Christian Religion Derived from the Literal Fulfillment of Prophecy*. Keith (1792-1880), a Church of Scotland minister, wrote several books on Biblical prophecy. Martha, a spiritual woman, wrote many times in the coming years of her strong religious beliefs.

This letter from Martha provides historians one of the first indications that Anna *Bamie* Roosevelt had a physical condition which caused her great pain and hindered her movement. Little Anna was a little over one year of age at this time. *Bamie: Theodore Roosevelt's Remarkable Sister* states that "she had been dropped in her bath as a very small baby, and her spine had been injured."[71] Several family sources indicate that at age three she could barely walk, and her father carried her everywhere. Other sources, including Theodore Roosevelt's (Sr.) journal indicate Bamie had suffered Pott's disease, leaving her with a curved spine. This form of tuberculosis occurs outside the lungs and affects the vertebrae, a kind of tuberculous arthritis of the intervertebral joints. As an adult Bamie often touted the dropped baby story; however Pott's disease appears to be the real cause of her affliction.[72]

Beginning in early May, Thee took what could only be considered a business trip across the Midwest. He visited a number of cities by train and sent letters home to Mittie quite often.

Pittsburgh May 13th 56

Dearest Mittie

It seems as if I have been travelling ages since I left you, I have been so continually on the go. I was very much surprised to hear from Mr Emlen on my arrival in Phil[a] that Mary was on the point of starting for New York. I posted immediately to 366 Walnut St and had a very pleasant little talk with Mary & Susan, but found my expected valise all packed with Mary's things. Hilborne had lost the key of his or I think I might have taken it as a substitute.

I reached Susans between five and six and passed a delightful evening there, indulging in not less than six cups of tea. D[r] Jones [also] passed the evening there. About ten o'clock Hilborne and myself started out with my trunk between [us] and carried it to the La Pierre house before we found a carriage. I never appreciated the length of the walk before. At eleven the cars started but from a very unnecessary detention did not arrive here until six this evening. All today through the most beautiful scenery that any railway in our cou[n]try traverses.

I met some acqua[in]tances on the route among whom was a Mr Steele from St Paul who Jim knows, with whom I have passed this evening. He is a very pleasant companion.

Mr Mc Cauley of this place a friend of Mr Jackson's asked me to take tea with him tonight which invitation I certainly would have accepted had I not fasted since breakfast time. The cars stopped nowhere for dinner. Mr Mc Cauley wishes me to drive out with him tomorrow and I will do so if I finish my business in time. I leave tomorrow afternoon for Cincinnati.

It seemed almost like a second parting from home to leave them all in Phil[a].

They were all so much interested in all the little incidents connected with either Bammie [yourself] or your mother.

I amused them by an account of your mother's losses in the spectacle line and how mildly she gave herself up to listening to the sermon. I hope you are still improving and look forward quite anxiously for your first letter. I would preach a little homily again upon the necessity of care did I not know you would laugh at me for it, and so I have to trust to your remembering your promise to me.

You must not forget it for one moment while I am away.

Little Bammie seemed positively glad to get rid of me when I went away and I know so well has shown no contrition for her conduct since.

Give her a kiss from me as I know that is the only punishment her grand-mother will let you inflict.

I have not changed any part of my dress since leaving you and you can imagine how I would enjoy a warm bath tonight (before going to bed) in ourown bath tub. I intend trying to get one here but am afraid it is too late and even if it is not know I will not enjoy it. What would I not give for one like I used to take at the Water barn last summer?

Both my miserable apologies for candles are burning down in their sockets Mittie and although I do not feel sleepy I know I ought to go to bed. I wish I could kiss you for good night I wonder if you would say "I'm so sleepy Thee".

Remember me always Mittie darling
Your loving husband
Theodore

In Philadelphia, Thee visited several relatives. George Emlen was James Alfred Roosevelt's brother-in-law. George was a wealthy Philadelphia merchant. Thee also visited Susan West, his sister-in-law, and her husband Hilborne. Hilborne's sister Mary West Roosevelt was visiting them as well. Dr. Joseph Jones of Liberty County, Georgia, brother of the Rev. Dr. Charles Colcock Jones, studied medicine at the Medical College of the University of Pennsylvania. He graduated in 1856 and returned to Liberty County to practice.[73] The Jones, Elliott, and Bulloch families had remained friends for several decades. At this time, Hilborne also attended medical school at the Jefferson Medical College of Pennsylvania.

Thee and Hilborne carried Thee's trunk to Lapierre House Hotel, one of the most prominent in Philadelphia at the time. Many publications touted it "as the most luxurious hotel in America."[74] In 1903, Theodore Winthrop wrote:

> At sunrise we were at the station in Philadelphia, and dismissed for an hour. Some hundreds of us made up Broad Street for the Lapierre House to breakfast. When I arrived, I found every place at table filled and every waiter ten deep with orders. So, being an old campaigner, I followed up the stream of provender to the fountain-head, the kitchen. Half a dozen other old campaigners were already there, most hospitably entertained by the cooks. They served us, hot and hot, with the best of their best, straight from the gridiron and the pan. I hope, if I live to breakfast again in the Lapierre House, that I may be allowed to help myself and choose for myself below-stairs.[75]

Cincinnati May 15th 56

Dearest Mittie

I had hoped to write you a few more lines from Pittsburg but was obliged to start scarce having time to write Jim a scrawl which I wanted him to get immediately.

The latter part of the time there was spent with M[c] Cauley to whom I before alluded; he insisted as soon as I had concluded my business in taking me in his carriage to see the "ly[i]ons" of the place. One was the nail factory compared to which the manufacture of sausages from alive pigs was nothing. The bars of iron were supplied as rapidly as men

167

Lapierre House, Philadelphia, circa 1865.

Jefferson Medical College, Philadelphia.

could supply them and in a few second's time dropped down nails ready for use.

The rolling mill adjoining this was the most beautiful.

To see enormous hunks of white hot iron rolling out like fiery serpants and the people all handling them as if they had charmed lives.

We also visited the flint glass factory and saw them manufacturing bottles with a miraculous speed. I blew a bubble of glass about three feet long and a foot through of which I enclosed a little specimen which I presume was much smaller before it reached Jim, to show the extreme thinness. Some was so thin that it almost floated in air.

Mr McCauley was extremely polite to me during my stay; I wish you would ask Jim to mention it to Mr Jackson as I know he will like to hear it; and of course he only showed me the politeness on Mr Jackson's account.

Since my arrival here I have received your little note and read it over more than once my own little darling one. I do hope that cold will not be a bad one, I wish I was with you to see that you took good care of yourself.

I am just as busy as I can be all the time, so that I am scarce able to write even these few lines, but on the long trips in the Rail R^d cars, alone among the crowd, I do a great deal of thinking about myown little home and often try to fancy what the different inhabitants are engaged doing. I will travel all tonight again and reach St Louis as I have hoped so as to spend sunday there.

Yours Ever
Theodore

Despite the information presented by Thee about his visit to Pittsburgh, identification of the rolling mill, nail factory, and glass works was impossible. *The History of*

Allegheny County, Pennsylvania, Vol. 1,[76] had no mention of a Mr. McCauley, but did list more than five nail factories and numerous glass manufacturers including, two that specialized in flint glass. The term, "flint glass" refers to a better quality and clarity of glassware. Perfected in England, glassmakers added powdered flint to the glass formula to improve clarity. Further research revealed a Mr. William McCully who owned five glassworks and several other businesses in Pittsburgh. Surely, this was the man Thee met who so kindly showed him some of the many factories of the city, all of which he no doubt owned.

William McCully never had much formal education and learned the glass trade as a young boy while working in a glass factory. By the time Thee visited Pittsburgh, McCully owned the Pittsburgh Glass Works, Sligo Glass Works, Empire Glass Works, and Phoenix Glass Works. He employed almost 500 people. The various works produced window glass, vials, demijohns, jars, flint glass, and black and green bottles.[77]

WM. McCully & Co. Glass Works
return address stamp.

St Louis Saturday night
[May 17ᵗʰ, 1856]

My own Dearest Mittie

I do long to see you tonight I am so glad to think that this is the farthest limits and that now every day will bring me nearer home. To day commenced with a heavy rain and all the incidents connected with it partook of a gloomy character. I had been looking forward to a quiet sunday in St Louis and upon arriving at the Planters House found no room without <u>one</u> occupant. I was given some hopes of getting one after dinner and as your letter was to be directed there I determined to wait a short time at least. Fortunately, as in all my stoppages I was soon so busy as not to have much time to dwell on my troubles. Mr Merir who I called to see at his store said he would offer me a room in his house was he not just "turned upside down" by the painters I am disposed to believe this speech intended, as there was no possible call upon him to make it. I had once taken tea at his house in Bremen.

After dinner I found there was no chance for my having a room to myself and I could not make up my mind to pass sunday with anyone else in my room and so wandered out to another hotel in which I am now ensconced.

Just before leaving the Planters your letter came which improved my spirits materially, it was so pleasant to feel that one person was thinking of me probably at the very moment that I was reading it for I knew you must miss me then; it was just between six and seven o'clock.

I was very sorry about your cold and I do hope it will not get any worse, but I will not talk to you any more about taking care of yourself as I hope to be with you a few days after this letter and be able to insist upon your doing so in person.

171

I will not probably write you again unless something which I cannot anticipate should interfere with my reaching you by next saturday. You must be very glad to see me when I come.

I am sorry about the Tuckers but it did not come with a very severe shock as I had all the time thought our arrangement rather an unsettled one and had not formed the very highest of opinions of Mr Tucker.

I hope Lizzie Emlen was perfectly satisfied with the arrangement, would she not sooner have her servants down stairs as she has the young baby? There is one comfort about it all that Lizzie ^{Ellis} always seemed to think our present rooms the pleasantest.

The Emmetts I suppose are the sister and mother of the Dr Emmett who spent one evening with us and whose wife invited us to a "tea-fight" once.

One of these days Mittie we must take a trip out here together not at the race-horse speed at which I have been going but as I went when I was here before.

Even now I cannot help being struck by the beauty of the scenery. The most beautiful was along the valley of the Juniatta which you may remember hearing me describe as having passed through with Rob in a canal boat. There are plenty of beautiful spots by the banks of the Ohio along which the RR^d runs for miles, but what gave everything its especial beauty to me was the way in which the flowers seemed to grow while you looked at them and the grass sprung up apparently while we were passing over it. Today there were numerous wild flower bouquets in the hands of the different people in the cars.

Do give a very great deal of love to mother from me I hope she is better again. Give my love to the others of the family and to yourown mother.

172

I have left little Bammie out, for I know long before this she has ignored the existence of a father.

Good-bye my-own dearest wife

Yourown Husband
Theodore

As Theodore continued his journey west, he wrote to Mittie about the beauty of the Ohio River Valley and the Juniata River area. The Juniata is a tributary of the Susquehanna and is located in central Pennsylvania. Upon reaching St. Louis, Thee tried to check in to the Planters House, the most expensive hotel in town. He had expected to stay there, as noted by his mail being delivered to that address. However, the hotel was full and he did not wish to "share" a room. The Planters House, which opened in 1817 on 2nd Street, occupied at this time a larger structure at Fourth and Pine which had opened in 1841. The newer structure had 300 rooms on four stories with shops and offices on the ground floor. The room rate per person included four meals a day. "Professor" Jerry Thomas served as the head bartender and was the first to write a cocktail book, which was published in 1862.[78]

Juniata River near Huntingdon
by John Hows.

On the Juniata by Currier and Ives.

New York May 17th

My own dearest Thee

I feel as tho I could not wait another minute to see you - Jim [Roosevelt] said the other night that he thought you would be home before the time you had appointed namely saturday week. I miss you in every thing - Mother received a letter from Anna this morning mentioning your visit to them on monday - I ^{have} received no letter from you as yet - I felt quite disappointed not to get one by Jim yesterday evening for I had surely expected one - I am in a great deal of trouble at present - I dismissed Bridget [Bamie's nurse] this morning - to leave on the first of June and I sup pose I shall have to advertise for a nurse - and that immediately I am going to try and get Mary Roosevelt to help me - I wish you were here my darling one I hope you will never leave me again. I dreamed again that you were attentive and loved some one else. Mother yesterday went to the first meeting of the General Assembly (old school) in Dr Phillips church - and was delighted - by {___} this morning she read the accounts of both the meetings in the morning ~~prayers~~ papers - and is now getting ready for church this morning -

Thee Lizzie Ellis has staying with her that cousin she found last summer living in or near New Rocheile - four children accompany her - the piazza is one wild scene of broken toys, dirt, confusion and tears, each one gets hurt constantly - and worst of all the nurse is a rude country boor - only think they have been <u>there since monday</u>, Brother [Daniel Stuart Elliott] is perfectly quiet plays his flute almost all the morning but is very comical. Mr Hutchison paid us two visits one when we were not at home - he thinks it is very strange that you do not take me to Europe - he says I want a complete change of air - he thinks as Father is rich you and I can do any thing we want - all merely depending upon inclination one way or the other, I hope I will hear from you to day - I have worked all your shirts dearest - Bamie is very sweet but has bad nights that is she wakes very often - she never eats any thing now -

Your own wife
Mittie Roosevelt

St Louis Sunday 1856
[May 18th, 1856]

Dearest Mittie

Every thing looks bright again out side and while I look out at the beautiful sky and hope you are getting well under an equally propitious one I cannot help trying to communicate my thoughts and feelings to you even if only for the feeling it gives me, as I can scarce hope that my letter will reach you much before myself. The birds are all singing delightfully around and while my prospect is by no means a very entertaining one prinᶜipally composed of bricks and mortar there is one little spot in which a fawn is enclosed that allows me to realize that I am still in the "great west."

We had quite a good sermon this morning from a Mr Rice who I went to hear principally because I was under the impression I had heard your mother speak of him. Next sunday I hope we will be able to go together, for I have fully made up my mind that you will be quite strong and robust by the time I get back. next saturday! it does not seem long when I reason quietly upon the subject, only six more days but somehow when I know I could reach you in two I feel very strongly disposed to do it. My business has given me in some particulars too a little more trouble than I had expected, and I find myself about to enter into an arrangement here which bids fair it seems to me to be advantageous but which I would like very much to consult Jim a little about. However I have got to do as I think best and trust entirely to myown judgment. I am perfectly well satisfied that the trip eventually will prove to be a very advantageous one, but in some particulars I think Jim expected larger immediate results.

I was on the point of longing for you to be with me here this lovely afternoon but upon looking round the room I fear you would not be very grateful for the wish. The walls of my room all have the sombre look often caused by age but I fear in this particular instance caused by a want of regularity in the attention paid to her duties by whoever has charge of keeping them clean. The bureau was intended to represent mahogany perhaps but a smoky look is all that remains, and I am obliged to sit every time that I brush my hair in order to get a glimpse of myself in the glass that hangs over it, being evidently intended for a youth four feet high.

I turn to describe the bed with still more painful feelings as reminiscences of last night spent there creep over me. In the first place I had to take the oath of the water that the sheets were clean and then had an uneasy feeling all night which I tried to apply to a lively imagination running upon certain small animals of which the appearance of the bed was suggestive. I had never thought of all this as anything especially disagreeable until I thought of it in connection with you, but I am afraid my poor little wife would not feel equal especially at present to putting up with the occasional discomfort of Western travel. I do hope however she will try to accustom herself to taking matters as easily as possible, for if I should have to go again I would want her and I hope she would want to be my companion. And now dearest one I must bid you good bye until we meet in New York, Oh for one glimpse into 33 E 20th St. to see how you all are passing the afternoon!

Your Husband
Theodore

One final 1856 letter gives an update on where the family resided and stories related to friends and family. Martha wrote to Mittie much later in the year from Philadelphia, where she then resided with Susan and Hilborne.

Philadelphia Nov. 21

On wednesday morning my dearest Mittie I received your very interesting letter - It was before Hill went to the medical College, and he and Susy both asked me to read it out. I did so and you would have been amused to see how much interested we all were - Susy says your letters are always interesting - When we came to that part about Mr Hutchison and the accident we all had one feeling - pity for him - I know it made him feel most awfully - I suppose the accident is almost magnified into a crime in his eyes - I suspect you and Anna thought immediately "Mursay"!!

[slang for Mercy] Now as Mr Morris' wedding is over you will have some respite from the gaiety. Anna will find it very dull in Philadelphia after all of that fun and frolic - Was Lieut Bent agreeable? (M H D) I anticipate Anna's return to hear her account of every thing - I have been thinking a great deal of dear James - I hope he loves that lady - of all things I think marriage without love must be the most uncomfortable. It must be particularly so, to one of James' genial and affectionate disposition - I intended writing you yesterday darling, but I went to Church in the morning, and Virginia and Dr King dined with us and stayed until nine o clock nearly in the evening - They appeared quite delighted with their visit and were very pleasant - Virginia expects to be confined the first of February and is quite busy making up her little things - She has just finished furnishing a nursery basket, which she lined and fixed herself - She says Marion [Dunwoody] is in excellent health and has improved in appearance most wonderfully - That she has every thing her own way, and that your uncle John does not thwart her in anything - The consequence is that every thing relative to the house etc is stylish and bountiful - I went directly after I received your letter on wednesday morning to the Depository and enquired of Mrs Sturtevant what your work would cost - She said the linens would be one dollar thirty seven and a half cents a piece and the quilt $3.50^{cts} When they are done, shall I have them sent by the express, or keep them until some of us go to New York? - If Anna can bring the bonnet I should like her to bring it - Thank you my darling for the nice present - I am concerned to hear that dear little Bamie, eyes are still inflamed - Do when you write tell me if her eye teeth are nearly through - Perhaps they keep up the inflammation - Poor little darling! I do feel very uneasy about those eyes - I do not like those white specks appearing on the pupil - Darling how sad the news about

Mary Cooper - Poor young thing! I hope she may live - I am afraid dear child you will scarcely be able to read this note - My eyes, not good at the best, have been unusually bad lately from cold taken in them - They remind me constantly of my dear little baby - Oh how I wish she could get well of all of her ailments - Susy and Hill send much love - write me when ever you can - I am always delighted to get your letters -

Your affectionate Mother
M Bulloch

Tell dear little Maiden I long to see her I know she must have looked nicely in that white muslin.

Identifying persons mentioned in the Bulloch letters often leads to fruitless searches of books, archives, online resources, and other reference materials. The more information learned about a person sometimes made the search easier. However, searching for Dr. George Morris had for years proved to be a lost cause. Despite added details such as his sisters' names (Josephine and Fanny), his residence in Yonkers, his ties to South Carolina, and his European trip in the early 1850s, he proved elusive. Only in this letter, where Martha mentions his wedding, did we (the authors) identify the man, as his date of death was uncovered in a later letter. George came from an old South Carolina family and was born on 29 December 1829 at The Grove, St. Paul's Parish, Charleston County, South Carolina, and christened George Washington Morris. He had at least two younger sisters, Josephine Matilda born in 1831, and Sabrina, apparently called Fanny, born in 1833. On 23 October 1856, he married Alice Matilda Watts (1832-1891) in Oaklands, Roanoke County, Virginia. It is possible that Mittie and Thee attended the wedding.[79]

Martha also commented on Mary Cooper, actually Mary Cowper Stiles Low, who married Andrew Low of Savannah in 1854. Mary gave birth to Catherine Mackay Low in 1855 and an unnamed child on 8 November 1856, who died one day later. Apparently, Mary was quite ill. She did recover and had three more children including Mary in 1859, William MacKay in 1860, and Jessie in 1862. Mary Stiles Low died in 1863. Many years later, her son William married Juliette Gordon, the founder of the Girl Scouts of America.

Martha, Susan, and Hill visited with Dr. William Nephew King and his wife, Caroline Virginia Way. William had already studied medicine at the New York College of Physicians and Surgeons, followed by a three year stay in Paris where he studied surgery. In 1858, he graduated from Hahnemann Medical College in Philadelphia, where he studied homeopathic medicine. He was also an allopathic physician, a system of medicine that combats disease by using remedies, such as drugs or surgery, which produce effects that are different from or incompatible with those of the disease being treated. William's schooling explains their residence in Philadelphia at this time. Virginia expected the birth of their second child in February of 1857. Their first child Mary Hartford was born in Roswell in 1852. However, family records do not list another child, a boy named for his father, until 2 January 1858. The fate of Virginia's unborn child, mentioned in Martha's letter, is lost to history.

Chapter VI
1857

The World in 1857

On 4 March, President James Buchanan, a Democrat from Pennsylvania, took office. Only two days later, the U.S. Supreme Court ruled Africans cannot be U.S. citizens. In *Dred Scott v. John F.A. Sandford* the court ruled (7–2) that a slave who had resided in a free state and territory was not thereby entitled to his freedom; that Africans were not and could never be citizens of the United States; and that the Missouri Compromise (1820), which had declared free all territories west of Missouri and north of latitude 36°30, was unconstitutional. The decision pushed the country ever closer to civil war.

On 12 March, Elizabeth Blackwell opened the New York Infirmary for Indigent Women and Children, the first of its kind to care for the city's unfortunate. On 23 March, Elisha Otis installed his first elevator at 488 Broadway in New York City. Citizens of New York enjoyed the opening of Central Park, often visited and enjoyed by the Roosevelt children in the coming years.

In April, Gustave Flaubert published *Madame Bovary*. William Makepeace Thackeray published *The Virginians: A Tale of the Last Century*, a historical novel and sequel to his *Henry Esmond*.

Sewing machines became readily available all over the United States, and the latest fashion fad, the bustle, was patented by Alexander Douglas. Joseph Gayetty marketed toilet paper as a mass-produced product which came rolled and dispensed from a box. The product proved a financial failure as most Americans refused to pay for the product when old newspapers and catalogs could be used at no cost. The year also saw the introduction of pink lemonades where natural juices such as grenadine, cherry juice, red grapefruit juice, grape juice, cranberry juice, strawberry juice, and pomegranate were added to lemonade to make it pink. A more important patent proved to be the Brown truss, a type of bridge truss, used in covered bridges.

On 24 August, the Panic of 1857 occurred and continued as one of the most severe economic crises in U.S. history. Additionally, the panic started the first world-wide economic crisis. The sinking of the SS *Central America* contributed to the panic as New York banks were awaiting a much-needed shipment of gold. Then banks and businesses failed; the railroad industry experienced financial declines and laid off hundreds of workers. American banks did not recover until after the Civil War.

The 1857 Letters

The beginning of 1857 found Mittie again without Thee and missing him terribly. The next two letters centered around family events including a wedding. Mittie, left on her own with only her mother for adult company, entertained and made social calls on numerous people. Quite often, Roosevelt family members including her sisters-in-law Lizzie Emlen and Mary, brothers-in-law Jim and Rob, and her mother-in-law Margaret, whom she calls *Mother,* played a role in her solitary life's events.

My own dear Thee

I was really ashamed to send that letter to you yesterday - but know my dearest could excuse, shall I say almost every thing so my darling is not very lenient - When will you come. I cannot do without you Mother does everything in her power to interest me But when night comes I would give anything just to throw my arms around you and kiss you over and over - I hope I shall get the telegraph Monday telling of your safe arrival in New Orleans I feel anxious to know about the voyage if you were very sea-sick etc - I hired a carriage on last Thursday (Lizzie & Mary had Chrystie) to pay a few visits - Ginnie Mitchell had called again to say good bye - and I know you would not like my not going to see her - she leaves on this Monday. Thee you gave me no idea of how very elegant Mrs Smiths house is inside I think it more magnificent than any I have ever seen in New York. both Ginnie and Mrs Smith were very cordial and pleasant - Sister Mary and Weir wanted me to go with them to the Charity ball at the Opera house. but I did not go. they were going in full dress to be on the floor had they been going as meer lookers on I should have gone but would have felt lonely without you mixing in with the company - Rob Lizzie and Miss Thompson went I heard from Rob they had enjoyed themselves very much - he had met Mrs {Lot___} he asked her to dance (there were two bands) and said she looked very much as if she wanted to altho she refused. he also met the Thomas and in fact every body he knew. Every body seems to have gone - I have called upon Mrs Garrelson and the Primus from New Rochelle who have come in ~~from~~ for the winter they seemed very

183

glad to see me. I called at the Hollinders too - I have not caught a glimpse of Tommy Morris lately tho I heard of him as going to this ball I told you last night Family and Mrs Morris were to spend the evening with me - we had quite a pleasant evening. I laid the supper table my self entirely - Mother thought it looked very prettily - Jim and Father did the honors of the table. Lizzie and Miss Thompson could not come in being too tired from the previous nights fatigue - Rob I sent in for he came when we were nearly done supper but was very radiant and pleasant - when we left the room I offered Jim and Rob some of <u>your cigars</u>! they staid and I believe smoked Rob staid some time after the others left and gave me quite an animated account of the ball and also of a party given by Mrs Ward on the first of the week by the way Thee Mrs Ward called here when I was out one morning - left a message - saying she had no card with her but inviting us to spend the evening with her - and that for particulars I must send in to Mrs Robert Roosevelt and this she would explain - I thought it was a very impolite way of making an acquaintance, however I sent in to Lizzie's and found it was to be a large Musical party. I wrote a formal regret giving as an excuse your absence from the city.

Darling I cannot write any more to day as it is saturday - my back pains and I wish to try and get rested before time today for dinner - Bammie when ever she wakes in the night calls out "Papa" "Papa" I have told her that you have gone in the big ship with Uncle Jimmie she says "oh" she is every day more interesting - her eyes still have the white spots - but are very much better of the inflammation I will write again on monday.

your own affectionate wife
Mittie Roosevelt

Captain James Dunwoody Bulloch, Mittie's half brother, now commanded the SS *Cahawba*, a large side-wheel steamer under the ownership of the New Orleans Steamship Company. During his regularly scheduled trips from New York to New Orleans, James met and fell in love with the 26-year-old widow Harriott Cross Foster (1829-1897) of Plaquamine Louisiana, located near Baton Rouge. Daughter of U.S. Army Major Osborne Cross[80] and the former Julia Louise Duvall von Schaumburg, Harriott had three siblings. Her sister, Annette, married Captain S. Grosvenor Porter, brother of Laura Porter Roosevelt, Cornelius' wife. According to the 1850 U.S. Census, Harriott lived with Jessee and Mary Hart of West Baton Rouge with her new husband Joseph Foster. Harriott and Joseph had married on 19 December 1849.[81] Little is known about Joseph Foster including his death date, although several sources list him as a planter.[82] The U.S. Census of 1850 shows Joseph's occupation as "none."

James married Harriott on 23 January 1857 with Thee in attendance, as he must have considered this not only the marriage of a "brother" but also that of a friend. Two days later, Thee wrote to Mittie about the wedding and like many of us do today, forgot a new year had begun and dated his letter incorrectly.

Mississippi River Jan 25th 56

Dearest Mittie

I find myself obliged to retrace mysteps to New Orleans and write this in considerable doubt whether I will not be obliged to return at last by sea with Brother Jimmie. The rivers are blocked up with ice and unless I hear positively that it has broken through I will not run the risk of spending an extra week on board the boat going up.

The wedding has passed off delightfully and I have enjoyed everything to the full limit. We started up the river found our pasages and state-rooms all engaged, and ourselves decidedly lions. At ten next morning we arrived at Plaquamene and having an energetic agent on the spot succeeded in getting two two horses vehicles ready by two in the afternoon when ^{we} left for Mr Heart's place. The roads were execrable but the party was a pleasant one and we were all as fresh as larks when we arrived at 10 <u>PM</u>. There we received a very hearty welcome and in about half an hour a haunch of venison a quantity of birds hot coffee wild ducks and fixings were arranged for us to fall on.

Next morning I was introduced to sister - Harriott. She has light hair blue eyes and the ordinary peculiarities of a blond, but is dependent more on expression for her pleasant appearance than on anything else. Her figure is very tall but not awkward and she is what I think would be termed a fine looking woman by this casual observer. She calls me brother Thee and I think is one we will all learn to like exceedingly. They were married at one in the morning so as to have it over before the company arrived; the bride's dress was very simple when married and she came on in the evening in a very pretty blue dress of some material unknown, wearing her pearls which she desired me to thank you for. I went out on horseback on her favorite horse in the afternoon went through a cane-break and after visiting the sugar houses returned in time to make the salad which I claimed my right as one of the family to do. They had two dishes of each lobster and chicken and celery to match and with ^{two} black assistants I set to work; while I was engaged mixing the salad I told one of them to mix up the celery with the lobster & chicken, when I had brought my salad to a consistincy imagine my horror on turning round to find that was but one dish a conglomeration of chicken lobster

186

and celery. The blackey had mixed them all up together. It was two late to remedy it and Mrs Hearts being one of those nice old ladies that take things easily she agreed in the propriety of putting on the dressing and saying nothing about it. I received twenty or thirty compliments upon my dressing some having eaten ^{it as} chicken some as lobster salad. I was perfectly quiet about it till next morning. Next day we started off with three carriages for our own party and an ox cart drawn by three pair of mules which was meant for the baggage. As it soon got so heavy going as to make it doubtful if the horses could carry us through we all took to the oxcart except brother Jimmie and the two ladies. You can imagine what a lively ride we had. We stopped and had a dinner of cold venison birds etc. again which they carried with them out on some boards in the woods with several bottles of first rate claret. Mittie you have never known what southern drinking is. I certainly never have, it beats anything you can conceive of.

[Incomplete]

Many historians consider the winter of 1856-57 to be one of the most severe in recorded U.S. history. By late December, all across the midwest and east, many rivers had frozen, and even the deep south suffered from an unrelenting cold snap. Thee's disrupted midwestern travel plans continued until after he returned home, as a major blizzard hit the east coast including New York.[83]

Months passed before the next letter in the collection. In this letter, Thee wrote to Mittie, who was visiting an unknown location, probably Philadelphia. As Mittie did in January, Thee spent his time alone with family and entertaining friends.

Dearest Mittie

I showed mother your account of Bammie and she seemed fully to agree with regard to trying Dr Peppers' treatment, while she was glad that he seemed to approve of Dr Chesseman's treatment.

A poor ragged bare-foot little boy came into the store yesterday and begged for just fourteen cents to make up the amount necessary to go in the steamboat to Hartford. I told him to work for twenty minutes and gave him in William's charge. The sympathies of the men were excited for him however and they raised the fourteen cents. I found him just as he was leaving and told one of them to go down and see him started in the boat. The boy then wanted to get his shirt first and took the man with him up to the five points, where he ran down into a cellar and when our man tried to follow him he came within an ace of receiving a flogging.

This is a sample of the amount of charity generally displayed by giving to street beggars.

I took Mrs Myers another drive yesterday and asked Col. Myers to meet us at our house and gave as an inducement that Lizzie Ellis would come in and sing for us. The Col. was ordered up to Troy yesterday and I would only persuade Mrs Myers (not to disappoint Lizzie) to stop and take coffee but not spend the evening.

We had a very pleasant time manufactured some lobster salad and took it with coffee. Lizzie sang some of her songs and she will give you an accurate account of the very satisfactory way in which she got on with Mrs ~~Meggs~~ Myers. Lizzie did or intended to call on her yesterday. I had intended to have some ice-cream for the benefit of Mr & Mrs Myers but sent ^{it} round to Mary instead and joined them in consuming it, which they did with great gusto.

This afternoon I take Mrs Lott to drive.

I have not received any letter from you today and am looking anxiously for it

Your Affectionate Husband
Thee[84]

Bamie's condition had deteriorated by the spring of 1857. The family consulted numerous doctors, many of whom were homeopaths. A large black, heavy brace was designed to "strengthen" her spine. The doctors required that she wear it 24 hours a day. This left Bamie to spend her life in her crib or cot. Thee entertained the small girl for hours at a time, according to Bamie's memoirs.[85]

New York May 31st. 57

Dearest Mittie

I have passed as you may imagine a very quiet sunday. During stray intervals I have read the sermon delivered by Dr Dewitt on the reopening of the old reformed Dutch Church. I for the first time learned from this what Anna has asked me once or twice. It is from what the name of "reformed" arose.

It was with regard to the real presence which Luther retained his belief in and which caused the others to break with him.

The D^r calls up all the associations connected with a church in which our fore-fathers had worshiped and incidentally mentions ~~that~~ the corner stone was laid by Issack Roosevelt in 1767.

Dr Adams preached this morning on the "great gladness" mentioned by the bible as shown by the apostles after the ascension of christ. He explained it by showing that through his ascension they saw their highest hopes made certainties.

There could be "no shadow of a doubt left in their minds after they had seen Christ ascend."

This afternoon was communion, one week earlier than usual for which the reason was given out last sunday. Dr Adams spoke of taking this in remembrance of Christ and then mentioned how much feeling might be excited by what was in itself a small matter. That ^{he} had once known a father to carry for months about his person a little sock belonging to a child he had lost.

A little child sat in our pew this morning that had lost one of its eyes. A person evidently the father was with it and it was almost painful to see the way in which he took care of it. I could not help thinking all the time that this might be in store for us too, poor little thing I never think of Bammie without pain. It seems such a dreary dreary life that is in store for her. We must try to teach her as soon as we can to fix her hopes of happiness far above this little world of ours.

I dined with mother and read your last letter loud to mother and father, the letter said you had forgotten him when I read the love you sent to "mama." I went down there again this evening at nine o'clock and found them both going to bed.

I sent up sweet breads yesterday for my breakfast and tea today and eat both those meals in lonely magnificence.

Last night I called again at the ninth Mr Morris but was informed by the servant none but the family were admitted. I probably ~~would~~ might have got in by sending in my card but I thought it best to err on the other side. I then went up to Fanny's, she thinks they know now all about the manner of George's death. She called there herself yesterday and says they seem much more miserable than the first time she saw them. It seems possible that George may have involved himself before his death but I do not believe it at

190

all. Fanny and Sue both inquired after you.

Tell Anna her gloves are being made; I will order a pair for you tomorrow; give my love to sister Harriot although she does not deserve it after leaving me to keep house all alone.

Jim now sees that my desire to go west was a very advisable one and would be very glad to have me go now if Mary was well. Of course Mary's sickness would have prevented under any circumstance but it proves the correctness of my own conclusion. Business is too quiet to be agreeable or profitable.

June 1st. I have received your two letters and am very glad to hear that Bammie is improving and you enjoying yourself although I must say I do not altogether envy you some of your little parties of pleasure. Of course you will apply this to "prejudice" on my part against Miss Lilly.

I am very sorry to hear that Harriot is sick and hope she is taking more care of herself than I could persuade her to.

> With much love to all I remain
> > Your Affectionate Husband
> > > Thee

Clues in the previous letter lead the reader to the conclusion that Mittie visited her half sister Susan West in Philadelphia in May of 1857. There she would have consulted doctors for Bamie, probably with the help of her brother-in-law Dr. Hilborne West.

During this period, a lady never left the house without putting on gloves. Ladies often wore gloves within the house as well. An old saying declared it took three countries to make one glove, Spain to provide the most soft kid (leather),

France for the cut, and England for the stitching. A glove maker measured, fitted, and created each pair of gloves for the wearer. They had to fit perfectly. Ladies had several pairs, kept in glove boxes, to meet the requirements of each occasion.

James Dunwoody Bulloch and his new wife Harriott established a home in New York after their marriage. New York's harbor served as home port for Captain Bulloch. Harriott established ties with the Roosevelts, as well as the remaining Bulloch family. They accepted Harriott as "sister" very quickly. Harriott's excursion to Philadelphia with Mittie and Bamie may have been the first time Harriott met Susan and Hilborne West and Martha, Anna, and Irvine Bulloch.

As he had many times in the past, Thee bemoaned Mittie's absence but still managed to keep up social appearances. Many of those with whom he visited remain unidentified. However, Thee's visit to the Morris family occurred in a time of grief as Dr. George Morris, newly married in the fall of 1856, died in April of 1857 possibly while in South Carolina. George had inherited The Grove, a plantation, and had run up significant debt before his death. His wife, Alice, delivered a baby boy on 13 December 1857.

The Isaac Roosevelt that laid the cornerstone for the Dutch Reformed church would have been the son of Jacobus (1692-1776), founder of the Hyde Park Roosevelts. Franklin Delano Roosevelt descended from this line. Isaac was Thee's great-great-great uncle. Thee was descended from Johannes (1689-1750), founder of the Oyster Bay Roosevelts.

The next letter illustrates the close connection between Thee and Brother Jimmie as they continued to see each other socially. This is the last letter in the collection dated 1857.

New York June 4th 57

Dearest Mittie

I left Brother Jimmie this morning fully intending to go on in the two o'clock train today and I presume before this he is with you.

We had a very pleasant dinner together last night and afterwards went down to see the Ellis' as Gus had sent some money by Jimmie for them.

Charley Carow was there with Miss Ludlow, he had just driven her in from her place and was going to take her to the yacht race to day. He is one of the members of the club. Mrs Lott told ^{me} her husband insisted upon her going although he could not accompany her.

My horse still remains laid up so that my afternoon drives are put a stop to. Annie need not fear my ^{not} enjoying her company after those I have been taking out and as for you, you never allow me to get accustomed to driving you out of New York, leave alone getting tired of you.

I am very far from the mood to write you an interesting letter in, an emphatic swelling had made its appearance on the right side of my neck and face just where you swelled up. I don't know whether it is mumps or not but it is not very enlivening to one's spirits whatever it is. I don't expect to be sick with it at all but it is possible and if so I will telegraph Jimmie to bring you on with his wife. There is no prospect that this will be necessary however.

No letter from you came today but I hope to receive one tomorrow

Your loving Husband
Thee

Do not think I am sick at all for my whiskers hide the lump and Annie would suggest that if it hurts me to open my mouth. Why open it?

Chapter VII
1858

The World in 1858

Those attending the 25 January wedding of Great Britain's Queen Victoria's daughter Princess Victoria to the Crown Prince Frederick William of Prussia heard Mendelssohn's *Wedding March* played at Chapel Royal, St. James' Palace. The Queen chose the piece, written in 1842, for Mendelssohn's suite of incidental music to accompany Shakespeare's play *A Midsummer Night's Dream*, for her daughter's wedding march. Thereafter the piece became extremely popular for weddings around the world.

Other overseas events included the 11 February vision of the Virgin Mary to 14-year-old Bernadette of Lourdes, France. On 13 February, Sir Richard Burton and John Speake explored Lake Tanganyika in Africa and excited Europe with their stories of the area during the coming years.

The volatile political situation in the United States continued to simmer. On 8 May, John Brown held an anti-slavery convention in Chatham, Ontario. Brown, an American abolitionist, believed armed insurrection was the only way to overthrow the institution of slavery in the United States. In 1856, he led the Kansas campaign, where he and his followers killed five pro-slavery supporters in what became known as the Pottawatomie massacre. Brown's actions came in response to the sacking of Lawrence, Kansas by pro-slavery

Illustration from sheet music of
Mendelssohn's Wedding March

forces. Brown's convention consisted of a series of clandestine meetings at Chatham's First Baptist Church. He planned to establish an independent republic within the United States followed by a guerrilla war to liberate the South from slavery. Brown's visit to Canada was an attempt to recruit blacks who had fled there in the wake of the Fugitive Slave Law (1850).

Inventions and advancements of the year included a pencil with an attached eraser patented by Hyman L. Lipman of Philadelphia. The first use of fingerprints as a means of identification was made by Sir William James Herschel of the Indian Civil Service. On 5 August, Cyrus W Field completed the first transatlantic telegraph cable, and on 16 August, Britain's Queen Victoria telegraphed U.S. President James Buchanan. On 15 August, regular mail service to the Pacific coast began. Later that year, Hamilton Smith patented a rotary washing machine, and R. H. Macy & Company opened their first store at 6th Avenue in New York City. There is little doubt Mittie and Anna became some of their earliest customers.

Men and women alike discussed the contentious political situation. On 11 May, Minnesota was admitted as the 32nd state, another state in the free category. In June, Abraham Lincoln accepted the Illinois Republican Party's nomination for Senate saying "A house divided against itself cannot stand." Following his nomination, Lincoln engaged in a series of seven formal political debates with the incumbent Stephen A. Douglas. At this time, each state legislature elected two U.S. senators. There was a popular vote for senator; however, it had little effect on the outcome of the race. The main issue of each debate was slavery. On election day, the Illinois Democrats won 40 seats in the state House of Representatives, and the Republicans won 35. In the state senate, Republicans held 11 seats, and Democrats held 14; therefore Senator Stephen A. Douglas won reelection by the legislature, 54-46. These debates, their transcripts reprinted in papers across the nation, catapulted Lincoln into the national scene and presented him as a viable candidate for president in the following election.

The 1858 Letters

While many of the Bulloch/Roosevelt letters survived, there are large gaps in the collection. Anna and Martha continued to live with Susan and Hilborne, but each seems to have spent the summer with Mittie and Thee at Tuckers in New York. Irvine continued his education, possibly finishing the year at the University of Pennsylvania in Philadelphia.

Feb 10th 1858

My dearest Mittie

Late afternoon I received your dear letter and the two you enclosed to me. We were delighted to hear from you darling I did not write to you on last monday as I had intended doing for I knew you would hear of us through Brother Jimmie. We had such a delightful visit from him. Do tell Brother Jimmie a Mrs Peachim[86] (that is the way the name sounds I do not know how to spell it) goes out with him on Friday she is the Aunt of his friend Mrs Cash. I promised to mention it to him - Clara Rosa came to see me a few days ago and begged me to go to the Opera with her tonight to hear Robrt for the last time. I am going to wear my blue chiné with the low neck waist pink flowers in my hair, only a few married ladies wear bonnets in the dress circle. How could Johnie [John Ellis Roosevelt, age 5] slap Bamie I feel as if it was the most cruel thing I have ever known the little darling to get a slap when I would do any thing in the world to save her from any pain or annoyance

198

however slight. Tell Bamie Auntie uses her little table to keep hers and Grandma's flowers on at night one of my white hyacinths is nearly in bloom. Mother told you about Miss Dicksons party - We had a very pleasant time, the supper was bountiful two large tureens of terrapin two of oysters, fried oysters and chicken salad in any quantity, a profusion of flowers and all the creams in formed shapes according to the flavor. Last Saturday afternoon I went with Dr Ford to the Germania concert - I have just invited Miss Bourn and her friend Dr Ford, to spend next thursday morning with me, Mary Boardman, Miss Dickson and Miss Coleman and a few others make up a very small number I know it will be intensely stupid but I felt obliged to return their politeness to us - Robert Troup has become something of a favorite with me lately so I have invited him too - Mother has promised to be down in the parlor to help me entertain, if Thee were only here I should not have the least doubt of the evening he would not let the girls be stiff! Mother is so glad Bamie is to drive at lizzie's on Saturday any little change is good for her. I am reading Quits with great interest - I like it exceedingly, of course it is not equal to the Initials but so very entertaining - As soon as I finish Quits I am going to read White lies - Do tell Bamie that this morning Margaret is going to take a soft feather duster and dust the "back niger boy"- Tudie sends love to you all she says she has been better since the time you came and brought little Bamie to cheer her up. About my edging, I am afraid you have taken in too much I was so amused to hear about {_____} again - I think the lace I have I will use for the cuffs, get the quantity I marked by the pair, if the materials match - I dont know what you will do about the money as Thee sent on to Mother the money she meant you to keep to use for us whenever we gave you any little commission - we will make with this arrangement - Do when you get chintzes get me a dressing gown of blue, lilac, or pink just as you fancy - When you write will you send me a small sample of your blue chintz with the price, the one like we bought for brother Jimmie afterwards I want Tudie to see it. I have at last found out something about Sir Galahad! The quest of San Great [sangreal or sangraal[87]] has the Search for the Holy Grail. The holy Grail was the cup of the last supper taken into England by Joseph of Aramthea - Where it was kept until it was lost on account of the wickedness of one of the priests or those who guarded it, from that time the Knights of the round table went in search of it - Sir Galahad the Spotless Knight gave life, honor, love, wealth in fact every thing he possessed to find the second cup, his devotion was rewarded the Holy Grail was borne before him as you find in Tennyson - It is all to be found in the seventeenth book of the Romance of King Arthur. Do give my love to Mrs Roosevelt and Laura, how is she now - I have written to Sarah Wallace this morning! Love from all. You can not imagine my own beloved Sister how dearly I love you and my precious little niece - Life is too short to be parted from those for we do really live - Kiss Thee for me. And now I must close this extremely wandering letter - When you write give much love to all the Greens for me I liked Sarah's letter much

Yours always aff[ly]
Anna

Anna and Clara Rosa (unknown friend) went to see Robert le Diable or Robert the Devil, an opera by Giacomo Meyerbeer first performed in 1831. The *Public Ledger* described it thus:

The Opera - the opera season which Mr. Ullman has given the Philadelphia public is drawing to a close. It has been brilliantly and fashionably attended and the performances have been worthy of the attendance. The manager has kept the public expectation alive with novelties, and the audiences are indebted to him for the production of opera seldom or never before heard in this city. To-night he announces the opera of "Robert le Diable," . . . .[88]

Based only superficially on the medieval legend of Robert the Devil, the opera's dramatic music, melodramatic plot, and spectacular stage effects once compelled Frédéric Chopin, to say, "If ever magnificence was seen in the theatre, I doubt that it reached the level of splendour shown in Robert. . . It is a masterpiece. . . Meyerbeer has made himself immortal."[89] It continued to be popular with audiences worldwide throughout the nineteenth century.

While Anna listed a number of lady friends, her male interests seemed to be Dr. Ford and Robert Troup. Anna attended the Germania concert with Dr. Ford, who is perhaps Dr. George W. Ford who graduated from the Jefferson Medical College in 1855. They attended the Germania Grand Orchestra concert at the Pennsylvania Musical Institute. On Saturdays the public could attend afternoon rehearsals. Evening performances could be attended for only fifty cents by subscribers to the Institute's concert series.[90]

Anna's reading interests continued to be mostly centered on popular novels of the age. In 1853, she read *Cyrilla: A Tale* by Baroness Jemima Montgomery Tautphoeus.[91] Now, she is reading the Baroness' *Quits. A Novel* and plans to then read the author's first work *The Initials. A Novel.*[92] *White Lies: a*

201

Story, Anna's next choice in reading, was written by Charles Reade, an Oxford scholar. By 1857 when he published *White Lies*, he had already published several other novels, many of which continue to be read as classics.

Many months passed. The Roosevelts and their extended families spent the summer at Tuckers. A letter from Rev. James Bulloch Dunwoody to Thee filled in details about their Roswell Dunwoody relations. And finally, the most important development of the year was never mentioned in the surviving letters until it happened. Mittie was expecting again, with the baby due in late October or early November.

Roswell Sept 21st 1858

My dear Friend
    You are perhaps blaming me for my continued silence. I have been anxious to write you and give the latest news respecting our affairs but have been prevented by a most singular and distracting affection of my eyes and nostrils which has rendered all correspondence unendurable for the last six weeks. In the beginning of August, I came to the conclusion from various considerations that it was indispensable to the interest of my daughter that she should again be sent to school. She was making great progress in some branches of her education under my tuition, while others equally important were totally neglected from necessity. Upon giving her a choice of several institutions of which I thought favourably she preferred to return to Bethlehem. Accordingly I immediately carried her thither.
    I was delighted to witness the cordial reception with which [she] was greeted by all her former teachers & by such of her fellow pupils as were still remaining at the Institute. I left her at the end of a week in excellent spirits & resolved

to make good use of her opportunity. Her letters give ample evidence that she is practicing her resolve and indeed my only apprehension is that she may become too ambitious & by undertaking too much endanger her health. I think she promised to be all that my fond hopes could desire.

Upon leaving Bethlehem [North Carolina] I went to Elizabeth-town or as it is now called Elizabeth city [North Carolina], to spend a few days with my fathers' well tried and most worthy friend Dr Magie. Upon hearing of my father's death he had written us such a tender and affectionate tribute to his worth that my heart actually yearned toward him. I found the good man enjoying a green old age, tenderly beloved by his people. His children four in number all grown up, & worthy of their excellent parents. His eldest son just married and very promising young lawyer. The second son just of age and preparing for the ministry. He was spending his vacation with his parents, highly intelligent and lovely & modest in his deportment. I learned to love him as a youngest brother. I spent five or six of the happiest days of my life with the dear friends who all vied with each other in acts of kindness and it was actually an effort for me to tear myself from their society. But the journey to the North was made at a time of unusual heat and drought and the constant irritations of the dust upon the eyes and mucus membranes of the nose produced a most painful state of those organs which has continued ever since I have suffered more than I can easily express have been unfitted for almost any kind of occupation. I have nearly filled my letter and told you nothing excepting of the family and its affairs. Well then we expect to divide our fathers estate by mutual agreement a method allowed by a recent decision of the Supreme Court of Georgia when all the parties are of age as is the case in the present instance. By this arrangement the Estate can be more speedily divided and the comfort of the negroes better insured than by following the ordinary routine. My fathers assets amount to about $51,000. My sisters [Marion] portions will be nearly $9,00 and will all be productive yielding her an income of from 12. to 1.5.00,00 I mean with what she already has. She will have a home with me as long as she pleases or I have one myself. So she will be perfectly comfortable as far as this world is concerned. I have taken my fathers house as part of my portion. It would have been burdensome to anyone of my brothers and thought it will be unproductive as long as I shall labour abroad yet it is a pleasant reflection that I am possessed of a comfortable and respectable home to which I can retire at any time should circumstances render it deliverable. Charley takes the farm as a part of his portion. We have put it down to him with the stock upon it worth about $700 at four thousand. My father himself in his will affixed the value of three thousand dollars upon the house and I will take it at that evaluation. It would be extremely low in any other place than Roswell but were we to put it up to sale would not bring that here. I have invited my brother John to reside in the old mansion until such time as I may need it myself. I have taken the care of Isaac's old age upon myself. William will probably purchase Welhaus from the Darien family and resume the practice of medicine in Marietta. There is land sufficient attached to the house to supply him with nearly all the necessities of life. He will give for the place $2.400 and will probably be able to sell the farm he owns at present for from 4,000 to 5,000 if he acts wisely he will have an income besides his residence and the produce of the ground of from $700 to $1.000 independent of any thing he may make by his practice and where by his wifes share of her mother's & father's property becomes theirs they will be extremely comfortable. The Col. [John, Jr.] is doing better for himself than he has ever done & if we can only prevail upon him to be quiet let well enough alone and go on steadily as he is he will soon be perfectly comfortable. Henry has a valuable plantation is a successful planter. If he takes my advice he will use all of his portion from his father other than negroes to cancel his debts at once. His factory and bank stock will nearly accomplish this. What will remain he can speedily pay from his income. He will then be worth fully $20,000 in lands & negroes and have an income of nearly or quite $2.000 I will have quite as much as I desire. I estimate my property at within a fraction of forty thousand dollars and income of from there to five thousand the first amount certain. Thus you see the prospects of the whole family are fair and we have much to be thankful for. It is my ambition to wind up my fathers estate in such a manner as will secure the affection of my beloved parents if they can look upon us from Heaven and without a heart burning on the part of our of the brethren. I will be here until the first Novem[r] After that at Barnwell C.H-S.C. where I have agreed to preach through the coming winter. Write me dear friend. All unite in warm love to you my sister especially.

Affectionately yours,

J. B. Dunwoody.

The Moravians opened the doors of their Salem Academy dormitory on 16 May 1804 and transformed into an all-girls boarding school. The Moravians established the school in 1772 with Moravian Elisabeth Oesterlein as the first teacher at the school. Moravians believed that women deserved an education comparable to that given to men, a radical view for that era. James' letter indicates Laleah, his daughter, had been a student at the Academy previously.[93]

Much of the letter focused on the estate of John Dunwoody, who died earlier in the year. John's estate included what is now known as Mimosa Hall in Roswell, Georgia, and the surrounding lands. During this period, the use of commas and periods in monetary notations were quite random. However, it is obvious that John left behind a considerable fortune. At 2015 prices, John's $51,000 equaled about $1,510,000.[94]

New York Oct 4th 1858

My dear Susy,

I have been so busy that I have not had time to write you even a few lines - We left Mrs Roosevelt on wednesday last. Mittie seemed to bear the removal very well - Since that time I have been almost constantly engaged assisting her in getting fixed and in hunting up a waitress for her The day you left, at one oclock I took a carriage and spent nearly the entire balance of the day going to the different places where they were advertised. I found, out of about twenty, one that I thought would answer - Engaged her she came and staid half of a day - On saturday I took a carriage again, and had another tramp. I have found another that I think will answer but she may go off tomorrow morning - Anna and Bamie came in on Friday. Bamie seemed quite pleased to get back - Anna is going to remain with Mittie - will take care of Bamie and do part of the chamber work - Anna is not going on to Phil[a] until the end of Oct. Mittie is anxious for her to remain - I got a long letter from Irvine lately - He said he had seen you and his brother Hill - and that you had gone to your house with him and had dinner gotten for him and John Stoddard, and that Hill had taken him to Hoyt to have his winter clothes made - He said he had had a conversation with you also about his feeling, that you gave him "English hearts and Hands" to read - It must have been troublesome to you to get dinner for those boys - dear little kind Susy, but it was just like you and Hill to take all that trouble. When Anna came to N York she did not expect to remain, but intended to go on with Stuart and Lucy to Phil[a], But Mittie thought she (Mittie) was too unwell to take the charge of Bamie at night, and she was afraid too that if Anna left her "By" would get into her old habit of requiring her to go to bed with her - This was particularly to be feared - as Mittie has to go to bed so early - Mittie is much better, goes down to breakfast and dinner, and can walk about the house - Mittie told me to say to you with her love - that she has sent for your pitcher to Hartford where they are made, and expects one daily. It shall be sent on as soon as it arrives - Berrian had a very pretty one, but it had a dent in it, and she would not take it -

Tuesday, Morn

All well Mittie continues to improve - James has arrived, but we have not seen him yet - I received a most excellent report of Irvine last night from Mr Arthur - no bad marks and only one last lesson - dear child, I do so much hope that he may do well - I am going to write to Tom King today, to make his check payable to Hill

I am going this morning to Berrians to see if your pitcher has arrived and to order it sent by express to 1524 Pine Street - Remember me affectionately to Mr Bruce if you speak to him - I hope Mr & Mrs West are well. I suppose after to day there will be no person left at Tuckers but Rob's family and Stuart, Lucy, and little Nannie - I think James will bring in Harriott to day. I have attended Dr Adam's church since I came to 20th St. He is a fine preacher - last sunday was communion - The church now numbers five hundred communicants. It was very solemn and interesting - I have only as yet attended evening meeting - good by dear Susy I hope your house cleaning etc. has not made you sick

- Mitties house-cleaning cost over $20 - this is simply the cleaning - not the putting down carpets, putting up shades, etc - write when you can without fatigue.

Your affec mother

M Bulloch

Love to Hill and yourself from us all - I asked By if she loved aunt Susie - she said no - a little anemated [annimated].

Irvine Stephens Bulloch, circa 1860

In 1857, in time for Christmas, English author Catherine Marsh (1818-1912) published *English hearts and English hands : or, The railway and the trenches.* The first volume had *by the author of the Memorials of Captain Hedley Vicars* tacked on to the end of the title. Catherine Marsh enjoyed wide circulation of her books and great popularity. *English hearts and English hands* presented "unimagined instances of fine character, and fine conduct amongst the working classes, and the soldiers."[95] Marsh emphasized good works based on faith and sympathy.

Another family wedding occurred on 1 June 1858, in Savannah, when Brother Dan, now using the name Stuart, married Lucinda Ireland Sorrel (1829-1903) of Savannah. We have no record of any Bulloch family members attending the wedding. Daniel's marriage into such an exalted Savannah family came as a surprise to many.

Daniel had fought a duel the previous year with Tom Daniell, son of a local Savannah physician. An expert shot, Daniel had tried to get Tom to apologize for throwing a glass of wine in his face and call off the duel. Despite Daniel's best efforts, both men had traveled across the river several days later to South Carolina where dueling had not yet been outlawed. Daniel's shot struck Tom directly in the heart.[96] The duel and Tom's death put Daniel in disgrace in Savannah society. When the wedding occurred, Charles Colcock Jones, a dear friend of Martha Bulloch's, wrote to Mrs. Mary Jones, "Miss Lucy Sorrel on tomorrow evening expects to espouse the name of Elliott. I wish her joy, but fear a disappointment. Were I a lady, I would certainly be very loath to marry one who had the guilt of homicide upon his skirts."[97]

In a letter written 3 May 1856, two years before the wedding, Laura E. Maxwell of Savannah wrote to Mrs. Mary Jones of Liberty County, Georgia,

> By the way, I hear Dan Elliott is going with him to Europe this summer, and they leave very soon. Mr. Stoddard informed Mr. Hutchison the other day that "Lucy Sorrel would marry any man as rich as he was." It seems that Miss Stoddard and Miss Sorrel are rival singers, and it is "diamond cut diamond" with them just now. . ."[98]

These bits of information from period letters and other sources provide much needed information about this match. First, Daniel *was* wealthy. He had inherited a great deal of money, stocks, and several slaves from his father. The money had been held in trust for him, with James Stephens Bulloch as his guardian, until he reached maturity. Newspapers of the time revealed that Daniel held 136 shares of the Bank of the State of Georgia in 1846 and 1847, valued at $136,000, approximately $3,128,000 in today's money.[99] The *Georgia Property Tax Digest of 1851* listed Daniel in Roswell where he owned only one slave. By this time he must have sold the others, providing him with additional revenue. In 1856, the *Savannah Republican* reported he owned 100 shares of the Central Railroad & Banking Company.[100] No value was given; however, few names on the list owned more stock than Daniel. That same year his reported holdings of Bank of the State of Georgia were listed at 55 shares and valued at $5,500.[101] Again, these were respectable holdings worth more than $158,000. Lucy had expressed the desire to marry a wealthy man. Additionally she had reached the age of 29 and was thus considered a spinster by Savannah society.

Daniel and Lucy traveled north at some point and spent the summer with his family at Tuckers. Martha returned to New York with Anna, Daniel, Lucy, and Mittie. Anna had planned to go ahead to Philadelphia with Daniel and Lucy but instead stayed with Mittie to care for Bamie, who was also called *By*.

Hilborne and Susan had welcomed Irvine into their home along with John Stoddard. This young man was most likely John Irwin Stoddard of Savannah and Liberty County, born in 1843 to John and Mary Lavinia Mongin Stoddard, making him about Irvine's age. John married into the Sorrel family after the Civil War.

Hilborne took Irvine to F.A. Holt & Brother, tailors located at 10th and Chestnut Street, Philadelphia, for his winter clothing. They specialized in "youth's clothing."[102] The firm can be found in city directories for many years during the antebellum period. Martha ordered a pitcher from Hartford, after Mittie refused to buy a dented one at J.C. Berrian, a household furnishings store located at 106 Broadway & 222 West 44th Street.[103]

Along with Robert Roosevelt and family, Lucy and Stuart and "little Nannie" remained at Tuckers. Little Nannie was Nancy E. Caskie (1851-1909) daughter of Robert Hutchison and his second wife, Mary Edmonia Caskie (1822-1852). Mary gave Robert one daughter, Nancy "Nannie" E. born 29 January 1851 about six months before her mother's death from tuberculosis. Nannie resided with her mother's family in Richmond, Virginia, for most of the year. Nannie had a new sister by Robert's third wife that summer. Ellen Laura Caskie gave birth to little Ellen Laura in March and succumbed to puerperal fever one week later.[104] As James Dunwoody Bulloch's first wife was little Nannie's aunt, he and his family had played an active role in her life. Unfortunately, at only 7 years of age, Nannie had suffered the loss of her mother and stepmother.

New York Oct 15th- 1858

My very dear daughter,

I received your letter of the 13th last evening, and was glad to hear from you - I know darling you have had a fatiguing time - I hope your new waitress may suit you. Mittie's seems to promise extremely well - She is very industrious neat and civil, her only fault is that she is too much amused by the conversation at the table. Mittie "does not be as funny as she can". Mittie, I may say has recovered her health, but oh how I wish she was over her trouble - Harriott has comfortable rooms in West 21 St and little Jimmy is the largest child of his age that I think I have ever seen - "By" has gone to spend part of the morning with him - Anna has been very busy shopping for Mittie - She does the fancy shopping, I the plain - Anna has received from Mr & Mrs James Caskie a most cordial and pressing invitation to visit, and spend some time with them - She has accepted the invitation, but has not appointed the exact time - That depends upon Mittie's confinement - Anna will return to Phil^a the last of Oct or first of Nov. After that if all turns out well she will go on to Richmond - She will probably go under Mr Hutchison's escort. She wishes you to send on her blue velvet bonnet with my things - I wish you darling to send me my cloak, fur cuffs, velvet bonnet and flannel petticoats as soon as you can, directed to 33 E. 20 St Mittie and I knew that the Depository had cut Bamie's pants shorter in the back than the pattern, but thought we had better not try to remedy that mistake, but just make them like the ones sent with that exception - we cant imagine why the box was not sent before - I am going to day to see if Barrien has sent your pitcher - People in this world seem determined not to perform their promises - I am glad that our little Lucy is having a pleasant time - Irvine says he is really in love with her - He was delighted with his visit home He is very fond of you and Hill, and of Stuart, Anna asks you please not to move any of my things out of her room, as she will probably be in Phil[a] but a short time and would rather appropriate some of her wardrobe to my things - Anna says Bamie deserves to be called "heartless By" for she does not hesitate to call her at any hour of the night to give her a drink of water, and yet in day light says she does not love her - Give much love to Lucy, Hill and Stuart - I am glad Stuart is going out to Annendale to see Irvine I think those kinds of attention encourage Irvine to act properly - Anna and Mittie send much love to your dear household - That you may be blessed for time and eternity in the sincere prayer

of your affectionate mother
M Bulloch

Martha's letter to Susan announced James Dunwoody Bulloch's first son. Harriott gave birth to little Jimmy, named for his father, on 29 April 1858 in New Orleans. Mittie's second pregnancy was Martha's reason for concern. Lucy and Stuart had continued on to Philadelphia to visit Susan and Hilborne. Irvine met Lucy so the family circle closed with all the new members being at least acquainted with each other. Why Irvine might have been in Annandale, Pennsylvania, remains a mystery. The small town is about 40 miles north of Pittsburgh.

New York Oct 22nd 1858

My very dear daughter

I received your letter of Oct 20th yesterday, only an hour or two before the trunk arrived in your order, we have not opened it yet, but know it is <u>all right</u> - Mittie and Anna have read your letter with attention and will have your bonnets fixed all nicely - They told me to say to you that to fix your velvet bonnet nicely required lace. Mittie says she knows a way in which it can be made very pretty and becoming to you, which she thinks will cost about ten dollars - let her know if you do not approve of this trimming. your feathers will be used also - The cloaks are very simple and pretty - The Raglan seem to be the only fashion, made of Beaver cloth without lining - prices from $17 to 20 and 25 - Harriott got a very pretty one lately at $17 - Mittie and Anna are going to get black, but you can get dark grey or any of the shades of dark brown quite pretty - Harriott's is brown - If you think best Anna will get Lily, also - I got a very pretty one for little Nannie Hutchinson of dark grey trimmed simply with black velvet at $10 - Anna & M will see to it that Dorsy puts nice strings to your bonnet & that it shall be unlike last winter's in the style of trimming etc - Dear Suzy I long to see you - Little "worldly minded" By is very sweet and sensible - I wish you could see how she plays in the evening now. Anna and Thee are her play-mates while Ann {?} is down at her dinner - They play that she is a little <u>ulse</u> wolf and her Father a larger "ulse" and that Anna is a watch-maker - This little wolf takes jewels to be mended to the watch-maker, But it all ends in nothing. The watch-maker never mends the things properly, and yet the wolves never eat him up, because she says they are good wolves - She is put to bed every day in the room adjoining mine, and when she wakes she blows a little whistle to let them know her nap is over. She is a very good child - I do not think she is quite as strong as when at Tucker's, but she has a good appetite and is very playful and happy - She is now busy with a wet cloth, and standing on a chair washing the sashes in her mother's room - Mittie looks quite well and has nearly got every draweruner closet in order - Last sunday Bammie & Mittie were up in my room. Bammie said Mama let us peep in all the corners - Every thing will be in such order that when Mittie is taken sick, every thing that can possibly be wanted will be found without the least difficulty - The kitchen, the dining room, the parlor, the bed rooms, with their respective closets - have all had their "corners <u>peeped into.</u>" I have been quite pleased in finding out where I could attend the noonday prayer meetings - There is an union prayer meeting principally of the Dutch Reformer and Presbyterian Churches held from twelve to one every day - It is held one week at a time in each Church - This week in Dr Pott's Church - They are very solemn and interesting - I was particularly glad of these day-meetings, as I could not well go out in the evening - Mittie & Anna had a hearty laugh about the "crying woman," and about the improvement in the waitress (wearing slippers). I hear from Irvine constantly - He was quite disappointed on saturday in not seeing Hill and Stuart, but consoles himself with the hope of going to Phil[a] on friday (this day) evening - I cannot judge from the tone of his letters whether he has much serious feeling. He still professes concern, but I think is putting off importance to a future day. A sad delusion which causes the ruin of many a soul - Poor little fellow! I wish God would in great mercy change his heart - but dear Sudy my faith is so weak, that my hopes are faint - The Savoir generally said, according to your <u>faith</u> be it unto you. Anna and Mittie unite with me in much love to Lucy, Stuart, Hill and yourself. If you get this letter tomorrow, tell Irvine I will write him the first of next week - Good bye darling - ever your affectionate Mother

M Bulloch -

NB I have opened the hat-box, and every thing is in good order - Mittie & Anna will take the bonnets to Dorsy

Godey's fashion plate showing fashionable cloaks from *Harper's New Monthly*, November 1858.

tomorrow or monday - They will also return Suzy's bows of ribbon to Le fonse {?} Little Jimmie has grown very much Harriott is to dine here this evening - I saw Lew West the other night he looked really handsome - He was dressed as scrupulously nice as ever- his <u>very</u> <u>nice</u> mother could have wished him - your affec mother

MB -

Mon last words - Anna says she has a silk skirt which she will give Lily - when the Dances commences please send the two bundles I left labelled one for Lawrence Corn {?} - and the other for Tom Sultions {?} to Mrs. Gartner and request her to give them to the two boys - I hope they will give the boys beside the accustomed suit from the society [Dorcas Society] - I would like to have my quilted skirt sent with Mitties things - Love to all -

Martha and her daughters wrote of fashion in the autumn of 1858. Anna and Susan were purchasing cloaks of beaver cloth, which was a woolen fabric which is milled and raised. Beaver cloth, used almost entirely for cloaks and outerwear, was napped and then pressed down to resemble beaver fur. It was also used for hats. The cost of these cloaks at $17 to $25 equaled about $357 to $525 in today's money, obviously making them a rather expensive investment. Even the cloak that Martha purchased for Nannie Hutchison at $10, or $210 in today's currency, indicated that Martha had some wealth or that the very wealthy Robert Hutchison left money for Nannie's care and upkeep. In years past, as Mittie and Anna had "come out" into society, Robert had purchased all of their clothing for the summer season. As this was 1848, James and Martha were perfectly capable of supplying the girls needs; however, numerous letters and sources of the period suggested Robert to be a very generous man.[105]

Milliner Helen A. Dorsey appears in the 1858 New York City Directory. Her shop was located at 683 Broadway, not far from the Roosevelt residence. During this period, a lady never left her home without a bonnet or hat of some kind. Often the previous year's bonnet would be restyled for the current year's fashions.

New York Oct 28 - 1858

My dearest Susy

Thee has promised to Telegraph to you this morning that Mittie has a fine little son. She went out in the carriage yesterday morning at ten oclock - Her object was to see about her's, your's, and Lucy's cloaks - She ordered the cloaks and attended some other little matters, and returned home about two oclock. She said she felt rather tired, so immediately after taking her lunch of bread and butter and ginger preserves, she laid down on her lounge to rest and take a little nap - Just at that moment Miss Wallace called and I went down to see her. Miss W staid some time so I suppose - when I returned in Mittie's room - it was about half past three oclock As soon as I got into the room she said Mother I am in great pain but perhaps it is only in consequence of the drive so I will try to be still and perhaps it will pass off - She did try but instead of its passing off it increased most rapidly - I sent immediately for Dr Chessman [John C.] but he was ill in bed and could not come. This was most appalling news, so I then sent to Hariott to know where Dr Emmet [Thomas A.] was to be found This of course occasioned some delay In the mean time the pains became so quick and sharp, that I sent Ann Butler off for Dr Markoe [Thomas M.] who lives some where near. I never was more relieved in my life than when Dr Markoe entered - All this time you must recollect when the different servants were flying about for D^r and for Susan Newberry the nurse, I was almost the whole time alone with Mittie - Anna had taken Bamie over to Lizzy Ellis'- I sent over for Mary but she was too unwell to come - I could not bear the idea of having no female presence with me, so sent for Mrs. Roosevelt and she came over - Mittie continued to get worse and worse until quarter to eight in the evening when the birth took place - She had a safe, but severe time - She is this morning as well as we could wish to see her - it is as sweet and pretty a young baby as I have ever seen weighed 8 pounds and a half before it was dressed - No Chloroform or any such thing was used, no instruments were necessary, consequently the dear little thing has no cuts or bruises about it - In the course of the night and morning the D^r has had it put to the breast three or four times, and says it must have not a drop of any thing else besides mother's milk - Mittie has behaved throughout the whole time like a sensible woman has objected to nothing that was right - I like Dr Markoe better than any Physician I have ever known under the like circumstances. Mittie says I must tell you she thinks the baby hideous - She says it is a cross between a terrapin & Dr. Young.

Dear Susy, I know you will feel with me that we have cause for great gratitude to God our good Father in Heaven for sustaining the poor feeble child in her great trial. How I wish that this great mercy could know her as a cord of love to her blessed Savior -

Dr. Thomas M. Markoe was only 39 years old when he delivered Mittie's second child, Theodore. In 1836, he graduated from Princeton and later the College of Physicians and Surgeons in 1841. Two of his children also became physicians.[106]

New York Nov 1ˢᵗ 1858

My very dear daughter,

I am determined if possible you shall hear from some of us every day - Thee wrote you I believe on saturday - Mittie continues as well as could be wished, and the baby (although like other babies) (he makes a little fuss at my nights) is a fine little fellow, and appears in perfect health. Mittie has not a great overflow of milk, has a plenty for him and it gives her as yet, little or no trouble - Susan Newberry is a first rate nurse - I think it will please you to know that I have not lost an hour's rest, and have had no fatigue whatever - Bammie is delighted with the Baby - She says she has two Babies now, little Jimmies and her own little baby. She says he is a cunning little {___} she hears him {___} in the night - he wakes up Bammie when she is asleep up stairs in her crib - I think they will name him Theodore. I have just returned from the noon-day prayer meeting - heard some interesting accounts of revivals and protractive meetings in Penn - The meetings are very solemn and interesting - Dear Sudy I enclose this account of the Skirt Supporters, for you to read and tell me if you can get them in Phil or if you would like me to get you one - They cost only $100 - your cloak has been sent home but your bonnet has not -Your cloak is grey - a very nice one - Anna has been very unwell but is better I hope Stuart and Lucy will not venture to return South until the weather becomes cool and it is quite safe - James writes that Mr. Palmer (Augusta's husband) who is now preaching in New Orleans, has had the yellow-fever, but is recovering. I sincerely hope he may get well - Harriott was here this morning says she cant go to see you for some time to come, but that she surely will in process of time - Mittie and Anna write with me in much love to all. Mittie says she would give any thing to see you, and when I hold the little soft baby I often think how much you would like to do the same - Give

220

a great deal of love to dear Stuart and Lucy - Tell Hill since I wrote you last I have secured a letter from Mr. Teft, so if he has not already written him, it is unnecessary to do so - Good bye darling - God bless you

Your affec. Mother
M Bulloch

Susan A. Newberry (1827-1871) was a 31-year-old widow with an eight-year-old son named William. Susan resided at 384 Sixth Avenue, probably a boarding house, as all of the home's adult residents were female. The 1858 *Trow's New York City Directory* listed her occupation as nurse.[107]

Skirt supporters began to be advertised in the late spring of 1858. N.C. Nelson of Concord, New Hampshire received her patent for her skirt supporter on 9 March of that year. Martha apparently had tried one of these supporters and recommended it to Susy. Advertisements for the supporters appeared in newspapers across the nation that year as well as in July's issue of *Harper's New Monthly Magazine.* The wire frame supporter simply fit around the wearer's waist, and the skirt was slipped over the supporter but not attached in any way. Petticoats were worn under the supporter. At $100 these were expensive investments, but considering the weight of all the petticoats and then a skirt with between 3 and 7 yards of fabric as were fashionable at the time, they were probably considered a worthwhile investment. One advertisement read:

> The Skirt-Supporter, which we illustrate separately and as worn, is a novel and exceedingly useful article, designs to relieve the person from the burden of the skirt. The weight of this, it will be seen, is borne by the projecting fender,

that is sustained upon the hips by netted pads. The value of this invention, in a hygienic point of view, can hardly be overrated. It is applicable to every description of skirt.[108]

Period illustration of a skirt supporter, *Harper's New Monthly*, July 1858.

The cage crinoline or hoop was patented in April of 1856. By 1858, half and full hoops or crinolines were coming into fashion. However, their use within the household and during the daily routine made the wearer uncomfortable and restricted ease of mobility. Few women wore them inside the home. Some continued to use the original style crinoline, a stiffened or structured petticoat used to hold out the skirt. Some continued to wear corded petticoats made by sewing cotton cord into rows around the bottom of the petticoat and then starching the entire garment.

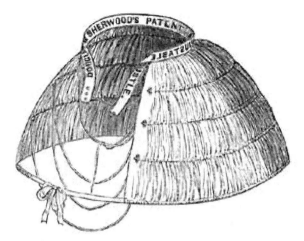

Period illustration of a half crinoline or hoop.

Period illustration of a full crinoline or hoop.

New York Nov 2nd 1858

Dearest Susy

According to my resolution to let you hear from us every day I now write a few lines - We are all well. Mittie's doing remarkably well. The baby sleeping better at nights and apparently in perfect health He gets a plenty of nourishment and Mittie suffers less from her new vocation of "nursing mother," than any person I have ever known. I am convinced there is more in skillful nursing, (I mean by the worthy nurse) in respect to the flow of milk etc than persons generally imagine. How I wish all who were dear to me could always have <u>Susan Newberry</u> at such times - Mittie has this morning hired a nurse for the baby, (day nurse) recommended by Mary Roosevelt - Mary in some of her charitable rounds found a woman who tho poor herself, had taken charge of one or two children who had been actually deserted by their parents - The mother had gone to California, & the poor children but for this woman would have perished - This is the woman Mittie has engaged as a nurse - She has other recommendations also, where she has been employed - Tell dear Stuart I received his truly welcome letter last night I am glad to find Lucy is so well. I hope the dear child may continue so, and that she may be as mercifully dealt with as our dear Mittie has been - I hope he may be directed by Infinite Wisdom with regard to his future plans - I do not like $10,000 debt, but perhaps if nothing is risked but little will be gained - I think debt keeps a poor young man so hampered that he cannot be happy - As it regards a removal to Texas, I have been thinking of one thing which perhaps does not have so much weight with dear Stuart as it would with me - I would not go to a place where I was sure of coining money, if that place were not blessed with the Gospel - I would not bring up a family where God was not recognized and worshiped. Better an other dearth than a famine of the Word of God - I would as soon think of going to a place where no water could be obtained as to a place where there were no religious privileges - In many parts of Texas I know these objects could not be urged - particularly in the towns, but I have my doubts, respecting the plantations and rural districts. Dear children I hope they may do well - Give much love to both of them - I have not seen Mr. Lew West very lately but I hear of his calling on Mrs. Minton, Mrs. Herop Harriott and other ladies constantly. He has been once or twice to Mrs. Minton's - I wish he would take a fancy to Miss Sophie - I think she is a very sweet girl - He visits Miss Smith occasionally also - I think he is interested in that direction - Anna encloses a list which she wishes sent with Mittie's work in addition to the other things she wishes you to send two packages of her envelopes and all of her writing paper - It was in her bureau or wardrobe.

Your affec Mother M Bulloch

Mittie's new nurse is not to come until Susan is dismissed.

Nov 3rd 1858

Dear Susy

All quite well this morning - As little Theodore is a week old this evening, I will not write you again, only occasionally, so if you do not hear frequently you must not be uneasy - I know you would like to hug up the sweet little soft thing - He is very quiet, but I think cries more than Bamie did - Mittie is quite motherly - likes to have him lying quite near her. I had no idea that Thee had a preference as it regards the sex. He is delighted at its being a

225

boy -Tell Stuart Thee says he always thought a man and his wife were the same person, and that when he sent his love to Lucy, he thought Stuart would take his share - Your bonnet has not been sent home yet - Anna had cold and the change of weather has prevented her going to see what Miss Dorsey means - I am glad the weather has changed - I hope now that dear Stuart and Lucy will not be detained longer than they wish to be - How thankful I am that the dear fellow & little Lucy did not remain in Sav during Sept and Oct.[109] Love to both of them and to Hill. Irvine is delighted with "sister Lucy."

Good bye dearest
your affec Mother
M Bulloch

Irvine writes me that he is delighted with his clothes which Hill assisted in purchasing for him, and says also, that he requires a warm coat for school and a vest & pants - I think if Hoyt has the English Tweed, it would be a good material for his common clothes - When he goes to Phil again will you dear Susy and Hill see to this matter for me? Tom King must send on my $3,00 [$300, commas and periods in monetary sums used interchangeably during this time] dollars now very shortly when I hope Hill will settle all of my debts in Phil[a] - I owe Hoyt, old Mr. West the boot maker, and young D[r] West - my respectable son-in-law -

yours etc MB

When Martha moved north, she left several slaves including Luke Moumar (or Mounar) on the property to care for her home and grounds. Jane Camp penned the next letter for *Daddy* Luke although it has been stated that Luke (including Luke's own reference to his abilities) could read and write, having been taught by Martha.

Roswell Ga 8th Nov 58

My dear mistress
            I have taken this opportunity to get a few lines written to you - It has been long since I wrote to you but it has not been any thing that prevented me The summer nights were so short that it was very inconvenient to commence to writing down. Mars [Master] Archy [Archibald Smith] is very good he gives me the refusal to come any time a day - Although I have not written to you Mistress I hope you will not feel that I think so little of you - Since you left Roswell it is not that you have been out of my mind one single hour - At night I would write but when the evening come around I feel pretty painful and sit down to rest but through the day I can get through my business written much life & spirit as I ever had - Great howdy to you my dear Mistress - thousand and thousand of howdy - I hope my letter may find you & all of the family well. Do Mistress by the first mail answer my letter if you please my dear good mistress - Do Mistress when you write me tell me what I must call Mars Irvin whether Mars Irvin, Young Master or Sonny - give him my love dear Mistress - Leah tell you heaps of howdy - Sally same old Sally one day up and three day down, cant tell you howdy enough also Grace & Peggy cant tell you howdy enough to the whole family - Henry and Hagar & Lawrence a smart boy tell you heap of howdies and also to Mars Irvin and the whole family - Jane & Lavina stand right down on the kitchen floor. I dont believe they grow one inch since you left they stand right scrawney bones - Hagar got another fine gall [girl] - Mars Archy and his family are very well but Young Miss Hellen trouble very much with the rheumatism - Do Mistress tell Mars Stewart [Daniel

Stewart Elliott] thousand of howdy for me and also his lady - If you please Mistress send some blanket for the old servants we are getting old and our blood thin and now you have a good chance to send it by Mars Stewart and let him send it on from Savannah to the care of Mars Tom [King] Dear Mistress what a happy thing to see Mars Stewart so far settled and as it makes me happy I know it must make you so and now for the Next thing to see him more settled and a happy man as the Children of God If you see Mars James [Bulloch] do Mistress tell him and his lady heap of howdy for me I hear he has a fine little boy I wish him my Joy and hope that God will enable him to prosper. Tell him I give up going with him to the navy now. I am getting over age - No more I am not so very well mistress but thankful I can go. For three weeks I was very sick but thankful I could go through my business - Aye Mistress we are now apart here but I hope we may travel together this good road which many did choose after this present life - Although the way is hard Mistress but I hope to die a trying - struggle through storms & roughness for heaven - Some days in my own weak feeling I feel it is almost impossible for me to get to heaven but some days I dont know whether it is a right feeling or no I lives up and hopes to see the kingdom of heaven - The white population I think are very good in the proportion is taken into the church. Every communion Mr Pratt has taken in what I call a good chance for our little place. I think Mars Barringtons family has had a great blessing on them. Mars Ralph join the church and so has young Mars Barrington oh what a great feeling I had when I look on them and feel as if they was my own family of people - Mars Pratt two daughters - Mars Tom King restored back to his seat what a blessed thing Mistress - Well Mistress comin round now to our colored population there is when I feel so weak and unworthy when I see the gentle grandchildren all

228

coming forward to the road to heaven and we are so wise as to hold on to this world of trouble and trial - Since you leave Roswell there has not been a coloured member taken in Mr. Pratts church - - There has a case been in our church which has give the church great trial and I had to stand before the session as a witness but you know Mistress I am not afraid to do my duty though I do not forget the bible which says bear not false witness against your brother. I tried to escape it mistress but I could not - When the clerk of the session examine around to find out the witnesses he asked me if I know any thing about it - I told him no, that I was in the country & the case here in Roswell - And when he ask me if I never hear anything about it I could not tell him no because it was public talk and I had to tell him all I heard about it or tell a lie and I could not tell a lie except being condemned [Luke referred to the trouble about the misconduct of Mr. Dunwoody's Abram. He had been excommunicated.] Do Mistress tell Master West ten thousand of howdy for me and also Miss Susan and let me know how the family is, very particular how Master West is. Tell Miss Annie thousand of howdies for me also Charlotte [Luke's wife] cannot express the howdies she send to Miss Annie Miss Susan Master West and also to you dear Mistress - Charlotte beg you Mistress to kiss Mars Irvin 4 times for her and also Miss Annie. Charlotte have been very sick this summer - the last of the summer she have been very poorly indeed - She tooken very sudden with a violent fever - pain in her head and nervous all over she lay up two weeks & three days and never did the first hand stir. Mrs Smith was very kind - She was very affectionate in the sickness with us both. The bible tells us "friend in need and friend indeed" we have been blessed with friend. My dear friend Dr King I made a visit to him and he give me medicine for her to take every hour night & day and if she did not get better to bring her over in a cart to William where he could see her all in good friendship he told me not to be disturbed about any payment at all - From Sunday evening till monday morning she has been getting better and better till now Mars W^m tell me not to let her get down so again but he will give me medicine for her & {___} and I know how to give it. my dear Mistress fare you well my dear Mistress and mother if I never see you again in this Life may we meet in a better. I remain your faithful servant as long as I got a blanket to sweep the dirt from round the gate of any body that has got your blood in them - I sent Dr Kings bill- Mars John was to pay it but the very day he died the bill was given to me and I have it and thought it best to send it to you not knowing what might happen - Dont trouble yourself about it as I took great pleasure in paying that little bit - I can make enough to buy my sugar and coffee

Your affectionate servant

Luke Mounar -

Luke's letter to Martha told the town's gossip and news. For today's reader, it illustrates the great affection Luke and many of Martha's slaves held for her and her family. Luke showed his great respect by calling the adult white population by the terms *Master* and *Mistress;* however, it should also be noted that with only two exceptions, Luke called each by their first name. The two exceptions are the Reverend Pratt and Mrs. Archibald Smith.

Luke lived under Martha's care at this time. She sent him money, probably through John Dunwody, her brother-in-law. Despite this care, Luke earned money for himself by working for the Smith family and the Camp family, and perhaps others. Luke's comment about Master John's death referred to the death of John Dunwody. Jane Dunwody had passed in 1856. The two were buried side by side very near the grave of James Stephens Bulloch in Roswell's original cemetery (now called *Founders*).

Roswell's Presbyterian Church organized in April of 1839 with fifteen white members and seventeen slaves. Luke Moumar was likely one of these original members. Martha and James Bulloch and Susan Elliott signed as original members.[110] Once the church was constructed, each family had a specific pew in which they sat. Their enslaved Africans sat in the balcony.

New York Nov 19-1858

My very dear Susy I sent your things this morning in the same trunk in which you sent my cloak etc. The key tied in front I hope you will receive the trunk safely - Mittie thinks your bonnet quite pretty. Miss Dorsey said she could not get velvet strings to suit, so put a rich ribbon - It was sent back to Miss Dorsey two or three times before it pleased Mittie - The cloak is a very plain looking one but it is made of the very best ribbed Beaver Cloth - The one I wrote you of, which Harriott had purchased for $19 dollars was too short so she has changed it for one costing $20. It is not as good a cloth as yours, but looks more dressy, being black - Mittie is quite well - the baby also - Bamie continues fretful - Thee takes care of her at night in the room adjoining mine - I think she sleeps a little better at nights - Anna went to Richmond on wednesday morning with Mr. Hutchison - She seemed very unwilling to have {or leave?} Bamie - I suppose Irvine is with you - Tell him I have not had time to write him of late - first very busy in helping Anna in her preparations to go and then in obtaining servants for Mittie. She has had to get a new waitress as the one I got in Oct has left and a

231

chamber-maid and seamstress in the place of Johanna who leaves her also the last of this month - I enclose a letter from Tom King - Also one from Luke I thought Irvine would like to read that from Luke - I heard a very fine Thanks - giving sermon from Dr Adams yesterday, which you will see in the "Times" for this morning, with other sermons by some of the Clergy of this City - After sermon Thee and I went to Mrs. Roosevelts to a very handsome lunch - As it was Thursday the children were there also. They were seated around the table & the grown people stood - Bamie went and seemed to enjoy it very much - When I began to prepare to write I found I had but this half sheet - I suppose Stuart and Lucy are gone - I must close - Good bye darling love to all from your affectionate mother

M Bulloch

Dr. Adams served as pastor of the Madison Square Presbyterian Church. Martha attended this church while in New York City. Dr. Adams delivered a "Discourse on the Blessedness of Tears" on Thanksgiving Day which was reprinted in its entirety on the front page of the New York Times the following day.[111]

New York, Nov 20th-1858

My dear Susy,

Thee forgot yesterday to forward your trunk by the Express and it still stands by the hall door. He promises me faithfully to attend to it this morning - I told him I was very sorry as I knew you stood in need of your cloak. Mittie has not been downstairs yet but is walking about in her room the nursery, the entry and bathroom - The baby quite well - Bamie as usual - I believe I told you Thee takes her at night

- While I think of it darling I will mention that the skirt for Lily is that reddish brown brocade of Anna's - You will find it in some of her things - I hope before this time Hill has received the check from Tom King - You will see in Lukes letter which I sent you, that he asks for blankets, and that he has paid Dr Geiger a bill of four dollars, (which by the way I have no recollection of owing) I shall write Mr. Smith to refund Luke and buy the blankets for him - when my money becomes due on the first of January - We have not heard from Anna since she left - I hope dearest you are well. I am afraid you have had fatigue and trouble in getting Stuart and Lucy ready for their departure - - I am afraid too that Irvines visits which appear to give <u>him</u> unbounded pleasure may impose on you some additional burdens. Mittie writes with me in much love to Hill and yourself I wish you could have been with me at the noon day prayer-meeting yesterday - It was a very interesting meeting. The principal topic enforced, was the duty of praying for others - That we must pray not only constantly, but importently and we must feel the value and importance of what we pray for - That until we do, we need not expect our prayers to be answered - Good bye darling - May our Heavenly Father bless you in every respect - For time & for Eternity -

Your loving Mother
M Bulloch -

New York Dec 1858

My dearest Susy,

I have been so very unwell with the influenza, that I have not seen Mrs. West but once since she came to Phil. On monday morning Mrs. West and Mary called to see us - I was surprised as I did not know she was in New York. Thee knew it, but never thought to tell us. Since that day (monday) the weather until today has been very bad, and I have not been able to leave the house - My cough is still very bad but I have less fever and am altogether better - Mittie has influenza also, but a slighter attack than mine - I have been proposing to Mittie to go home but she cries at the bare mention of it, and says of course she cant object if I really want to go, but she thinks with a young baby, and Bamie such an invalid and sufferer, that she ought not to be left alone. I will tell you the routine of one day which will answer for every day - We get up and have breakfast - At ten, or half past ten Dr Davis comes to adjust the apparatus - Then stories must be told or stories read all of time during the operation to keep her from crying - Under her arms her back and her chest are bathed first with water, and then alum and water to prevent chafing - Then the abscess has to be washed with castile soap and water - and greased - Then under her arms etc. are powdered - Then the D^r puts on the apparatus again - She then has her lunch, and is put to bed to take a little nap - Sometimes she sleeps, sometimes she does not not. At one she is taken up and changed, takes her dinner at two, then goes out a little while if the weather is good - When she comes in again it requires constant effort to amuse her and keep her quiet. In the evening about half past seven she goes through the same process with the apparatus as in the morning except that Thee fixes her instead of the Dr Then she is put to bed and I rub her little legs until she goes to sleep - Last week we were very much amazed by Ann Butler {?} getting in a pet [upset/angry] and suddenly leaving - That was on this day week (Thursday evening) While she was washing the rubbed places Bamie screamed out and Mittie asked Ann in the mildest imaginable way not to be rough - Ann immediately said <u>I am not rough</u> flung the towel at Bamie and said you may wipe yourself - I believe Mittie then said I am surprised

234

at you Ann. Ann then said well you may get another nurse as soon as you have a mind to, and flounced out of the room - The next day (Friday) we had a hard time - On saturday she (Ann) went into Mittie's room and made an apology, and said she knew she had spoken very uncivily - Mittie has agreed to keep her until she can get another nurse no longer - They have advertised and Mittie is constantly going down to see applicants. She has a very nice nurse for the baby. The woman Mary recommended - The baby could be placed entirely under her care now, only that his navle is not quite well - and Mittie prefers my attending to it. He is a fine little fellow and has become quite fat and large - He cries a good deal from colic, but is a vigorous natural child has much more spring than even poor little Bamie had - The little thing Bamie is standing by my knee now, and says "she will take my letter to the post ossis" - She has placed the stamp on the envelop as you may perceive She is gone now to eat her dinner, so I can finish my letter - I am afraid you will hardly be able to read it.

Friday morning

I received your note yesterday dearest Susy with Lucy's enclosed. I perceive in that, that my notes of wednesday and yesterday you had not then received. I hope you have gotten them by this time I also, on wednesday morning sent Delia's breadth of silk. Mittie received the box yesterday and says I must tell you and Hill that she is very much obliged to you - Pay for Mittie's soap out of my money, and she will return it to me. The amount is $8.40 cts - I sent the check on wednesday - Poor little Bamie is just the same the abscess not broken yet I think she was not as fretful yesterday as on wednesday - I shall be so glad to see you darling - Mittie says it would not inconvenience her for you to come here & told me to say so to you - but I think if you only stay one night it would not be worth the trouble of bringing up your baggage into the third story - And beside she has just had a large wardrobe made and painted in that room and it smells of paint - But if you do not mind that darling I am sure she would like to have you - Good bye dear Susy Love to Hill - I gave poor little "By" your message -

Your affectionate
Mother M Bulloch

The apparatus worn by Bamie at this time was designed to straighten her spine. Bamie called it the "terrible instrument." In *Bamie: Theodore Roosevelt's Remarkable Sister,* Lilian Rixey related that in the winter of 1858, Theodore Roosevelt discovered Dr. Charles F. Taylor who proposed a series of exercises to help Bamie. The year must have been 1859, for the previous letter tells of Bamie still using the apparatus in December after baby Theodore's birth.

With the new regimen, Bamie would do a series of exercises during the day while confined to her cot to make herself stronger. By the end of the summer, wearing a new light weight brace or harness she could get around by herself and moved to a room on the third floor where all the "big people" lived.

On November 19, Martha wrote to Susan of Anna's trip to Richmond by train on Wednesday 17 November. She was probably escorted by Robert Hutchison, as unmarried women rarely traveled alone. Only one letter remains from the trip, from Anna to Thee.

Richmond

My dear Thee

Yesterday I received your half pages containing the blue fringe for which I am much obliged to all who had any trouble about it. The first package came long ago - You can not think what a splendid time I am having - This morning I would not have a moment to spare but Mr Caskie sent me up from the breakfast table to write. He says I must tell you that on Tuesday 14th he is going to give me a large party and that you must come on to see my "triumph" his own words, he says a little trip would do you good and you shall have the very best of wines and a fine supper - Apropos of suppers, on last Tuesday night Mrs John Walker (brother Jimmie knows her) gave me a most beautiful party if the society had not been so charming I do really think that supper would have finished me - Large dishes of Canvass back ducks, most daintily cooked partridges (I mean quail) - Turkeys in all kinds of fabulous forms - Saltads I had only read of before and when among the stews I include gumbos, oysters in cream, and terrapin! wont your heart bleed to think that I stand in a group of seven gentlemen and was considered a belle! hollow sound to a famished heart - Mrs Caskie has just come in and says I must beg you to come, but that I must tell you that she will not let me go back with you unless you will stay here as long as they want you to - On monday evening I was invited very sociably to the Mitchells - Tennie asked me and said very sadly when she invited me that she could not possibly give me a party this month - The report is that she was engaged to a young man who died last summer, I do not know that this is so it is only what I have heard I passed a delightful evening there Julia looked so elegant and her mode of entertaining was so refined that it was impossible to put her origin lower than the Howards! Jennie was as lovely as the Peri[112] and it was wonderful to behold her on this side of the gates of Paradise! Do give my love to Hattie and ask her if she received a little needle book from Mrs Caskie? How very popular brother Jimmie must have been since so many of his old friends pay me attention for his sake - At Mrs Faulker's party Mrs Heath and Mrs Alfred Jones introduced themselves and paid me all kinds of attention as my brothers friends. Mrs Fitz-Hugh Mayo (a perfect beauty) has called for me and chapperoned me to a large party entirely on brother Jimmie's account and dwelt in such enthusiastic tones on his fascinating manner ways and looks that Mr Mayo eagerly engaged me for imaginary sets of Lancers - going in to suppers for all the rest of the winter and when I told him knowing I would be here he seemed to think his life would become a blank with my departure - Do write to me soon - Love to Mother and Mittie - Kiss both of the little darlings how happy you must be to have them so near you at night - Love to brother Jimmie and Hattie and do ask her how many teeth little Jimmie has - I have had to enter into the most minute detail in my descriptions of him to dear old Mrs [Mr?] Caskie - Fondly dear Thee I would love to have a letter from you I am

your affectionate Sister
Anna L Bulloch.

Anna visited the Caskie family in Richmond. This was probably James (1792-1866) and Eliza Kennon Randolph (1797-1864), the parents of Ellen Laura Caskie Hutchison (1836-1858), Robert's third wife who died after childbirth earlier that year.[113] James and Eliza had six remaining children, none of whom are mentioned in this letter. Unfortunately, none of the other Richmond residents mentioned in the letter have been identified.

Chapter VIII
1859

The World in 1859

While political turmoil continued across the United States, another state joined the Union when Oregon became the 33rd state on 14 February. On 28 February, the slave-state Arkansas' legislature required free blacks to choose exile or slavery.

Other developments included the 23 January eruption of Hawaii's Mauna Loa volcano. The eruption continued for 300 days. On 25 April, construction began on the Suez Canal. In June, the Comstock Silver Lode in Nevada was discovered. Additionally, a western boundary dispute between the U.S. and Canada's Oregon Treaty led to the so-called *Pig War*.

On the cultural scene, Bryant's Minstrels debuted *Dixie* in New York City in the finale of a blackface minstrel show on 4 April. Later in the month, Charles Dickens' *A Tale Of Two Cities* saw publication in the literary periodical *All the Year Round*. Weekly installments ran until 26 November. After presenting his evolutionary theories in public speeches for several years, on 24 November, Charles Darwin published his *On the Origin of Species*.

Abolitionist John Brown and 21 followers seized the government arsenal at Harpers Ferry, Virginia, on 16 October and held it against counterattack for two days. After his capture, Federal forces executed Brown as a traitor. He became a martyr and hero to many in the North; however, John Brown's raid escalated tensions between the North and South to a degree not previously reached.

The 1859 Letters

Tuckers
Saturday Afternoon July 16

My dearest Susy,

I have been wanting to write you ever since you left this place but some how never could make it convenient - I received your sweet letter several days since, and intended writing yesterday but pretty soon after breakfast, heard a little noise in Anna's room & found Mrs. & Mr. Roosevelt had arrived to spend the day - We were delighted to see them - Mrs. R is quite improved in health - The day you left I felt really bereaved and home-sick about you - I thought you did not look well the evening before you left. They tell me it is conceit on my part, but I know better - I hope dearest Susy you will enjoy your cessation from the cares of house-keeping and that the fine air at Rockaway may invigorate and do you much good - I am glad too that you will enjoy a little respite from Mantau makers. I cant bear to think of the haggard course through which Mrs. Lewis had you. I have been very busy of late assisting Mittie to get ready for a visit to the Sharon Springs. She and Thee expected to go a few days since, but they were Telegraphed that there were no vacant rooms - It is uncertain therefore when they will go - The trunks are packed, and they are now waiting for good weather and to hear that they can get rooms - Little Theodore has been very unwell of late, but seems better now - He has had a violent cold, in addition to which I think he is cutting several teeth - He is however so much better, that Mittie will leave him with less reluctance than if she had gone at the time first appointed. Darling it seems to me that you had a narrow escape in the omnibus the day you left N York - By your letter however I infer that you were not in danger yourself, but that your dress trunk was - How glad you must have been after the fatigues of the day, to rest & have such kind friends - Do give our kind regards to them all - No picnics since you left, but an incessant row of some sort or other - Last saturday afternoon there was a man drowned some where near the rocks on which we used to sit. He took a heavy-supper just before he went in the water, and it is generally supposed he had a fit in the water, or he would not have drowned as he was a good swimmer I think the occurrence made even the most thoughtless pause for a few moments and reflect on the uncertainty of life - All appeared in some degree awed and the usual saturday night dancing was suspended - The next day (sabbath) we had communion in the little church which we attend. We had solemn and delightful exercises, including a very good sermon from Mr. Prime, brother to {__ius} Prime - In the afternoon on sunday Bamie [age 4] seemed at a loss for amusement so I gave her a piece of paper and pencil with which she wrote you a letter -

She read it to me and this is as near as I can recollect the letter -

Dear Aunt Susy and uncle Hill
Bamie writes you a letter - you and uncle Hilly don't know what is in it but you got a long time at Rockaway and you must read it odis and odis Dear Aunt Susy here is a picture of Tedo [little Theodore], and here is a picture of Rockaway - Bamie -

She really thought it was writing and was surprised that I could not read it - I received a letter from Stuart lately which I enclose - I wrote him immediately - and sanctioned the disposal of Luke [Moumar] to Mr. King -

Mittie and Anna send a great deal of love to Hill and yourself and Irvine has just been in my room to say that I must be sure to give his love to you both - Lew is well does not know I am writing - Your affec. Mother M Bulloch

Little Tedo's milk crust is better, but he suffers with boils - Direct to the care of
>   Wm Tucker
>   New Rochelle
>   NY -
I have concluded not to send Stuart's letter - It is a mistake about little John, having the milk crust Stuart mentions that he is quite well and very pretty.

>   MB

The Roosevelts, Wests, and other members of the family spent the summer at William Tuckers' resort on Long Island, near New Rochelle. Today, an area called Tucker's Point is quite popular for tourists. Mittie and Thee planned to visit Rockaway, New York, an up and coming tourist area advertised in several New York papers in the late 1850s.

Martha's reference to Susan and the mantua makers used a period term for seamstresses that specialized in ladies' dresses. Susan and Hilborne were planning a visit to Sharon Springs, New York about 50 miles west of Albany. The small spa village welcomed about 10,000 visitors each summer during the mid-1800s.

Martha mentioned Stuart's letter and his newborn son John for the first time. Named for his grandfather and

Stereoscopic view of Sharon Springs, New York.

Stereoscopic
view of
Magnesia
Springs Resort
at
Sharon Springs,
New York.

243

his father, John Stuart Elliott arrived in March of 1859. At this time Stuart and Lucy resided either in Savannah or near Marietta, Georgia.

Mrs Mitchill says she leaves on the first of September.

Tucker's August 16-

My dearest Susy

I received your letter of the 11^{enth} inst, and need not say how glad I was to get it - We are all well - Bamie has missed her fever and is getting well - Tedo has cut two teeth lately, and is labouring with two others, but he is doing very well, and is a sweet little fellow. I have lately received a letter from Lucy - Stuart is a little better but is still very unwell - but I will inclose the letter to you. I have written her today, and begged him to employ medical aid - The first rooms I wrote you about were not Mrs Corneil Mitchill's, but a room at the disposal of old Mrs Mitchill. Her daughters Anne & Mary Louise went to Niagara and their rooms were vacant several weeks. Indeed they have not returned yet The last rooms I wrote you about were Mrs Corneil Mitchill's which are to be vacant for the first of Sept - These I am going to secure for you - I will give Mrs Tucker your message about Towels etc - I have lately heard from Mr Hutchinson - He says he is quite well but is still thin - Rob Lew West, and Irvine have just been to Rockaway in the Yacht - They were delighted with their visit - Irvine was sick while he was there and says they were all very kind to him - I will see Mrs C Mitchill at dinner and know exactly when she expects to leave - I would write you longer darling but having just written a long letter to Lucy feel tired of the pen - How I should like to have gone to church with you - Love to Hill & yourself from Mittie, Anna & Irvine

Your affec mother M Bulloch

244

My dearest Susy

In my last letter to you I told you that Mrs Corniel Mitchell was to leave the first of Sept. I would not write you possitively about her rooms until I had heard their intention from her own lips - This morning she came to my room and told me she was very sorry to disappoint us, but that her Father {Mr Reid?} had persuaded her to remain the month of Sept. at Tuckers consequently the rooms would not be vacated - Now there is no other room vacant but the one which is opposite to ours - The room which was formerly called the "Office". It has been furnished as comfortably as any of the other rooms and I think is not more public and is nearly or quite as good a room as our front bed-room, which Anna occupies - A lady and her husband have occupied this room the greater part of the summer but had to leave on the account of the illness of her sister - Mittie and I were consulting about the matter this morning and we think you might spend a few weeks there tolerably comfortably - Let us know what you think of it - We are all well darling - Little Tede still has milk-crust and is troubled with his teeth - He is not at all sick tho', and is one of the brightest little fellows I ever knew - Bamie has been very unwell but has missed her fever seems to have a good appetite and is improving very much - About a week since she complained so much of her apparatus, that Thee and Anna took her to New York, and sent for Dr Chesseman who had recommended a different kind of apparatus, and different physician - The physician is a Dr Taylor. Immediately on seeing Bamie he took her measure and said he would have an apparatus made for her as soon as he possibly could - They had to remain in NY until friday evening when they brought her back with her new apparatus on. I like it much better than the other. It is much more comfortable, and we all hope will be more efficacious. Dr Chesseman said it was constructed on more enlightened principles - I think you would like to see how much more pleasant it is to her than D^r {D__sis}. I have not heard lately from Stuart and Lucy - I hope poor Stuart is better - the fair is to come off next week - I must not forget to tell you that Rob has exchanged his old Yacht giving some boat, for a very nice one indeed. He has a man too to do all of the hard work, so that the gentlemen now will only have to sail her - Lew is quite pleased - I often wish Hill could be with them - I suspect it will kick Irvines heart when he has to leave in a fortnight from this - nothing new except that Mr Sam Mitchell is engaged to be married to a Miss Smith boarding at the Neptune House -Susy darling have you read those accounts of the great revival of religion in Ireland? It is indeed a most wonderful work of grace I wish I could see something of the kind here - One sabbath at Tuckers makes one feel like weeping to think that there is so little love and fear of God - write me dear Sudie when you can - Anna Mittie & Irvine send much love to you both Give my warmest love to Hill - I must stop as the dinner bell will soon ring -

Your affectionate mother
M Bulloch

Tuesday morning Aug 23-
{___I} got a letter from Stuart yesterday He has sold his place near Marietta & gone down to Sav - He has been elected to fill some situation in the State Bank He is much better - nearly well of his pain and cough - All well this morning dear Susy -

Your affec Mother MB

These three letters provided a glimpse into the family situations in 1859. Bamie continued to suffer from her ailment, little Theodore began cutting teeth, and Stuart received an appointment at the Bank of the State of Georgia. In these letters, Martha first mentions Stuart's illness.

The *Brooklyn Evening Star* on Friday 2 September reported a horrible accident that occurred at Tuckers and involved the Roosevelt family. While we have no additional letters from this year, the Roosevelt and Bulloch women would have been present at the ladies' fair when all of this transpired.

> As the yacht Edda was nearing her harbor at New Rochelle, about half past eight o'clock Wednesday evening she was struck by a sudden squall, capsized, and Miss Catherine Waterbury, daughter of Lawrence Waterbury, Esq., and Miss Littlefair, her governess were drowned.
>
> There had been a ladies fair at the house of Mr. Tucker, on the little island in the sound in the town of New Rochelle, and Mr. Robert Roosevelt had gone down the shore a short distance to Throgg's Neck, to the house of Mr. L. Waterbury, in the yacht Edda, for the purpose of bringing up to the fair Mrs. Gregory, a sister of Mr. Waterbury; Miss Catherine Waterbury, a girl of twelve years of age, daughter of Mr. L. Waterbury; and Miss Littlefair, her governess.
>
> The Edda is a trim sloop yacht of fifteen tons, thirty seven feet long, painted white, and is one of the New York Yacht Squadron. Mr. Roosevelt had with him a man named Ned to assist in managing the boat. The party had

proceeded on their return with a light wind under full sail, until within about twenty yards of their destination.

The night was dark, and Ned was steering, while Mr. Roosevelt was on the bow looking out for the rocks and giving directions to the helmsman. Suddenly the squall came up, and to avoid the rain which evidently impended the ladies took refuge in the cabin. The next instant the wind struck the full sails of the yacht, careening her over to her beam ends, and in another moment the vessel had capsized, while Ned was in the act of getting Mrs. Gregory out of the cabin, precipitating the two men and Mrs. Gregory into the water, Ned succeeded in getting Mrs. Gregory on the side of the yacht, and Mr. Roosevelt swam about trying to find either of the other females, but without success. The small boat was still floating right, side up and finding the search fruitless, the survivors took to the small boat and made for the shore.

The merry party at the fair had meanwhile been all unconscious of the fearful scene which had been enacted during the last hour within a stone's throw of the scene of their festivities, and the appearance of the two men bearing the dripping form of Mrs. Gregory was the first indication they had of the painful circumstances. The boarders at Mr. Tucker's instantly manned and launched the life boat, and for hours pursued a fruitless search for the bodies of the unfortunate females. The squall had subsided in a few moments; but the yacht had filled, drifted off, and soon after sunk in fifteen fathoms of water, so that it was impossible to rise her until morning. The search was, however, continued during the night, in the vain hope of finding either of the missing ladies, saved by some fortunate circumstance, or their bodies as a last mournful consolation to their friends. All that could be found was a few remnants of their clothing.

Yesterday morning, by the aid of wreckers, the yacht was raised, and the body of Mr. Waterbury's daughter, thus suddenly transformed from the health and bloom of childish innocence to the cold embrace of death, was found in the cabin. Up to last evening, when our reporter visited the scene, the body of Miss Littlefair had not been recovered. A reward of one hundred dollars has been offered, and the search was being vigorously prosecuted.

There can be no doubt that the affair was purely accidental, as with such a light breeze as permitted all sail to be up until the boat was within twenty rods of her anchorage, no human forethought could have anticipated such a squall. . . . .

Chapter IX
1860

The World in 1860

A speech by Abraham Lincoln on 27 February at New York's Cooper Union pushed him further into the limelight and directly led to his nomination and election to the Presidency. Many saw Lincoln as a symbol of the frontier and hard work. The Republican Party convened in Chicago on 16 May and selected Lincoln as their candidate. A new party, the Republicans recognized the split in the Democratic Party as their path to winning the White House. The Democratic Convention, held in Charleston, South Carolina, the previous month, had been divided over the slavery issue and ended amidst turmoil. At their 1860 convention, Northern Democrats had selected Stephen Douglas, an ardent supporter of slavery who also supported popular sovereignty. *Popular sovereignty* gave new territories and states the right to decide for themselves whether to be free or slave. Southern Democrats left their convention without choosing a candidate, and met again six weeks later to decide on the sitting Vice President, John C. Breckenridge of Kentucky.

To further complicate the election, a group of aging politicians and distinguished citizens, calling themselves the Constitutional Union Party, met and nominated wealthy slave holder, John Bell of Tennessee. The Constitutional

Union Party believed the best way to confront the difficulties the nation faced was to take no stand at all on the issues that divided the north and the south.

The votes of the Electoral College split among the four candidates. Lincoln received only 40% of the popular vote and won 180 electoral votes to narrowly win the crowded election. This meant that 60% of the voters selected someone other than Lincoln in the November general election.

Other events of the year included the beginning of the Pony Express on 3 April. Using a relay of horses and riders, the express began mail service between St. Joseph, Missouri, and Sacramento, California. On 19 July, the first rail line reached Kansas. On 20 September, the Prince of Wales, later King Edward VII, became the first British royal to visit the United States.

After the November election, the South erupted. On 20 December, South Carolina seceded from the Union. On 26 December, U.S. Army Major Robert Anderson, under cover of darkness, concentrated his small force at Ft. Sumter, located in Charleston, South Carolina's harbor. Two days later, once-enslaved Harriet Tubman arrived in Auburn, New York, on her last mission to free slaves. She evaded capture for eight years on the Underground Railroad while escorting others to freedom.

The 1860 Letters

The beginning of 1860 found Mittie and the children in Philadelphia with her mother and sisters. Mittie, again pregnant, expected her third child in February. Apparently, Thee took Mittie and the children to Philadelphia by train for their visit and then returned home to continue his usual pursuits. This letter contains our first look at Thee's charitable efforts.

New York Jan 22^d 60

Dear Mittie

I have at last finished my days labours, I should rather say pleasures, and although only eleven o'clock it might as well be the night before Christmas for the amount of noise that there is in the house. The table with its green cloth, the curtains, the book case all look as home like as usual and I try to imagine Bamie and yourself tucked in as usual at this hour of the evening up-stairs.

Mother sent her love to you but <u>particularly</u> to Bammie. I gave hers to "Grand ma".

Tell Tedore I miss his assistance sadly in helping me get out my clothes and kiss both the children for me, "all three together."

I had a very pleasant trip on secured my order on the way, and just reached the train in time. One of those numerous acquaintances that George Morris used to laugh at me for having so many of took his seat by me and I amused myself by drawing the little there was in him out during the twilight. He has purchased a ticket to Trenton for fifty cents and paid for another one from there to New York one doll and forty five cents. Hill will explain how much cheaper this was than paying as I did three dolls through. The gas was soon lit when I was able to continue in the Harper my travels through Costa Risa through the pen of Mr Meagher.

I had scarcely put the key in the door at the corner of Broad Way & 14th St. before father came out to see if it was me as they were expecting me.

Mr Mrs & Miss Hoy were there in addition to our own family in whom Grove is included. Miss Hoy is to me a very ugly young lady with a very pretty figure. I was immediately supplied with so much supper that I found no more than time to give mother a very succinct account of our trip without devoting myself to Miss Hoy.

Mother sympathized very much with your mother and seemed much gratified by Bammie's remembrance of her.

All were in very high spirits Grove walked up home with me regretting frequently that he had not known where you and Annie were going to start from. He had suggested to Mother to send up for the Bananas and oranges for which there was a good deal of laughing at his expense as mother of course did not find them. He stayed with me until twelve o'clock and will dine with me tomorrow evening.

This morning I went to the sunday school and the day was so bright that it brought out a very large attendance George Peet told with a very smiling face that his sister had the Scarlet fever.

When I told him I was afraid of the other boys catching it and would not be able to let him stay he cried most piteously.

Dr. Adams gave us the sermon of the season, text St. Luke XII 47 & 48 verses. It would have done Dickens good to have heard a contrast to his pictures of most preaching to fashionable audiences. It will be worse for those whose first words were those of prayer, whose whole training is the inculcation of the truths of the Bible, who always have that book where they can see its teachings, than it will be for Sodom and Gomorrah and the day of judgment unless they come out on the Lords side.

And then he pointed to the Lords supper an ordinance commanded by God and by receiving which we would show our faith in him. But this would be only an acknowledgement of the many and very responsible duties which we owed to him. Much had been confided to us and much would be expected from us. I went away feeling that I might devote all the time and much more than I was now doing to God's service and I would still fall far short of any hope of salvation except through his divine mercy.

Mr Caulkins the visitor came home and dined with me.

Mr Craven called and sent his respects to you. He described his experience at the Water Cure down-east this fall and how he was at last cured by the use of Peruvian Syrup in a very amusing way, actually remembering the point to the story.

At half past one I started off again and after a very satisfactory time at school found one of the boys turned out of Mr Collins class hanging round the streets. I gave him a tract on condition that he would go home and read it which I found an hour or two afterwards he had done by dropping in and examining him on the contents. I laid myself out to see how many I could persuade to meet me at the Mission church in the evening who would not have come otherwise. About ten came I thought a pretty good afternoon's work. One was a very peculiar case; Mrs. Guins {?} the mother of the hump back whose husband died a short time since seemed sinking into a kind of melancholy and never left her room. To use her own expression was "kinder upset." I used every argument of religion in vain; her husbands desire expressed in my presence on his dying bed was of no more use only bringing tears.

Atlast I asked if in consideration of the kindness I had shown her she would grant me a personal request. This gained my point and she told me after the service that she was very glad she had come.

My last visit was to mother at half past nine this evening. She said she had almost given me up and then asked me to sit down and tell her "everything".

I had asked her for two oranges the night before for the boys whose limbs are paralyzed and of course she wanted to hear about him.

Laura and Cornel came in and I had two pieces of pie, covered over with white stuff, and some chedar cheese.

Give my love to Susan and Annie and believe me

Your Husband

Thee

Confidential. Mittie it is very important that you should lie down as much as possible to avoid the risk which otherwise attends the trouble you described to me. Tell your mother to get Hill to call in Dr Meiggs if he neglects it.

Enclosed is a letter from Sue Morris. Miss Robbins sent her love to you today.

While traveling by train, Thee often entertained himself by talking with total strangers, as he did during this journey before returning to the quiet of his newspaper. With the December 1859 issue, *Harper's New Monthly Magazine* started a three part travel article about Costa Rica by Thomas Francis Meagher, complete with illustrations.

Thee wrote of Dr. Adam's sermon on Luke 12:47-48.[114]

> Luke 12:47 And that servant, which knew his lord's will, and prepared not himself, neither did according to his will, shall be beaten with many stripes.
> Luke 12:48 But he that knew not, and did commit things worthy of stripes, shall be beaten with few stripes. For unto whomsoever

much is given, of him shall be much required: and to whom men have committed much, of him they will ask the more.

Thee, no doubt, recognized he was one of the latter to whom "much is given" and seemed to act accordingly. His charitable actions often focused on orphan boys or young boys and men who needed direction and help in life.

In 1854, Nathaniel L. Clark published a booklet describing his contacts with Peru and the benefits of the Peruvian Syrup. He advertised his syrup in many newspapers and even *The Old Farmer's Almanack* as a cure for dyspepsia. The product continued to be sold until the late 1800s.

Thee wanted Hilborne to call Dr. Charles Delucena Meigs (1792-1869), an influential American obstetrician known for his opposition to obstetrical anesthesia and who advanced the idea a physician's hands could transmit disease. Meigs graduated from the University of Pennsylvania's medical school in 1817 followed by specialized training in obstetrics and was for a long time the acknowledged leader in this branch of medicine. In 1841, he became professor of obstetrics and diseases of women in the Jefferson Medical College, where Hilborne was a student.[115] Thee, like most men of the era, understood the risk of death to the mother, child, or both during childbirth. Although this birth would be Mittie's third, Thee was no doubt concerned.

Washington Feb 2ᵈ 60

Dear Mittie,

We arrived in Baltimore without any incident except the purchase of a pr of moccasins by myself, which I indulged

257

myself with from an old love for the article and because I really require slippers of some kind.

I transacted my business and then before going to the hotel called on Elliott Johnston to explain my apparent neglect in not answering his letter.

His brother Joe received me in the most friendly manner and after walking back to the hotel with me inquired when I would be at home to see his brother Elliott. I told him I would be engaged until ten o'clock. Hill said he was going to the French Opera and I started out to see Miss Meredith and Mrs Howland. They were out and after paying a short visit to my friend Smith I found he was going to a supper party and not liking to be left to the miseries of the seniors went to join Hill at the opera. At ten I returned home and found a card from Elliott requesting me to join him at Guy's the individual for Terrapin and Canvas Back duck.

I would have liked to bring you home a specimen of the terrapin, you would have eaten it even with the prospect of a bottle of soda as the consequence.

This morning we reached here in a very pleasant frame of mind, received very good rooms and started out Hill with Mr Rapello and I to attend to my business.

We both agreed not to indulge in any society so I have seen no one out of the hotel and in it I have but two or three friends all gentlemen.

Bill Pennington is here and professes himself rather regretful that his father has the labors of speaker on his shoulders.

Mrs Gwin gives a ball tonight which might be worth seeing but not in consequence of any additions it receives from this house, an uglier, more remarkably dressed set of women I never saw. It almost took away my appetite for dinner to look at them.

This house has been enlarged and much improved but still retains the look it had when we were here together, the long hall and little parlors opening now into a larger one.

Hilborne and myself will be waked tomorrow at nine o'clock and leave for Mount Vernon at eleven if the boat is not prevented from running in consequence of the ice. I hope to combine my visit to Alexandria with it and get back in the evening but this seems questionable.

Elliott Johnston has promised to send by me his receipt [recipe] book entire to you and requested to be remembered. I was very much pressed by both Smith and himself to spend several days in Baltimore on my return. Both of them invited me to dinner.

As we approach the South, tell Anna that we begin to perceive the effects of the remarkable inventive genius of her pets. The wardrobe in my room is a specimen; it is very large beautiful and made of inlaid walnut. On opening it however no pegs were apparent and after much search we discovered them screwed onto the door of the room instead, in large quantities.

Hill is in fine spirits and of course makes a very genial companion, the trip so far in a pleasurable point of view is a decided success.

As far as business is concerned it has not been in consequence of any want of effort on my part but the fates have not this time smiled on me quite as much as is there wont.

I went all over the top of the Treasury Building through the snow this morning, sometimes sliding thirty or forty feet down the roof and only wanting my Alpine Stock to remind me very much of my Swiss experience. I gained the desired information with regard to the glass but did not gain a decision in my favor, indeed cannot make them decide at all.

I hope you will be able to decipher this letter but it is written while I am surrounded with blooding fire-eating looking set of men talking smoking chewing and spitting; not to mention that the ink seems from its consistency to have been some left in Noahs inkstand and was since exposed to the air.

Your husband
Theodore

Thee visited with his friend Bill Pennington, son of Speaker of the House, William Pennington (1796-1862). William, a Republican, represented New Jersey in the 36th Congress in 1859-1860. After two months of being unable to reach a majority decision on who should be Speaker of the House, members finally elected Pennington. He ran an unsuccessful campaign for reelection to the 37th Congress in 1860 and died of an accidental overdose in 1862.

Thee visited Washington on business, as he apparently consulted on the glass for the renovations of the Treasury Building. After a fire in March of 1833, the current Treasury Building was constructed. By the late 1850s, the Treasury needed additional space, so the building was undergoing an expansion and renovation. After the Panic of 1857, construction had been halted except for completion of the South Wing.[116]

New York March 14 60

My dearest Susy

I hope this letter may find you much better than when I left and the rest of the dear family well. I arrived here

260

U.S. Treasury Building, Washington, D.C.,
photograph taken before 1861.

on saturday about four oclock after a very pleasant journey-
Mary and Mr Roosevelt were very kind and attentive - My
{___} soot [foot?] received no injury whatever Little Hilly
was as gay as a lark, & Jimmy time was occupied with short
naps and grave conversations with Jane. We took a carriage
at the wharf, which took some time to make its way through
the lower part of Broadway - However tedious things have
to come to an end at last so after a while, much to little
Jimmie's delight we found ourselves at No. 1 E 20 St. Mary
and Jimmie got out and Hilly was taught the gallantry to
escort me to 33 E 20 St. Little Hilly rang the bell which
was soon answered by Ann Butler, followed closely by Bamie
- The little creature was perfectly delighted to see me and
followed me up stairs into her mother's room - Dear little
Mittie would have been sitting up, but for a severe pain
in her face. She did not know whether it was caused by
a slight defect in one of her jaw teeth or whether it was

not a neuralgic affection - All of saturday evening we were applying laudanum poultices to the part, and bathing it with warm laudanum - Just before bed-time she seemed to suffer so much that I advised her to take 20 drops of Mᶜmunn Elixer she soon after went to sleep and in the morning (yesterday) I found her quite easy - To day she is in her usual health - She says she has been literally not sick at all since the first day of pain - Except this pain in her face - she has been a well person - The baby is a fine healthy little fellow, but small - I think he is decidedly pretty for a young baby, and the most quiet child I have ever known except Bamie - Mittie has asked me two or three times if you were pleased at its being named after you - Bamie is devoted to it - I am afraid Mittie will not have milk enough - her heart begins to over flow with love for it - I think it is going to look like Mittie has a small head shaped like hers - Bamie sleeps on her little bed in my room - I found her very much improved in health - and she is certainly one of the sweetest little children I have ever known. She knows all of her letters perfectly, large and small, & can spell in words of three and four letters - She is as busy as ever, always wanting to assist somebody - Tede is still toothless {?} is in good health and eats his full share of food - I did not go to church yesterday and as I heard Hariott was not well, took Bamie with me in the afternoon to see her - She has a sweet little plump baby - very good and sweet looking - She says James is devoted to it - Little Jimmie is as bad as ever with his mischief - I did give her your message but [will] see her again shortly and {__}. Hariott was doing very well but the day Mittie was sick, she sent to ask Hariott where Mrs Newberry was, <u>She</u> directly (had not been out before) rushed over to Mittie's had beds etc all arranged, and sent for the Dʳ At three she found Mittie was getting quite sick, but she knew all was right, and as Mary and Mrs Roosevelt were with Mittie, and her baby was at home she went back - That evening she was taken with her old complaint and had to send for Dr Emmet. She is better but not well - Tell dear Anna I have just received her letter, will write her next Tell her Mittie was delighted with the slippers and little shirts and Bamie of course as much pleased as Mittie - Mittie told her last night to show them to Laura, and when she took them out of the drawer she reprimanded her Mother for not turning in the bows just as aunt Anna had sent them -

Good bye darling as I shall write Anna shortly I will write no more at present - Anna Butler is to take the dresses today to Lafuse [Lefevre[117]] how sorry I am for poor Mr. Chambers. You must not write to me at all. I know what it costs you - Mittie seemed almost to think hard that we did not write her when we heard about the baby - and Jimmie thought hard that we did not notice little Jessie's birth - Love to dear Anna & Irvine and to the busy Dr from

your affectionate Mother
M Bulloch

Tell Anna Bamie received the Vallentine & ring - It is a cherished object.

Martha traveled back to New York with Silas Weir and Mary Roosevelt. Mary was Hilborne's sister. In 1860, Silas and Mary had three children, Cornelius, age 13, Hilborne, age 10, and James, not quite two. The younger two traveled with Martha and their parents. Martha's return was welcomed by two new mothers. Mittie gave birth to Elliott on 28 February, just after the arrival of Harriott and Jimmie's daughter Jessie Hart. While Mittie named her son for Susan, Harriott named her daughter for the riverboat captain and plantation owner she lived with for several years before marrying James.

Patent medicines contained all sorts of formulas purported to solve a variety of ailments and were very popular during this period. Many of these like McMunn's Elixer contained narcotics, just as McMunn's Elixer actually contained opium. These medicines were therefore quite addictive, and yet, not illegial. It was readily available and was used by men, women, and even given to children.

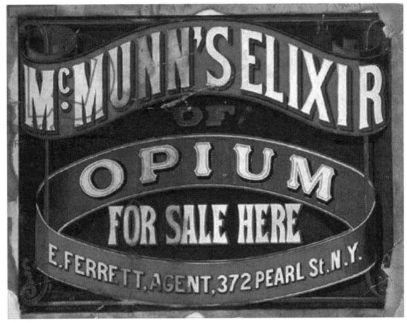

Advertisement for McMunn's Elixir

Fog April 4th 60

Dear Mittie

I begin a letter, finishing it will be a different matter. Everyone around me seems, as I feel, perfectly miserable and at any moment I may be obliged to give up even the spirit that suggests sending you a drive from Halifax.

Give a kiss to Bamie from me._

5th Imagine me suddenly obliged to leave the cabin and finding even fresh air did not revive me make a rush for

the side of the ship convinced for once that I was sea-sick.
The balance of the evening I did not feel equal to entering
the cabin and only now as we approach Halifax does my
evening revive.

I have not been too sick to make acquaintances and find
quite a pleasant set on board. Mr [M___] who is engaged
to Miss Nelson and one or two others were my original
acquaintances.

Young Bartlett and the Greek came down to see some friends
off in Boston and Bartlett was particularly cordial.

My companion in the state-room is a thoroughly english long
nosed individual painfully good natured and commonplace.

I could not help contrasting the relative enjoyment of little
Teedie in my room with his white top knot on bringing me
an indefinite supply of boots and this youth in the little
stateroom, in which I stay until after ten o'clock this
morning hoping he would go out first.

I remembered Bammie's morning visits also but suppose
her time is so much occupied taking care of the rest of the
family that she does not miss them.

Tell her not to forget the care she has promised to take of
Teedie during my absence and to see that Elliott does not
starve.

There are a most motley crowd on board, the worst specimens
however will leave at Halifax where we will take on board
another supply. It is eleven o'clock at night and we are still
ten miles from there or I would make an effort to see Tom
Renny and Maggie.

The women on board look at present even more cadaverous
than the men but I feel at present particularly willing to
apply the text advising us not to judge others.

Tell Jim that I left my silver pencil at the store and request
him not to throw it away because the pen does not suit him.

Give a great deal of love to mother from me and tell her I will write to her from England.

And now Mittie I must say good bye requesting to be remembered to all my friends for if there is a time when I would like my friends to remember me it is when undergoing the misery of a sea voyage

Your Melancholy Husband
Thee

New York Wednesday April 18 / 60

My dearest Susy

I received your letter of the 16 yesterday morning - It amused us very much and I was glad to hear you were better & that Irvine was studying - I begin to be so anxious to see you all that I shall certainly return the last of next week or the beginning of the week following if nothing providential prevents - We went yesterday to see the woman who is engaged to be Mitties wet nurse - Her infant is only a week old and she is still in bed, but Mittie and I both liked her, and the Matron says she has an abundance of milk - She <u>could</u> come when her baby is two weeks old, but Mittie says she prefers her remaining three weeks in the Asylum - If she stays three weeks she cannot be here before this day two weeks. This may delay my return a few days longer, as I think I had better wait until she comes - However - I am not sure but what I shall return on saturday week, whether she comes or not provided I find as she gets up from her confinement that she will suit. Lafevre [see endnote #117] promised me that your box would go yesterday and as she sent yesterday morning for the articles I had here I presume it goes today, at any rate - When you try on the dresses if you find they fit, I can pay your bill for you right away, as I

A fashionable evening gown and bonnet in 1860
from *Godey's Lady's Book*.

A fashionable day gown and bonnet in 1860
from *Godey's Lady's Book*.

have funds and it would save the trouble and risk of sending it. Let me know about this matter, and tell Anna to do so likewise - As it regards bonnets Mittie says she has been out so little, she has seen nothing - but we will go shortly to Miss Dorsey's and make enquiries I heard Lissie Emlen & Mary say that they are not worn large, but Lissie Ellis said they have a peculiar fit in front, and were worn without caps - We have had Quaker weather here also - It rains almost incessantly - How amusing Dr Lewis is, I should like to have heard him. I hope Dr Henry has recovered - Mittie is quite well, is not quite as much troubled with the pain in her chest and shoulders when she nurses as she was a few weeks since. The baby grows finely, and is a sweet quiet little thing - The truss does not appear to annoy him at all - nothing makes him cry but hunger He will not bear that for a moment. Teedie and Bamie are well. I found no difficulty at all in reading your dear letter, I know even what your little strait marks mean but I do not want you to write - I know it fatigues you - I am truly glad Hill is well again. I do think it is too much to teach in sabbath school and practice medicine also. I have written to Mr Tifft for my Dividend - I have written also to Luke a long letter - and to Tom King to settle up to the present time with Mrs Campbell for Byron and to give Luke five dollars The balance which he owes me is to be sent to Phil^a If you receive a letter from him to me enclosing a draft on M^{c}divit & co, just put it one side until I come - I went last sunday to hear Dr Hoge - I went with H Pratt and sat in Mr Wilson's pew - It was a beautiful sermon on the loving kindness of God - I am going again I live for next sunday morning to hear Dr Spring - I am so very glad that Irvine studies - Tell him to persevere, and I hope he will yet be a good scholar - I am very glad too he has had his teeth fixed - and I hope darling that you did not suffer much in having yours fixed - Remember to let me know whether

I shall settle yours and Annas bill with Lafever - Give a great deal of love to each member of the family - I can say truly that the house in Pine St 1524 contains four persons whom I love -

Yours affectionately
M Bulloch

Mittie sends love - Would you like me to get your bonnet here? I could take it back with me to Phil very well as my trunk will be so empty it can hold several band-boxes.

Elliott weighs nearly eleven pounds

Irvine studied at the University of Pennsylvania, beginning in 1860. He lived with Hill, Susan, and Anna at 1524 Pine Street. The site is now a brownstone apartment building built in 1900.

Valenciennes April 29th 60

Dear Mittie

I found myself obliged yesterday to change my route with some regret and pass my sunday here. It has proved however a very great pleasure.

The trains did not connect at Mons and I had three hours to see the many curiosities of that old town. First came the Cathedral and here I must say that my little charity for the catholics is fast oozing out.

Before all the different images were poor little children kneeling and while I was present the recitations in latin commenced. It made me almost sick to see the disgusting representations of our Savior represented by a statue flesh colored with the crown of thorns and all streaming with blood.

The alto relievos which are very old and proportionately disfigured and noted are simply amusing.

He is in one of those on the cross represented as supported by a very large person with immense whiskers and surrounded among others by the Pope in full canonicals and three little children standing in a tub.

Under one of them that represent the passion or rather one scene of it was a short prayer headed by a paragraph which I copied for you it is as follows, after stating the indulgences. "These indulgences are available forever and applicable to souls in purgatory." The cathedral itself is remarkable being a net work of marble to the top.

The town is surrounded by fortifications and just outside of them those pleasant walks that surround most of the old fortified towns.

They have turned the water in the moat to the only use that will probably ever be made of it now, washing clothes and acres of land were covered with the clothes drying.

I enquired if there was a protestant church in the city and was informed that there had been one but a long time ago it was destroyed; I thought it might be impolite to ask whether one of my guides forefathers had assisted at the demolition.

Here I have been enjoying a European sunday (I imagine I see your mothers expression of face). An immense crowd were coming from the cathedral as I entered it and on inquiry I found they were attracted by the military band which performed there in the mornings and gave a concert somewhere else in the afternoon.

It was a lovely day, the first one I remember having since I started, and I took a long walk on the ramparts. Everything is just budding, the grass is beautifully green and just to sit on the banks of the sluggish Scheldt was delightful after the continued occupation I have had lately. The shops were open all day but in the afternoon the little decorum of the morning was done away with and all the games from the playing ball of the higher orders to the pitching pennies of the lower were entered into by the whole presentation of young people. I never saw so many children in my life; every street and above all the parks were crowded with them.

Yesterday I had to take a driver to go from Nannce to Floreffe on business and returning fearing I might not have another opportunity asked him to stop where I could buy a pair of sabots or wooden shoes for my child. I got a pair worn by the better class of peasant and he said if my little child had never had them she would think her fortune made, evidently pitying her extremely for having so long been deprived of the luxury.

I hope Bammie will take the same view of them, they are certainly curious.

I leave here at seven o'clock tomorrow morning and only arrived at ten last night so that I will not be able to see again that manufacture with which this town must be principally associated in your mind.

I have written until my candle threatens to leave me to go to bed in the dark and must now close expecting to fill the balance of this sheet tomorrow in Paris.

Good night. I have for bed clothes a feather bed.

May 1ˢᵗ Paris.   Dear Mittie here I am so quietly ensconced in a comfortable french hotel after a very busy but owing to the delightful weather pleasant day. Before I forget it I must tell you that Uncle Tom's Cabin was played yesterday (sunday) evening in the theatre at Valenciennes. Relieve you mother's mind with the information that this part of a European sunday's occupations I did not enter into.

272

This morning I was obliged to stop at a little Rail R^d station five miles from my destination Aniche. There was nothing to be hired and I had determined to walk it when a very polite frenchman insisted upon my taking a private cabriolet. The owner of the Glass factory drove me back so that I found it more agreeable than I had anticipated. The vehicles and horses would amuse you, the first weigh an indefinite amount and the last are built proportionately clumsily. Six miles an hour is an unheard of speed here.

My shirts have just come home but I find everything so much higher that I am only buying enough to carry me home. The good old Parisian pieces are all done away with or it requires one to live here sometime to get the run of them again. None of my old acquaintances are still in existance.

The difference in costume of the women has been very remarkable in the last few days. Even the fish women of Brussels had their fancy white caps while the Germans wore only their dirty looking head gear.

I am glad once more to come back to the french style.

As I have a good deal of figuring to do before I go to bed I must now say good bye, hoping to receive a letter from you before I write again. Thee

Thee's journey to Europe dealt with business not pleasure. But of course, he had leisure time to spend seeing the sights. In Valenciennes, on the Scheldt River in northern France, he visited the Basilique Notre-Dame-du-Saint-Cordon known for its *alto relievo* or high relief sculptures. Valenciennes' glass makers were among several in that area of Europe. In Floreffe, Belgium, and Aniche, France, glassmakers made window glass, stained glass, and glass bottles. After the creation of the first glassworks in 1823, Aniche became the

French capital of the window glass industry and went from 4,000 to 7,500 inhabitants in 1900. All of these glassmakers' factories were destroyed during World War I.

A sabot is a clog or wooden shoe from France or surrounding countries such as Belgium. These whole feet shoes began to be produced in the 16th century and were most commonly worn by the lower classes. Sabots were durable and comfortable when worn with thick socks.[118]

A pair of sabots

New York May 7- 1860

My dearest Susy,

Your sweet amusing letter we received on saturday I will settle Lafever's bill darling and bring you the receipt - I have been very unwell since I wrote you - My cold has been a severe one. On saturday afternoon I had to go to bed, and did not leave my bed until about mid-day yesterday - About 3 oclock on saturday I was taken with a chill which was followed by fever which lasted all night saturday night - I am much better now, but still the cold in my head is very annoying - I take quinine to prevent the recurrence of the chill and fever. I have just heard this morning that Lissie Emlyn [wife of James Roosevelt] has gone to Phil[a] If I had only known it in time I think I should have tried to go with her, but I suppose it is best as it is as I should hardly have been able to do so - It seems one of Lissie's uncles is to bring her back - if so, I will return under his care - Mrs Roosevelt told me she thought he would return home about this day week - Mittie has her wet nurse at last - a real Bog - bottom - Poor child! This has been a great trial to her altogether and it seems as if to enhance the trial, she has had much more milk lately than usual - The family all advised that she should depend upon herself and the bottle, but the D[r] insists on the wet-nurse. - Tell Anna the nurse says; mi babys name is Patrick - she says her husbands name is Samual Smelly, but her name is Annie Sheron - that she does not go by her husbands name at all but I suppose Patrick will rejoice in the name of Smelly - A name very suggestive of the want of soap and water, and plenty of clothes to change - She seems like a well-tempered woman and has a fine breast of milk - We are today trying to get a place for Patrick and have a great hopes of succeeding - Mittie advertised & several have applied and offer to take good care of him and nurse him and give him as much as they give their own babies - Mittie will keep a good look out for she is very tender-hearted and conscientious about the little baby -

After dinner

Darling I feel so much better since dinner - I had been dieting for several days, and took medicine too, but today as I had no fever I took some soup, and some beef steak - I really feel strong again. Mittie and I are now planning about

Mrs Sherons clothes - we hear there are some ready made clothes in Amity St - and will go in the carriage tomorrow to make the purchases Mittie will advance one months wages - seven dollars, of which has to be paid for Patricks board - the remaining five has to purchase her wardrobe - A small sum to go upon in these days of extravagance! - I am glad my dear Irvine has had scarlism so lightly - I hope now he will make good use of his time during this last session - How very warm it has become, but I shall so soon return home that I think you need not send any of my things - I suppose you have received Lucys letter, which I sent to Anna - I have not been well enough to write her since. Poor Lucy! I do pity her from the bottom of my heart I will write her shortly. Bamie is well again - She has just been up to tell me goodby as she is going into the square - I wish you could have seen her - she looks so prettily with her little missoil sack on, and her little new leghorn [tightly woven straw] hat. Now here comes Tede with his little white sack and a leghorn hat trimmed with black velvet and the edges all turned up boy-fashion - His milk crust is all gone and he is almost a little beauty - Little Elliott is not so well - his vaccination is at its height, and he has on his hands and feet an infection The D^r has not seen him today but I suppose it is of little consequence - Bamie was quite annoyed about the little mouse - Goodbye dear ones I hope to see you all very shortly -

Your affec
Mother
M Bulloch

[No early photographs of Anna *Bamie* Roosevelt have been found. This may be due to the difficulty of photographing a child in a brace or the Roosevelts' reluctance to have Bamie photographed during that period of her life.]

Theodore *Tede* Roosevelt, about age 2.
Courtesy of the Theodore Roosevelt Collection

Theodore *Tede* Roosevelt, about age 2.
Courtesy of the Theodore Roosevelt Collection

Written in the bar room with an office pen!!

West Point Aug 19th 60

Dear Mittie

I will write to you although your ability to read it is a different matter.

I scarce know where to begin but knowing your methodical temperament will start where we parted. The road was beautiful just on the bank of the river with, in many places, rugged rocks rising like the palisades for the first twenty miles.

Generally however it was through a very highly cultivated county dotted with pretty little country villages. Annie was in extacies of delight. For the first time in my life I really appreciated the beauty of the Hudson forming as it did the all important features of the landscape.

I have just discovered that this paper has lines invisible in the light with which I am writing.

Four miles of our road was over immense stones and so rough that it was rather a question whether the wagon would hold together, indeed it did brush at last although not badly.

We arrived a little after eight o'clock and found Miss Bunson, Mrs Stuart, Mrs Cuyler and Stephen King and Nina ready to give us a warm reception.

John was ready to take the horses and informed me that there was not a room vacant.

Henry Campbell offered me half his room and Anna has a nice room for one night only.

Henry Campbell's room is entirely filled with two single beds and two chairs, but as you may imagine I see it but seldom.

Anna has been since obliged to share a {___} Pollard's room, one of Mr King's party. We have been all over the Point and through the numerous rooms that we visited together on that eventful day. The cadets drill admirably and this evening they seemed very devoted when the band played to hundred for their benefit. We went to church on the Point in the morning and heard a very good sermon although I almost regretted that I had not gone to a chapel opposite here built by Weir the artist who had settled more money on his children and on their death appropriated it to this building. A Mr Cornelius Roosevelt Duffy who claims relationship preached in it.

We took tea tonight accidentally with Colonel Hardie who has called on us. They seemed disposed to be very polite to us and a Mr Sidney Hardie seems to be an old friend of Annas. She is enjoying herself extremely and will probably not be ready to leave until next friday morning, in which case she could not get to Morristown until quarter past five at which time please get Irvine to have Welch meet us.

We will leave saturday morning for our little trip as I feel as if I could not pass the children without a short visit. Kiss them all for me and give them a great deal of love. Tell Bammie I hope her eye is quite well, I saw a little girl of Mrs Cuylers who she saw last spring at mothers the day of a procession. I long to see little Teedie's curls again.

I feel as if this scrawl is unintelligible and am strongly disposed to tare it up.

But if you could only see the difficulties under which it is composed you would excuse all its many imperfections and only wonder I had had the hardihood to write at all

Your Husband
Ther. Roosevelt

Cornelius Roosevelt Duffie (1821-1900), who preached at the West Point Chapel, was related to Thee through his mother's line. He and his father were prominent

New York Episcopal ministers. The West Point chapel of this period (now called the Old Cadet Chapel) was a Greek Revival stone church built in 1836. Robert Walter Weir (1803-1889) painted the altar mural entitled *War and Peace*. Weir served as Professor of Drawing at West Point.

The Old Chapel at West Point from *New Outlook*[119]

Colonel William Joseph Hardee (1815-1873) served as Commandant of Cadets from 1856 to 1860. A highly respected officer from Camden County, Georgia, Hardee had lost his wife in 1853. In 1855, Secretary of War Jefferson Davis advised Hardee to publish *Rifle and Light Infantry Tactics for the Exercise and Manoeuvres of Troops When Acting as Light Infantry or Riflemen,* popularly known as Hardee's Tactics. This manual became the best-known drill manual during the coming war. He is also said to have designed the so-called Hardee hat about this time.

Colonel William Joseph Hardee.
Photograph by Matthew Brady circa 1860.

Hardee Hat[120]

West Point Aug 21ˢᵗ. 60

Dear Mittie

 Annie says I <u>must</u> stay until monday next. She says she will take all responsibility for your disappointment in waiting to start until Tuesday next. Colonel Hardie has promised to have a drill for her and she seems altogether so happy that I have not the heart to say no again although I have told her that I would very much prefer not waiting. I never saw Annie so anxious to do anything, and she will probably never have such another opportunity to be lionized. You know civilians are thrown very much in the back ground so that it is not quite a place after my heart.

283

If it was not for John "with his large mouth" and my ponies I would feel quite lost.

I only write this at twelve o'clock at night to inform you of our change of plans but will try to write you a long letter tomorrow and get Annie to do the same.

I feel a dreadfully homesick feeling tonight but hope to take a more cheerful view of things tomorrow.

I will tell Bamie all about the soldiers tomorrow, in the meanwhile kiss her good night for me also little Tedie and Elliott.

Your Husband
Thee

West Point Aug 22nd 60

Dear Mittie

Annie refuses to write; she offers to if I will not but really seems to think so much more of the excitements of the Point that I know you would probably not hear from either of us.

I have just been interrupted by John Carone who you may remember married his landlady's daughter and to whose wife I am to be introduced.

We have been this morning to Weirs studio and he claims on mother's side a relationship with me, his pictures are beautiful. The party consisted of Colonel Hardie Dr Campbell (military) Colonel Saxton and myself with Annie the Misses Hyatt and Miss Laura Hooper.

I know quantities of officers and feel very much at home in their tents, but Annie appreciates the life here much more.

I wrote and telegraphed you yesterday that she would stay until monday.

I tried to persuade her to let me go and remain herself under Mrs Stuart's care, which Mrs Stuart was anxious for, but Anna would not. I have never seen her so determined before.

We went over yesterday to the indian falls and had a very pleasant time although caught in two or three showers. Annie was under Colonel Hardie's charge while I took Miss Grosvenor, Johny Reid's friend. She is very intelligent and I regret now more than ever that Johny don't get her if he can. She is certainly far from handsome but entirely a lady in her manners.

I will take Miss Hardie out driving this afternoon as Annie is going with a party to the point. I console myself for Annie's neglect as well as I can and although a civilian find some who will take compassion on my loneliness.

We have not made as much of the walk on the point as I would have desired but the excitement of parade draw everyone.

The hotel is well kept but the company changes continually and of course cannot be so pleasant for a long stay. I know crowds of people, but they are all like myself birds of passage.

It is absurd to see the tents of the cadets with their rows of dirty Shoes and indeed all their dressing arrangements exposed to view.

The ladies, or rather some of them, visit the officers' tents with a perfect looseness and I found a group compound in part of Mrs & Miss Ella Porter quietly sitting on one of their beds this morning.

I have been expecting a letter from you daily remembering your determination to do better in future after my return from Europe but I suppose the good resolution would not hold when the trial came.

I would like very much to hear about the children and have found one here that reminds one very much of little Tedie.

Tell Bammie that they harnessed horses to the cannon and fired then so near us that Aunt Annie thought she would be shot.

My little ponies were very much frightened when a number of soldiers ran at them just as if they were going over them.

They ring the bell for dinner and as I must change my coat before going for Annie who is never ready. I must say good bye

Your Husband
Thee. Roosevelt

While Colonel Hardee escorted Anna, Thee occupied himself with a visit to Indian Falls on the Hudson River and a drive with Miss Hardee. Colonel Hardee had four children, Anna age 17, Sarah, age 15, William, Jr. age 12, and Elizabeth only 10. Perhaps Colonel Hardee saw Anna, now 27 years of age, as a possible mate and mother to his four children. *Colonel Saxton* may have been Rufus Saxon (1824-1908) who served valiantly in the Civil War, earning the Medal of Honor. He graduated from West Point in 1849.

Martha failed to put the year on the next letter. As Irvine attended the University of Pennsylvania beginning in the fall of 1859, this letter could have been written either 1859 or 1860. However, the contents of this letter and the following letters indicate they were all written in 1860, as throughout this series of letters, Martha was in Philadelphia, and Susy was in New York.

Indian Falls by William H. Bartlett

Oct 16, Tuesday afternoon

Hill has just told me dear Susy that he is going to write you this afternoon, so I told him I would write a note also. We are getting along, but although the Tiny does not complain I can see he feels your absence very much - But since he & Delia came I feel so set up, that I almost look with pity on the other households Delia commenced her duties on saturday morning - She and the other two are ironing today, but at odd times she has nearly finished the [carpet of the laundry - I think they all go on pretty much as when you were here - I had to get a yard and ¼ more of the drilling for Hills drawers and Emily says she will finish them very soon - She cut out and carried home yesterday 2 pr of the sheets, and will take the rest of the sheets shortly. I have a great deal of sewing work to do, and Emily will not be able to do it so I am going to have the sewing machine on friday and saturday next. I have attended the noon day prayer-meeting very frequently of late - Today Mr Crowell presided - We had a solemn and interesting meeting - Some persons sent in Thanksgivings that their prayers and the prayers of that meeting have been answered in the conversion of children, friends, etc. & not Emily.

It is encouraging to think that God will answer prayer. I felt today that it was pleasant to be at that meeting with Gods children. I shall attend whenever I can - I suppose Mittie and Anna have returned from West Point.

Dear Children! give my tenderest love to them. Tell them to write me. Tell them that George Eve called today on Irvine at the University and George asked where Anna & Mittie were. Irvine said he looked very seedy, as if he had just emerged from the back-woods - - Irvine spoke today, and in order to look very impressive wore his new College suit. A rough suit - Hill's new clothes fit him very nicely - The man brought one shirt on friday evening - Hill tried it on.

It was rather tight but very nicely made - He promises they shall all be right -

Good bye darling Susy
Your ever affectionate
Mother M Bulloch

I long to see the sweet little children.

Oct 18 afternoon

Dearest Susy,

Your Tiny writes you so often that there is nothing new in our monotonous household - The last occurrence is that old Ann brought 12 yrds of merino to make herself a skirt - 6 would have been an abundance, but she said the shopkeeper told it was a remnant and very cheap. Yesterday Hill forgot to go to Rose's for dinner so she went and let Rose impose upon her four lbs of veal cutlet Hill says he expects to have breakfast of it for three or four days to come. She is a good, silly old thing - Delia is never idle and Hannah does very well - My room is lovely so clean - Hill's also - - Love to M & A

Your affect Mother
M Bulloch

While Tiny has not been identified, Hill's family employed Delia Murray, age 24, and Hannah Crone, age 20, and Mrs. Ann Doolin, age 58, all born in Ireland. Irish domestic servants were very common during this period and until the beginning of the twentieth century. The Great Irish Famine (Potato Famine), between 1845 and 1849, was a period of mass starvation and disease. The famine led to a period of great emigration from Ireland between 1845 and 1852.

Wednesday morning 31st Oct

My ever dear Susy,

     I received your sweet letter this morning, and after reading it gave it to Hill who was looking over his morning paper, and handed him also his little note - We are truly glad darling the D^r thinks you will get better - what a blessing it will be if you get well - Even the utmost prospect is truly cheering - I was talking to Hill the other day about the orphan state in which "<u>House</u>" will be left without either you or I to take care of the basket of keys and Rose's and Thomson Block's books - He says he can keep house perfectly well himself - He thinks he is equal to you and rather superior to me - I have told Delia about over casting the napkins, and she says she knows exactly how to do it - Hill has had two of his new shirts done up to see how he likes them - He tried one of them on for me to see how they fitted I thought they fitted a little too loosely - but when I came to see one of his old ones on I thought the new fitted best - He reads to me in the evenings (dear fellow!) I never liked Thomas Carlyle until I heard read his "Hero & Hero worship" - It is a good true book and I like it. Hill writes you so often that I did not think it necessary to write often, besides you know I have been busy - I have nearly finished now - only some night caps etc. to make - I got Mrs Lewis to make a muslin delane and I think she has bothered me as much as she ever did you - In the spring she lost my pattern so now she cuts her own way and it is guess work of the worst kind - Mr Hutchison has not come yet - I suppose the weather now prevents - I have not heard from dear Stuart since Lucy's letter - It makes me feel very unsettled - I do not know when Mr H will go south, but I suppose not before the middle of Nov - I do not think it would be safe to go before that time. I shall be ready to go at a moments warning - I don't know what to do about a winter bonnet - If when I see Mr Hutchison and find out when he is going would it be best do you think to have Dorsey make it or get it here? - Oh how sorry I am to have to leave home but I must go - should the poor darling not get well, I should always reproach myself if I did not-Oh Susy darling I hope God will hear our prayers - Spare his life if it be his will, but above all things grant him true sorrow for sin, and justification through the atoning blood of Christ - How often was our dear Redeemer afflicted to when he was upon earth and he never refused - Do you remember his prompt answer to the Centurion? "I will come and heal him." Well, he is the same yesterday today and forever - As you say the answer has to be in his own way and his own time. I am sorry to hear that precious little By has been unwell again - I am sorry on account of the debilitating treatment - That together with the warm weather must make the poor little thing very weak - Tell Anna with my love to her and dear Mittie, that she must let me know whether I am to carry her new linens to New York when I go - I hope dear Anna is better than she was when we separated - How sweet dear little Teedie & Elliott are - With much love my dearest Susy

Your affec Mother
M Bulloch

Hill read Scottish writer Thomas Carlyle's (1795-1881) *On Heroes, and Hero-Worship, and the Heroic in History* to Martha, in which Carlyle compared different types of heroes. The book focused on the idea that all heros were flawed and had to deal with difficulties in their own lives. Carlyle's works were often quoted by those who defended slavery. However, by this time, Martha and her daughters appeared to believe the end of slavery was coming and that it should end.

Much of Martha's last two letters dealt with clothing. Everyone in the household kept busy preparing clothing for the coming winter. Martha had a dress made of delaine, a high-quality, worsted fabric used mainly for dresses. She busied herself with making other simple garments including night caps.

Lucy's letter, which was not saved, most likely gave news of the birth of her and Stuart's second child, Matilda Moxley Elliott, born 4 October 1860. Although family members mentioned Stuart's illness in previous letters, this letter indicated its serious nature. Stuart suffered from tuberculosis. Martha desperately wished to travel south to Georgia to be with her son; however, the uneasy state of the nation's affairs at the end of 1860 added complications to any such journey. By going south, Martha seemed to realize she might not be able to return. Additionally, she would be leaving her youngest son and her three remaining daughters in the north.

Events of the years between the beginning of 1854 and the end of 1860 forced many changes for the Bulloch women and the Roosevelt family. Martha, Anna, and Irvine joined Susan and Mittie in the North. Irvine finished preparatory school and entered college. Anna traveled and carried on a brief romance with Colonel Hardee, commander of the U.S. Military Academy at West Point. Mittie successfully delivered three children, Anna, Theodore, and Elliott. However, economic events forced the Roosevelts to cut back on spending and hampered the growth of their business ventures. Susan's health improved, and Hilborne finished medical school and became a successful physician. James Dunwoody Bulloch married for the second time, and he and Harriott had two children. After numerous romances and extended trips to Europe, Stuart married Lucy and seemed settled in Savannah.

Throughout all these events, Martha continued as the strong matriarch of the family. Her words of encouragement and religious instruction carried the family forward. Family letters reveal her loving attachment to each of the family members, especially her seven grandchildren. Her only real concerns continued to be her remaining family in the South, especially Stuart, his wife Lucy, and their children.

While few lines of these letters revealed each writer's feelings about the political and social events of the last half of the 1850s, these individuals lived amidst growing tensions over slavery. The Bulloch ladies, James D. Bulloch, Stuart, and Irvine came of age in the South. Martha, Susan, and Stuart had owned slaves. Anna, Mittie, and Irvine grew up in a household supported by slave labor. They called many of these *Maum* and *Daddy*. Martha owned property in Roswell. Her extended Bulloch, Dunwoody, Stewart, and Elliott families still resided in the South, many of them on plantations.

At the end of 1860, the nation teetered on the brink of war. Martha's three *sons*, James, Daniel, and Irvine would need to choose on which side they stood. Martha's daughters, all living in the North, awaited what would come. The end of 1860 found these families united in love. The coming war would find them divided only by distance and allegiance.

Endnotes

1. Lilian Rixey, *Bamie: Theodore Roosevelt's Remarkable Sister* (New York: David McKay Company, Inc., 1963), 4; These letters noted the address as 33 East 20th Street, rather than 28 East 20th Street. The reason for the discrepancy has not been determined.

2. Walter E. Wilson and Gary L. McKay, *James D. Bulloch: Secret Agent and Mastermind of the Confederate Navy* (Jefferson, North Carolina and London: McFarland & Company, Inc. Publishers 2012), 22.

3. Personal Communication, Stephen Kinnaman's transcription of letter from Robert Hutchison to Miss Mary M. Caskie, Richmond, Virginia, dated 18 October 1848, on file at the Georgia Historical Society, Savannah.

4. Hilborne West of Philadelphia had attended St. Mary's Seminary of St. Sulpice, in Baltimore, Maryland, leaving there in 1834. He had studied to become a priest. St. Mary's was the first Catholic seminary in the United States. Hilborne left without finishing his studies. In 1858, he graduated from the Jefferson Medical College of Philadelphia and set up practice in that city. The Philadelphia City Directory of 1861, listed his practice at 1524 Pine Street. His thesis work focused on traumatic tetanus. It seems very likely Susan's wealth paid for his medical training and their living expenses during this time. Susan and Hilborne appear to have resided with his parents during this period.

5. Carrie's mother, Caroline Seymour Dunwoody (1816) died on 27 August 1838, when Carrie was only three years old. Carrie spent many years of her life at Hopestill but also resided in Savannah with her father Francis Robert Shackelford and his second wife Eliza Bloom.

6. Ebenezer Senior Rees and Mary Dews Rice Rees had died by 1854. The girls were in their early thirties.

7. Anna Glen Bulloch was a daughter of Archibald Stobo Bulloch, James Bulloch's (1765-1807) brother. This James Bulloch was Anna's grandfather. Wimberly Jones Hunter died in 1834, when Lydia was only five.

8. Sarah Jones Potter was a descendant of the Potter family who purchased the 3,000 acre Colerain Plantation, on the Savannah River, in the first quarter of the nineteenth century by taking advantage of foreclosure sales, lapsed mortgages, and unpaid claims along with a few outright sales. John and Catherine Potter raised four children, James, William Henry, Harriet Maria, and Thomas Fuller. James, whose father gifted him a large portion of the plantation, married Sarah Jones Grimes. They raised eight children Catherine Elizabeth, Mary Marshall, Sarah Jones [1835-1879], Maria Stockton, Emily Charlotte, John Hamilton, Frances Glen, and John Potter. James' younger brother Thomas also married a woman named Sarah, Sarah Jane Hall. James completed a new residence about 1855-57 at Colerain which he occupied with his wife and four unmarried daughters, Sarah, Maria, Emily, and Francis. Sarah would marry Richard Stevens Conover in Princeton, New Jersey, in 1855.

9. Under its third owner, Dr. Thomas Poullain, Scull Shoals consisted of several flourishing mills, boarding houses, stores, a large warehouse and store combination, a distillery, a toll bridge, and other enterprises. During Poullain's 41-year leadership (1827-1868), a devastating fire completely destroyed the wooden mill buildings in 1845. Poullain oversaw the rebuilding of the mill which, like Roswell's mills, produced cotton and cotton goods for both the Southern and Northern markets.

10. Fred would marry Eliza Mackay Elliott the following year. Eliza was Phoebe Elliott's (1833-1866) sister. At this point Leita Elliott has not been identified nor has their relationship to Senator John Elliott (Martha Bulloch's first husband).

11. Wilson and McKay, *James D. Bulloch: Secret Agent and Mastermind of the Confederate Navy,* 22-24.

12. Connie M. Cox and Darlene M. Walsh, *Providence: Selected Correspondence of George Hull Camp 1837-1907, Son of the North, Citizen of the South* (Macon, Georgia: Indigo Publishing Group, 2008), 373.

13. *Western Farmer & Gardener*, 1846, Vol. II:1:1846:100-101.

14. *The Southern Planter*, Vol. 64:1:1903:564-565. The Southern Planter Publishing Company, Richmond, Virginia.

15. *The Southern Banner* [Athens, Georgia], 22 June 1854.

16. Virginia King Nirenstein, *With Kindly Voices: A Nineteenth-Century Georgia Family*. (Macon, Georgia: Tullous Books, 1984), 91, 102.

17. The Rev. Francis Robert Goulding wrote in the *Savannah Republican* on 29 March 1871 that Major Minton had served under General Andrew Jackson in 1817 who presented him with the sword and epaulettes of a major for "gallant conduct."; Robert Manson Myers, *The Children of Pride: A True Story of Georgia and the Civil War* (New Haven and London: Yale University Press, 1972), 1626.

18. Scott Derks and Tony Smith. *The Value of a Dollar: Colonial Era to the Civil War: 1600-1865*. (Millerton, New York: Grey House Publishing, 2005), 383.

19. Tim Lockley, "Like a clap of thunder in a clear sky: differential mortality during Savannah's yellow fever epidemic of 1854." *Social History* Vol. 37:2:2012:166-186.

20. Ibid.

21. Ibid.

22. Berrien's young son, named for his father, died on 15 February 1855. Althea lived until 1891. She never remarried.

23. Sarah Blackwell Gober Temple, *The First Hundred Years: A Short History of Cobb County in Georgia*, (Atlanta: W. Brown Publishing Company, 1935).

24. William Gaston Bulloch was the son of John I. Bulloch, James Stephens' older brother. Anna and William were first cousins. James S. Bulloch had served as guardian to William G. Bulloch and his sister Jane after their father's death.

25. Wilson and McKay, *James D. Bulloch: Secret Agent and Mastermind of the Confederate Navy*, 25.

26. Melanie Pavich-Lindsay (editor), *Anna: The Letters of a St. Simons Island Plantation Mistress, 1817-1859 (Anna Matilda Page King)* (Athens: University of Georgia Press, 2002).

27. Hugh Fraser Grant, *The journal and account book, 1834-61, of Hugh Fraser Grant of Elizafield Plantation, Glynn County, Georgia* (publisher unknown 1983).

28. Myers, *Children of Pride*, 85-86.

29. Walter J. Fraser, Jr., *Lowcountry Hurricanes: Three Centuries of Storms at Sea and Ashore* (Athens: University of Georgia Press, 2006).

30. Huddleston and Koehler, *Mittie & Thee*, 207.

31. Cox and Walsh, *Providence*, 379.

32. Walter E. Wilson, *The Bulloch Belles: Three First Ladies, a Spy a President's Mother, and Other Women of the 19th Century Georgia Family* (Jefferson, North Carolina and London: McFarland & Company, Inc. Publishers, 2015), 93.

33. Cox and Walsh, *Providence*, 396.

34. Wilson, *The Bulloch Belles*, 92-93.

35. *Bulloch* was often spelled *Bullock* in historic documents; however, never by family members.

36. Walter E. Wilson - personal communication, 18 January 2016.

37. Willard Hotel - Franklin Pierce inauguration from *Frank Leslie's Illustrated News*, 1853.

38. Derks and Smith, *The Value of a Dollar*, 409.

39. Cox and Walsh, *Providence*, 632n681.

40. Myers, *Children of Pride*, 1559.

41. John Lossing Benson, editor, *Harper's Encyclopedia of United States History* (vol. 7) (New York, NY: Harper and Brothers, 1912).

42. Croton basin, running water from the Croton Reservoir.

43. Myers, *Children of Pride*, 1588.

44. Connie M. Huddleston, letter report "Bulloch Hall - 9FU255 Investigations at Site of Third Slave Cabin" dated August 2013. On file at Bulloch Hall.

45. Cox and Walsh, *Providence,* 659n1091.

46. Cox and Walsh, *Providence,* 657n1054.

47. Cox and Walsh, *Providence,* 628n626.

48. Cox and Walsh, *Providence,* 284.

49. Derks and Smith, *The Value of Money,* 383.

50. Andy Piascik, "Jackson v. Bulloch and the End of Slavery in Connecticut" at http://connecticuthistory.org/jackson-v-bulloch-and-the-end-of-slavery-in-connecticut/; Durwood Dunn, *An Abolitionist in the Appalachian South: Ezekiel Birdseye on Slavery, Capitalism, and Separate Statehood in East Tennessee, 1841-1846.* (Knoxville: University of Tennessee Press, 1997), 173.

51. Barton Myers. "Georgia Military Institute" at http://www.georgiaencyclopedia.org/articles/history-archaeology/georgia-military-institute.

52. Charlton Hines Way, son of William James Way and Mary Elizabeth Hartford Way, married Frances Williams, of Milledgeville, Georgia, about 1860. Charlton, a lawyer, served as a Colonel in the Confederacy's 54th Georgia Regiment and later as Counsel General to St. Petersburg, Russia, under President Cleveland.

53. Myers, *Children of Pride,* 1713-1714.

54. Myers, *Children of Pride,* 1532.

55. Donald A. Sinclair. Railroad Accident at Burlington in 1855, *Journal of the Rutgers University Library,* Vol. 10:2:2012:46-54.

56. Ibid.

57. Ibid.

58. William S. Forrest, *The Great Pestilence in Virginia; Being An Historical Account of the Origin, General Character, and Ravages of the Yellow Fever in Norfolk and Portsmouth* (New York: Derby and Jackson, 1856): Lon Wagner, The Fever. *The Virginian-Pilot.* 2005 as seen at www.portsmouthva.gov/history/fever/TheFever.pdf.

59. Huddleston and Koehler, *Mittie & Thee,* 146.

60. Forrest, *The Great Pestilence;* Wagner, The Fever.

61. Ibid.

62. Ibid.

63. Ibid.

64. Ibid.

65. Wagner, The Fever.

66. Ibid.

67. Cox and Walsh, *Providence,* 412.

68. *The Bible*, primarily Acts 9:36-42.

69. *The Bible, Acts of the Apostles* (Chapter 9, v. 36): Benjamin Quarles, *Black Abolitionists* (New York,: De Capo Press, 1991), 101: Bruce Dorsey *Reforming Men and Women: Gender in the Antebellum City* (Ithaca New York: Cornell University Press 2006), 258.

70. "A. T. Stewart's Dry Goods Store" as seen at http:// www.nydivided.org/popup/Places/ATStewartStore.php.; Christopher Gray "Streetscapes/The A.T. Stewart Department Store; A City Plan to Revitalize the 1846 'Marble Palace'" in the *New York Times*, 20 March 1994.

71. Lilian Rixey, *Bamie: Theodore Roosevelt's Remarkable Sister* (New York: David McKay Company, Inc., 1963), 4.

72. Edmund Morris, *The Rise of Theodore Roosevelt* (New York: Random House Trade Paperbacks, 2001), 796.

73. Myers, *Children of Pride,* 1573.

74. http://philadelphiaencyclopedia.org/archive/broad-street/.

75. *Great men and famous deeds Vol.III* (New York: P.F. Collier & Son, 1903), 602.

76. Errett, Russell, *History of Allegheny County Pennsylvania, Vol. I,* (Chicago: A. Warner & Co. Publishers, 1889), 555.

77. Errett, Russell, *History of Allegheny County Pennsylvania, Vol. I,* 555; Jay W. Hawkins, *Glasshouses & Glass Manufacturers of the Pittsburgh Region 1795-1910* (New York: iUniverse, Inc., 2009), 348.

78. William Hyde and Howard L. Conard, *Encyclopedia of the History of St. Louis, A Compendium of History and Biography for Ready Reference Vol. III* (Philadelphia: Louis H. Everts & Co., 1899),1742; http://stlouis.genealogyvillage.com/hotels. htm.

79. "Grove Plantation – Adams Run – Charleston County" at South Carolina Plantations as seen as http://south-carolina-plantations.com/charleston/grove.html; Kappy McNulty and John Melton Ferry. "Grove Plantation" (pdf 2007). National Register of Historic Places - Nomination and Inventory.; *New York Tribune* 4 November 1856 printed announcement of 23 October wedding of Dr. George W. Morris of South Carolina to Miss Alice M. Watts, daughter of General Edward Watts, at Oaklands, Roanoke County, Virginia.

80. Osborn's obit from the *New York Times* 17 July 1876: "Brevet Brig Gen Osborn Cross, whose death occurred in this City last Saturday, was a native of Maryland and a graduate of the Military Academy. He entered the United States Army with the rank of Second Lt of the 1st Infantry on July 1, 1825. He was almost immediately transferred to the 4th Infantry and again assigned to duty with the 1st Infantry on Sept 29, 1827. On the last day of December, 1831, he was raised to the grade of First Lt and continued to perform duty with his company until July 7, 1838 when he was appointed Asst. Quartermaster of the regiment with the rank of Captain. The position of Quartermaster becoming vacant in July, 1847, Capt. Cross was appointed to fill the position on the 24th of that month with the rank of Major. He was transferred to the staff of the Quartermaster General on Feb 26, 1863 and promoted to Lieutenant Colonel. On July 29, 1866 he was appointed Assistant Quartermaster General with the rank of Colonel and continued to hold that position until March 13, 1865 when he was breveted Brigadier General, and on July 29, in the following year he was placed on the retired list.": Osborn's Obituary from the *New York Times* 16 July 1876: "In this City, July15, Brevet Brigadier Gen. Osborn Cross, United States Army."

81. Ancestry.com references, other genealogical references, and numerous family trees all state the date of Osborne and Louisa Cross wedding as 15 December 1832. However, records found by Walter E. Wilson (*The Bulloch Belles*) show

an earlier marriage, dated 7 May 1827, in New Orleans based on a telegraph to Washington, D.C. dated 30 May 1827. Personal communication, 19 January 2016.

82. Wilson and McKay, *James D. Bulloch*, 26-27, Wilson, *The Bulloch Belles*, 94-95.

83. David M. Ludlum, *Early American Winters II 1821-1870* (Boston: The American Meteorological Society, 1968) "January 21-23, 1857. Just a few days after 'The Cold Storm,' amazingly, an even more frigid air mass descended on the Northeast and well into the mid Atlantic—what we might call today a 'reinforcing shot' of cold air. Except that this was more than a reinforcing shot. It was one of the coldest Arctic air masses ever to invade the eastern part of the country since our ancestors arrived on these shores. Although no records are available for the D.C. area, other temperature readings were as follows:
Northern New York and New England: -40 degrees (colder readings have since been seen here, but it was further south that the most striking temperatures were seen; Charleston, in (present-day) West Virginia: -24 degrees; Fort Monroe, on the Chesapeake: -0.5 degrees; Portsmouth, VA: -5 degrees; Petersburg, VA: -22 degrees, a reading thought to be atypical due to the thermometer's sheltered, partially snow-covered location, away from the water, under ideal radiational cooling conditions. Nevertheless, another nearby thermometer supposedly registered -20 degrees. These observations were taken under the auspices of either the Smithsonian Institution or the Surgeon General's Office and are now stored in the National Archives."

84. Collection contains, with the letter from 29 May 1857, a copy of bank note on bank of Portsmouth, VA, for fifty cents.

85. Rixey, *Bamie*, 4.

86. "Mrs. Peachim" was Mrs. John C. Pechin who sailed with Captain Bulloch on the S.S. *Cahawba* on 12 February 1858. Found in the *New Orleans Times-Picayune*, 21 Feburary 1858 per personal communication from Walter E. Wilson.

87. Sangreal or sangraal refers to kingly or holy blood, a term often used in reference to the Holy Grail or cup of Christ.

88. *Public Ledger* (Philadelphia, Pennsylvania) 5 February 1858.

89. Clive Brown, "Giacomo Meyerbeer," in *The New Penguin Opera Guide*, edited by Amanda Holden. (New York: Penguin / Putnam, 2001), 570–577.

90. *Public Ledger* (Philadelphia, Pennsylvania) 15 March 1858 and 24 April 1858.

91. Huddleston and Koehler, *Mittie & Thee*, 27.

92. *The Initials. A Novel* was published in London in 1854. *Quits. A Novel* followed in 1857 and was also published in London.

93. "Salem College: Our History" as seen at http://www.salem.edu/about/history/.

94. "Measuring Worth" at https://www.measuringworth.com/uscompare/relativevalue.php.

95. Lucy Elizabeth Marshall O'Rorke, *The Life and Friendships of Catherine Marsh* (London, New York: Longmans, Green & Co., 1917), 156-157.

96. The duel was widely reported in the nation's newspapers including *Southern Recorder* 24 February 1857, *Weekly Raleigh Register* 25 February 1857, and *The Louisville Daily Courier* 25 February 1857.

97. Myers, *Children of Pride*, 418.

98. Myers, *Children of Pride*, 214.

99. *Savannah Daily Republican*, 15 October 1846 and 17 April 1847; Scott Derks and Tony Smith, *The Value of Money*; A simple Purchasing Power Calculator would say the relative value is $158,000.00. This answer was obtained by multiplying $5500 by the percentage increase in the CPI from 1856 to 2014 at www.measuringworth.com.

100. *Savannah Republican*, 10 November 1856.

101. *Savannah Daily Republican*, 22 March 1856.

102. *McElroy's Philadelphia City Directory*, 1857 (Philadelphia: Edward C. and John Biddle, 1857)

103. H. Wilson (compiler), *Trow's New York City Directory for the Year Ending May 1, 1859.* (New York: John F. Trow, 1859).

104. Wilson, *The Bulloch Belles*, 105.

105. Cox and Walsh, *Providence,* 99.

106. *The Brooklyn Daily Eagle*, 28 August 1901.

107. H. Wilson (compiler), *Trow's New York City Directory for the Year Ending May 1, 1859.* (New York: John F. Trow, 1859); Susan Newberry (1827-1871) resided at 384 Sixth Avenue with her son, William, age 10 in the 1860 census. Also residing in the home were several other women, men, and children. Susan probably resided in a boarding house.

108. *Harper's New Monthly Magazine*, July 1858, 288.

109. Yellow fever struck Savannah again in the late summer and fall of 1858. William Harden, *A History of Savannah and South Georgia, Volume I* (Chicago, New York: The Lewis Publishing Company, 1913), 415.

110. Darlene M. Walsh (editor), *Roswell: A Pictorial History* (Roswell, Georgia: Roswell Historical Society, 1994), 39.

111. *New York Times*, 19 November 1858.

112. Peri (in Persian mythology) was a mythical superhuman being, originally represented as evil but subsequently as a good or graceful genie or fairy.

113. John Caskie (1790-1867), father of James Dunwoody Bulloch's first wife, Elizabeth Euphemia (1834-1854), and Robert Hutchison's second wife Mary Edmonia (1822-1852) still lived; however, his wife Martha Jane (1798-1844) had passed twelve years earlier.

114. *The Bible*, King James Version.

115. "Meigs Family History and Genealogy" as seen at http://www.meigs.org/charles219.htm.

116. *The Treasury Building: A National Historic Landmark* Department of the Treasury, Office of the Curator, Washington, D.C. 20220. Found online at https://www.treasury.gov/about/history/Documents/web%20version%20Architectural%20History%20Treasury%20Building.pdf

117. In 1860, there were three dressmakers named Lefevre in New York City. Florine lived at 610 Houston Street, Lucy at 330 Fourth Street, and Matilda at 71 W. 20th Street.

118. By Thesupermat - Own work, GFDL, https://commons.wikimedia.org/w/index.php?curid=7674325.

119. "The Old Chapel" from *The Outlook*, Vol.89:1908:939.; President Theodore Roosevelt became an associate editor in 1909 and published several articles in *The Outlook* (1870–1935).

120. By Hal Jespersen - Own work by the original uploader, Public Domain, https://commons.wikimedia.org/w/index.php?curid=5629394.

Bibliography

Benson, John Lossing (editor). *Harper's Encyclopedia of United States History, Vol. 7.* Harper and Brothers, New York, 1912.

Cox, Connie M. and Darlene M. Walsh. *Providence: Selected Correspondence of George Hull Camp 1837-1907, Son of the North, Citizen of the South.* Indigo Publishing Group, Macon, GA, 2008.

Derks, Scott and Tony Smith, *The Value of a Dollar: Colonial Era to the Civil War: 1600-1865.* Grey House Publishing, Millerton, NY, 2005.

Dorsey, Bruce. *Reforming Men and Women: Gender in the Antebellum City.* Cornell University Press, Ithaca NY, 2006.

Dunn, Durwood. *An Abolitionist in the Appalachian South: Ezekiel Birdseye on Slavery, Capitalism, and Separate Statehood in East Tennessee, 1841-1846.* University of Tennessee Press, Knoxville, 1997.

Errett, Russell. *History of Allegheny County Pennsylvania, Vol. I.* A. Warner & Co. Publishers, Chicago, 1889.

Farnham, Christie Anna. *The Education of the Southern Belle: Higher Education and Student Socialization in the Antebellum South.* New York University Press, 1994.

Forrest, William S. *The Great Pestilence in Virginia; Being An Historical Account of the Origin, General Character, and Ravages of the Yellow Fever in Norfolk and Portsmouth.* Derby and Jackson, NY, 1856.

Fraser, Walter J., Jr. *Lowcountry Hurricanes: Three Centuries of Storms at Sea and Ashore*. University of Georgia Press, Athens, GA, 2006.

Grant, Hugh Fraser. *The journal and account book, 1834-61, of Hugh Fraser Grant of Elizafield Plantation, Glynn County, Georgia*. publisher unknown, 1983.

—. *Great men and famous deeds Vol.III*. P.F. Collier & Son, NY, 1903.

Harden, William. *A History of Savannah and South Georgia, Volume I*. The Lewis Publishing Company, Chicago and New York, 1913.

Hawkins, Jay W. *Glasshouses & Glass Manufacturers of the Pittsburgh Region 1795-1910*. iUniverse, Inc., New York, 2009.

Holmes, James, MD. *"Dr. Bullie's" Notes: Reminiscences of Early Georgia and of Philadelphia and New Haven In The 1800s*. Cherokee Publishing Company, Atlanta, 1976.

Huddleston, Connie M. and Gwendolyn I. Koehler. *Mittie & Thee: An 1853 Roosevelt Romance*. Friends of Bulloch, Inc., Roswell, GA, 2015.

Hyde, William and Howard L. Conard. *Encyclopedia of the History of St. Louis, A Compendium of History and Biography for Ready Reference Vol. III*. Louis H. Everts & Co., Philadelphia, 1899.

Lockley, Tim. "Like a clap of thunder in a clear sky: differential mortality during Savannah's yellow fever epidemic of 1854." *Social History* Vol. 37:2(2012):166-186.

Ludlum, David M. *Early American Winters II 1821-1870*. The American Meteorological Society, Boston, 1968.

McElroy (compiler). *McElroy's Philadelphia City Directory, 1857.* Edward C. and John Biddle, Philadelphia, 1857.

McLeod, Rebecca. "The Loss of the Steamer Pulaski," *The Georgia Historical Quarterly* 3:2(1919):88.

Moore, John Hammond. *Columbia and Richmond County: A South Carolina Community, 1740-1990.* University of South Carolina Press, Columbia, 1992.

Morris, Edmund. *The Rise of Theodore Roosevelt.* Random House Trade Paperbacks, New York, 2001.

Myers, Robert Manson. *The Children of Pride: A True Story of Georgia and the Civil War.* Yale University Press, New Haven and London, 1972.

Nirenstein, Virginia King. *With Kindly Voices: A Nineteenth-Century Georgia Family.* Tullous Books, Macon, GA, 1984.

O'Rorke, Lucy Elizabeth Marshall. *The Life and Friendships of Catherine Marsh.* Longmans, Green & Co., London and New York, 1917.

Pavich-Lindsay, Melanie (editor). *Anna: The Letters of a St. Simons Island Plantation Mistress, 1817-1859 (Anna Matilda Page King).* University of Georgia Press, Athens, 2002.

Quarles, Benjamin. *Black Abolitionists.* De Capo Press, New York, 1991.

Rixey, Lilian. *Bamie: Theodore Roosevelt's Remarkable Sister.* David McKay Company, Inc., New York, 1963.

Robinson, Corinne Roosevelt. *My Brother Theodore Roosevelt.* Charles Scribner's Sons, New York, 1921.

Salsi, Lynn and Margaret Sims. *Columbia: History of a Southern Capital*. Arcadia Publishing, Charleston, SC, 2003.

Sinclair, Donald A. Railroad Accident at Burlington in 1855, *Journal of the Rutgers University Library*, Vol. 10:2(2012):46-54.

Temple, Sarah Blackwell Gober. *The First Hundred Years: A Short History of Cobb County in Georgia*. W. Brown Publishing Company, Atlanta, 1935.

Walsh, Darlene M. (editor). *Roswell: A Pictorial History*. Roswell Historical Society, Roswell, GA, 1994.

White, George. *Historical Collections of Georgia: Containing the Most Interesting Facts, Traditions, Biographical Sketches, Anecdotes, Etc. Relating to the History and Antiquities, From Its First Settlement to the Present Time*. Pudney & Russell, Publishiers, New York, 1855.

Wilson, H. (compiler). *Trow's New York City Directory for the Year Ending May 1, 1859*. John F. Trow, New York, 1859.

Wilson, Walter E. *The Bulloch Belles: Three First Ladies, a Spy, a President's Mother, and Other Women of the 19th Century Georgia Family*. McFarland & Company, Inc. Publishers, Jefferson, NC and London, 2015.

Wilson, Walter E. and Gary L. McKay. *James D. Bulloch: Secret Agent and Mastermind of the Confederate Navy*. McFarland & Company, Inc. Publishers, Jefferson, NC and London, 2012.

Wood, Betty (editor). *Mary Telfair to Mary Few: Selected Letters 1802-1844*. The University of Georgia Press, Athens, 2007.

Newspapers and Magazines:

Darien Gazette (Georgia)
Daily Georgian
Harper's New Monthly Magazine
New Orleans Times-Picayune
New York Tribune
Public Ledger (newspaper)
Savannah Daily Georgian
Savannah Daily Republican
Savannah Republican
Southern Recorder (newspaper)
The Brooklyn Daily Eagle (newspaper)
The Brooklyn Evening Star (newspaper)
The Louisville Daily (newspaper)
The New York Times (newspaper)
The Outlook
The Southern Banner (newspaper)
The Southern Planter
The Virginia Pilot (newspaper)
Weekly Raleigh Register (newspaper)
Western Farmer & Gardener

List of Persons

Adams, Theodore Dwight (1829-1901): storekeeper at the Roswell Manufacturing Company and assistant postmaster.

Baker, William Elliott, Reverend (1830-1906): born in Liberty County, Georgia, to John Osgood Baker and Frances Adeline Fabian Baker (sister of Rosina Fabian Minton).

Bulloch, Anna Louise (1833-1893): daughter of Martha and James Stephens Bulloch.

Bulloch, Elizabeth "Lizzie" Euphemia Caskie (1831-1854): of Richmond, Virginia, sister to Mary Edmonia Caskie, (second wife to Robert Hutchison) married James Dunwoody Bulloch in 1851.

Bulloch, Irvine Stephens (1842-1898): son of Martha and James Stephens Bulloch.

Bulloch, James Dunwoody (1823-1901): son of Hester Elliott and James Stephens Bulloch, married Lizzie Caskie in 1851. Often referred to as *brother Jimmie.*

Bulloch, James Dunwoody, Jr. (1858-1888): first son of James D. Bulloch and Harriott Cross Foster.

Bulloch, James Stephens, Major (1793-1849): grandson of Georgia's first governor, Archibald Bulloch, veteran of the War of 1812, invested in Roswell Manufacturing Company, built Bulloch Hall. Married first to Hester Amarintha Elliott (1797-1831) in 1817, one son James Dunwoody Bulloch (1823-1901) lived to maturity. Second marriage to his stepmother-in-law, Martha Stewart Elliott in 1832, children include Anna (1833-1893),

Martha "Mittie" (1835-1884), Charles Irvine (1838-1841) and Irvine Stephens (1842-1898).

Bulloch, Jessie Hart (1860-1941): first daughter of James D. Bulloch and Harriott Cross Foster.

Bulloch, Martha Stewart Elliott (1799-1864): daughter of American Revolutionary General Daniel Stewart. Married first John Elliott in 1818, children include John Whitehead (1818-1820), Susan Ann (1820-1895), Georgia Amanda (1822-1848), Charles William (1824-1827), and Daniel Stewart (1826-1862). Married second, in 1832, James Stephens Bulloch (her step-son-in-law), children include Anna Louise (1833-1893), Martha *Mittie* (1835-1884), Charles Irvine (1838-1841) and Irvine Stephens (1842-1898).

Bulloch, Mary Eliza Adams Lewis (1828-1902): wife of Dr. William Gaston Bulloch, a cousin by marriage.

Bulloch, William Gaston, Dr. (1815-1885): cousin to James Stephens Bulloch, resident of Savannah, Mittie's second cousin.

Camp, George Hull (1817-1907): New Yorker who moved to Roswell for his health and a position with the Roswell Manufacturing Company. He is assistant agent for the company in 1853 as well as Roswell's postmaster.

Caskie, Ellen Laura (1836-1858): resident of Richmond, Virginia, first cousin to Robert Hutchison's second wife and Lizzie Bulloch.

Although most Dunwoody family documents from this period use only one "o" in the name, we have used the more familiar Dunwoody spelling for consistency.

Dunwoody, Charles Archibald Alexander (1828-1905): son of John Dunwoody, married Ellen Rice (1827-1895) in 1852.

Dunwoody, Ellen Rice (1827-1895): married Charles Dunwoody in 1852.

Dunwoody, Henry Macon (1826-1863): fourth child of John and Jane Dunwoody.

Dunwoody, James Bulloch (1816-1902): son of John and Jane Dunwoody. A Presbyterian minister who served from 1845 to 1855 in Pocotaligo, South Carolina. He married Mittie and Thee. Married Laleah Georgianna Wood Pratt (1823 to 1853) who died about 1 October giving birth to a son.

Dunwoody, Jane Irvine Bulloch (1788-1856): wife of John Dunwoody of Roswell.

Dunwoody, John (1786-1858): planter in Liberty County, Georgia, before moving to Roswell, Georgia, married Jane Bulloch in 1808, brother-in-law to Martha Bulloch.

Dunwoody, John, Jr., Colonel (1818-1903): second child of John and Jane Dunwoody, served eight years in Georgia militia, fought in Mexican War (1846-1848), served as government surveyor in Kansas, and later in Confederacy, married Elizabeth Clark Wing.

Dunwoody, Laleah *Lilly* Georgianna (1844-1919): daughter of Reverend James and Laleah Dunwoody.

Dunwoody, Marion (1821-1885): fifth child of John and Jane Dunwoody, married for second time in 1851 to William Glen.

Dunwoody, Rosaline M. (1853 - unknown): daughter of Charles and Ellen Dunwoody.

Dunwoody, Ruth Ann Atwood (1826-1899): married to Dr. William Elliott Dunwoody, mother of three children by 1853.

Dunwoody, William Elliott, Sr. Dr. (1823-1891): son of John and Jane Dunwoody. cousin.

Elliott, Daniel Stewart (1826-1862): son of Martha Stewart and John Elliott, often referred to as *brother Dan*. Daniel Stewart Elliott officially changed his name to Stuart Elliott in December of 1853. The official notice did not give a reason for this change.

Elliott, John (1773-1827): planter, lawyer, and U.S. Senator. Married in 1795 to Esther Dunwoody (d. 1815), children included Caroline Matilda (1796-before1827), Hesther Amarintha (1797-1831), John (1801-1803), Rebecca Jane (1803-1804), John (1807-1813), Jane Elizabeth (1809-1829), Corinne Louisa (1813-1838) and Charles James (1815-1817). Second marriage to Martha Stewart in 1818, children included John Whitehead (1818-1820), Susan Ann (1820-1895), Georgia Amanda (1822-1848), Charles William (1824-1827), and Daniel Stewart (1826-1862).

Elliott, John Stuart (1859-1913): son of Daniel Stuart Elliott and Lucinda Ireland Sorrell.

Sorrell, Lucinda *Lucy* Ireland (1829-1903): married Daniel Stuart Elliott in 1858.

Elliott, Matilda Moxley *Maude* (1860-1910): daughter of Daniel Stuart Elliott and Lucinda Ireland Sorrell.

Emlen, George (1814-1853): resident and wealthy merchant in Philadelphia and brother-in-law to James Alfred Roosevelt.

Green, Elizabeth Sarah (1835-1916): student at Kennesaw Female Seminary in Marietta, (Myers 1972:1534).

Habersham, Mary Ann Stiles (1834-unknown): wife of Dr. Joseph Clay Habersham, Jr. of Savannah.

Hand, Julia Isabella (1834-1911): younger daughter of Eliza Barrington King Hand (later Bayard) and Bayard Hand (died 1838), granddaughter of Roswell King, lived in Rome, Georgia. Married Dr. Henry Mortimer Anderson in July of 1854.

Hutchison, Robert (1802-1861): Scottish born, wealthy Savannah merchant, married first in 1832 Corinne Louisa Elliott, Martha Bulloch's stepdaughter. Corinne and their two daughters died in the sinking of the steamer *Pulaski* in 1838. Hutchison married his second wife, Mary Edmonia Caskie of Virginia in 1848. Mary died of consumption in 1852. Hutchison remained a friend of the family and was executor of James Stephens Bulloch's estate. He married a third time, on 23 April 1857, Ellen Laura Caskie (1836-1858), who was the first cousin of his second wife.

King, Barrington (1798-1866): son of Roswell King and co-founder of Roswell Manufacturing Company, married Catherine Margaret Nephew. Lived in Barrington Hall, adjacent to Bulloch Hall.

King, Barrington Simeral (1833-1865): fifth son of Barrington and Catherine King.

King, Catherine Evelyn *Eva* (1837-1923) only daughter of Barrington and Catherine King, granddaughter of Roswell King (Roswell's founder), lived at Barrington Hall. Eva married the Reverend William Elliott Baker (1830-1906) a Presbyterian minister on 17 July 1856.

King, Clifford Alonzo (1842-1911): youngest surviving child of Barrington and Catherine King, grandson of Roswell King (Roswell's founder), lived at Barrington Hall.

King, James Roswell (1827-1897): son of Barrington and Catherine King, grandson of Roswell King (Roswell's founder). Married Elizabeth Frances *Fanny* Hillhouse Prince (1829-1881) in 1851.

King, Ralph Browne (1835-1900): son of Barrington and Catherine King, grandson of Roswell King (Roswell's founder), lived at Barrington Hall.

King, Thomas *Tom* Edward (1829-1863): son of Barrington and Catherine King, grandson of Roswell King (Roswell's founder). Married Mary (Marie) Read Clemens of Huntsville, Alabama, on 30 November 1854.

King, William Nephew, Dr. (1825-1894): son of Barrington and Catherine King, grandson of Roswell King (Roswell's founder), lived at Barrington Hall, William studied at the New York College of Physicians and Surgeons before studying surgery for three years in Paris.

Morris, George Washington, Dr. (1829-1857): plantation owner (The Grove, on the Edisto River) and doctor from South Carolina whom Thee met while on his trip to Europe.

Pratt, Nathaniel Alpheus Reverend (1796-1879): first minister of the Roswell Presbyterian Church and schoolmaster, married Catherine Barrington King in 1830.

Roosevelt, Anna *Bamie* (1855-1931): first child and daughter of Mittie Bulloch and Theodore Roosevelt.

Roosevelt, Cornelius Van Schaak (1794-1871): married Margaret Barnhill (1790-1861) in 1821.

Roosevelt, Cornelius Van Schaak, Jr. (1827-1887): married Laura H. Porter (1833-1900) in 1854.

Roosevelt, Elizabeth *Lizzie* Thorne Ellis (1833-1877): married to Robert Barnhill Roosevelt.

Roosevelt, Elizabeth *Lizzie* Norris Emlen (1825-1912): married James Alfred Roosevelt in 1847.

Roosevelt, Elliott (1860-1894): third child and second son of Mittie Bulloch and Theodore Roosevelt

Roosevelt, James Alfred (1825-1898): married Elizabeth Norris Emlen (1825-1912) in 1847, often called Jim.

Roosevelt, John Ellis (1853-1939): first child of Robert and Lizzie Roosevelt.

Roosevelt, Laura H. Porter (1833-1900): of Lockport, New York, married Cornelius Jr., in 1854.

Roosevelt, Margaret Barnhill (1799-1861): married Cornelius Van Schaak Roosevelt, Sr. in 1821.

Roosevelt, Margaret Barnhill (1851-1927): daughter of Robert and *Lizzie* Ellis.

Roosevelt, Martha *Mittie* Bulloch (1835-1884): daughter of Martha and James Stephens Bulloch.

Roosevelt, Mary West (1823-1877): wife of Silas Weir Roosevelt.

Roosevelt, Robert Barnhill (1829-1908): married to *Lizzie* Ellis in 1850, most often called *Rob*.

Roosevelt, Silas Weir (1823-1870): married Mary West in 1845.

Roosevelt, Theodore (1831-1878): married Mittie Bulloch in 1853.

Roosevelt, Theodore (1858-1911): first son and second child of Mittie Bulloch and Thedore Roosevelt, future president of the United States.

Shackelford, Caroline *Carrie* Matilda Elizabeth (1835-1927): daughter of Francis Robert Shackleford and Caroline Seymour Dunwoody, cousin to the Dunwoody children.

Smith, Ann Magill (1807-1887): resident of Roswell, married to Archibald Smith.

Smith, Archibald (1801-1886): resident of Roswell married to Ann Magill.

Smith, Elizabeth *Lizzie* Anne (1831-1915): eldest child of Archibald and Ann Smith, resident of Roswell.

Smith, Helen Zubly (1841-1896): third child of Archibald and Ann Smith, resident of Roswell.

Stiles, Mary Cowper (1832-1863): sister of William Henry Stiles II, daughter of William Henry and Eliza Anne Stiles of Savannah.

Stiles, William Henry II (1834-1878): brother of Mary Cowper Stiles, son of William Henry and Eliza Anne Stiles of Savannah.

West, Hilborne, Dr. (1818-1907): of Philadelphia, married Susan Ann Elliott in 1849.

West, Lewis *Lew* (1829-1867): of Philadelphia, officer in the U.S. Navy, younger brother of Hilborne and Mary West.

West, Susan Ann Elliott (1820-1895): daughter of Martha Stewart and John Elliott, married Hilborne West in 1849.

Enslaved Africans (Roswell):
Abram
Bess - formerly Anna and Mittie's personal maid
Daddy Brister
Maum Grace
Hagar
Henry
Isa
Isaac
Jane
Johnny (pretty)
Lavina
Lawrence
Leah
Daddy Luke Moumar (or Mounar)
Maum Charlotte Moumar
Peggy - Anna's personal maid
Sal
Sally
Sarah -sister of Peggy
Maum Sylvia

Roosevelt Family Servants (New York):
Bridget - Bamie's nursemaid
Ann Butler
Ann Dash
Garry
Margaret Dash
Nora - Irish nursemaid to Anna (Bamie)
Mary Ann

West Family Servants (Philadelphia):
Ann Doolin
Delia Murray
Emily
Hannah Crone
Rose

Appendix
Setting the Stage from *Mittie & Thee*

The Bulloch Family

The year 1853 began just like all those since 1849 for the James Stephens Bulloch family of Roswell, Georgia. Martha "Patsy" Stewart Elliott Bulloch, matriarch and widow, who lost her daughter Georgia Amanda Elliott, in 1848, and her husband James Bulloch, in February 1849, still dressed each day in the total black of deep mourning. Her eldest daughter Susan Ann Elliott had married Hilborne West of Philadelphia in January 1849 and now resided in that city with her husband's family. Martha's son from her first marriage, Daniel Stewart Elliott traveled in Europe with her former step-son-in-law and family friend Robert Hutchison. Poor Robert tragically lost his wife, Martha's step-daughter Corinne Louisa Elliott and their two small daughters in the June 1838 boiler explosion and sinking of the Steamship *Pulaski* off the coast of Palmetto Bluff, South Carolina.[1] Robert survived, one of only 59 souls to do so, while approximately 100 men, women, and children perished. One other young man called Martha *mother*, the son of James Stephens Bulloch and his first wife Hester. James Dunwoody Bulloch served as Lieutenant on the SS *Georgia*, a ship of the United States Mail Steamship Company while on furlough from the United States Navy.[2]

By the beginning of May, spring resided in all its southern glory. Trees and flowers bloomed as the days warmed easily to the mid-70s. The hustle and bustle of life could be heard in this small, upcountry mill village. Each day the large white-columned Greek Revival home at the end of Bulloch

Avenue filled with the sounds of her children's gaiety and the subdued noises made by their enslaved African-Americans as they carried out their chores. Martha enjoyed the company of her two daughters still at home, Anna Louise, age 20, and Mittie, age 18, and son Irvine Stephens, a boy of only 11, the remaining children of her marriage to James Bulloch.

It was here that our story of an enduring love and the birth of a future president truly began. To understand the many characters in this story, one must travel a bit further back in time and examine the intertwining roots of the family tree that brought about the events of 1853.

Mittie's story began with the complicated tale of her parents romance, oft told, yet undocumented. According to family lore, in 1817, in Liberty County, Georgia, twenty-four-year-old James Stephens Bulloch, business man, planter, and veteran of the War of 1812 proposed to eighteen-year-old Martha "Patsy" Stewart, daughter of Revolutionary War General Daniel Stewart. Despite her reputed love for this man she had known since early childhood, she did as the fashion of the time dictated and refused his offer. Tradition indicated she could expect another offer. However, much to her dismay, James instead proposed to her friend, Hester Elliott (b.1797), daughter of neighbor John Elliott. Hester readily accepted his offer and made wedding plans. Meanwhile, Martha, a noted beauty, received an offer of marriage from that same John Elliot, age 44, a Yale graduate, some 26 years her senior.

James and Hester (Hettie) married on 31 December 1817, followed quickly by the marriage of Martha and John on 6 January 1818. Both weddings took place in the Midway Congregational Church in Liberty County. Thus Martha became James' stepmother-in-law. Liberty County society saw

Martha's marriage as one of prestige and advantage for the couple.

History has not revealed the nature of James and Hettie's relationship; however, it was not uncommon for young women to marry for status instead of love. James was quite a catch. The residents of Liberty County and Savannah (Chatham County) already recognized this young man for his family connections. His grandfather Archibald Bulloch was the first *president* of Georgia and the man who first read the Declaration of Independence to the citizens of the colony. Additionally, James had by this time established himself as a gentleman investor, public servant, and factor in Savannah.

James and Hettie resided in Savannah on Broughton Street. Hettie bore James at least two children, of whom sadly only one lived to maturity, James Dunwoody Bulloch (1823-1901). Their first son, named John Elliott for her father, died at age two years and 10 months in Burke County, Georgia, in late September 1821.[3]

Though marrying a man old enough to be her father, Martha embraced the role of stepmother to John's three daughters who remained at home, Caroline Matilda (a 22-year-old spinster, who died before 1827), Jane Elizabeth (age 9), and Corinne Louisa (age 5). Perhaps an added attraction was the anticipation that John Elliott was a likely candidate for the United States Senate. Martha's first child, John Whitehead Elliott, was born on 7 November 1818. Her life changed greatly when the Georgia legislature elected John to the U.S. Senate in 1819. John took his young wife to Washington where she charmed residents with her stylish and gracious ways. Tragedy struck the family in November 1820 when her first-born son died. Another son, Charles William, born in 1824, would survive a mere three years. The infant mortality rate was high in the 1820s. Only three children from this union would live to maturity; Susan Ann (1820-1895), Georgia Amanda (1822-1848), and Daniel Stewart (1826-1862).[4]

Historical records show that the two families were much entwined, with James, John, and their wives often traveling together for business and pleasure. Years passed with James and Hettie residing in Savannah, while John and Martha split their time between his Liberty County plantation, their new expansive Savannah home, and Washington, D.C. and Philadelphia.

In 1824 with John's term of office completed, they returned south and rejoiced at the birth of son Daniel Stewart (1826). On 9 August 1827, John Elliott died prematurely in Savannah of dysentery he contracted while tending the slaves at one of his plantations. John's death left a grieving 28-year-old Martha with four small children from their union, including nine-month-old Daniel, and two stepdaughters, Jane Elizabeth, age 18, and Corinne Louisa, age 14, to raise. Compounding the family's grief was the death of three-year-old Charles, one month in early September.[5]

It seems this shared grief brought James, Hettie, and Martha even closer together. At age 55 and in robust health, no doubt expecting to live many more years, John Elliott died *in testate*. James became the executor of John's estate. Managing John's extensive plantation and other business holdings occupied a tremendous amount of his time in the coming years. That first year, both families lived in *full mourning*. Then, for half a year, the families continued in *half mourning*, attending only small social events and traveling little.

On 1 May 1828 following her father's death by not quite nine months, Jane Elizabeth Elliott married John Stevens

326

Law, a physician from Liberty County. Sadly, Jane enjoyed only eleven months of marital bliss. The *Savannah Georgian* on 18 April 1829 reported a fire at their residence. On 30 April, the *Georgian* posted Jane's death notice, documenting her death only 3 days after the fire. Jane's death, falling so soon after the fire, presumably at their home, leaves the nature of her death to speculation.

It seemed Martha's period of mourning would never end, as one month later on 27 May 1829, Martha's father General Daniel Stewart died at his plantation in Liberty County. Within a two year period, Martha lost her husband and young son, her stepdaughter, and her father.

Life went on. Martha inherited a substantial amount from her father's estate. Her personal wealth also increased with her inheritance from her husband's estate, insuring a comfortable life style. Steamship records of the times show that Martha traveled, sometimes with only her children and a few servants, to the North during the South's hottest months of summer and often to Charleston, South Carolina. At other times she was accompanied by James, Hettie, and their small son, Martha's step-grandson.

Hettie's health deteriorated, and at some point in 1830, James, Hettie, and their seven-year-old son moved in with Martha at her Savannah home. On 21 February 1831, Hettie died of what was described as a "protracted and painful" illness.[6] Life now found Martha and James, living as *brother and sister* [7] while raising children from three marriages. On 12 January 1832, her step-daughter Corinne Elliott married family friend Robert Hutchison.

One year and two months after Hettie's death, on 8 May 1832, James and Martha married. Savannah resident

Mary Telfair wrote to her friend Mary Few of Virginia that a good deal of buzzing was taking place over a match among members of the church. It was said that "the church would weep over such a marriage."[8] She described Mrs. John Elliott as a woman of exalted piety. But clearly she has misgivings about this upcoming marriage:

> . . . she married in the first instance a Man old enough to be her father and no doubt sacrificed feeling to ambition. She made a most exemplary Wife & (hardest of all duties) an excellent Step Mother. For four years she has acted the part of a dignified Widow which of all characters (Step Mother excepted) is the most difficult to support, and now she is about marrying her husband's daughter's husband — he has been living in the house with her ever since the death of his wife and I thought viewed by her with sisterly regard. I begin to think with Miss Edgeworth that propinquity is dangerous and beyond the relationship of Brother and Sister mutual dependence is apt to create sentiment more tender than platonic. . . It does not strike me as a criminal connection, but one highly revolting to delicacy. . .[9]

Mary Telfair went on to expound that the late Mr. Elliott's surviving daughter's feelings "were very much enraged." Telfair stated that this daughter, Corinne Louisa, was devotedly attached to her stepmother, but now refused to have any interaction with her brother-in-law.[10] Mary Telfair ended with "I feel sorry for Mrs. Elliott, she had in her first marriage to practice an Apprenticeship to self denial, in order to conciliate the good will of daughters as old as herself — by a noble and disinterested course of conduct she received their confidence and affection and fulfilled her duties as a wife as faithfully as if she had married from Love."[11]

This marriage brought about Mittie's birth, then the move to Roswell, and finally to the year 1853. In the intervening years, Martha and James lived in Savannah, on Liberty County plantations, and in Hartford, Connecticut. Their first child Anna, born in 1833, joined the family while in one of their southern residences. It was during their extended stay in Hartford, where James Dunwoody Bulloch, age 14, Susan Elliott, age 15, Georgia Elliott, age 13, and Daniel Elliott, age 9, were attending school that Mittie was born on 8 July 1835.

In the spring of 1838, Martha, James, and four of their children (Susan, Georgia, Anna, and Mittie) left Savannah for the "colony" at Roswell, Georgia.[12] Fifteen-year-old, James Dunwody Bulloch and eleven-year-old Daniel did not make the trip with the rest of the family, as both still attended boarding school in Middletown, Connecticut. James Bulloch had invested in the Roswell Manufacturing Company, newly established in the town, and had received acreage for a home as part of the deal. Located in Georgia's Piedmont region, Roswell sprang into being due to the efforts of Roswell King and his son Barrington. In the early 1830s, Roswell King had initiated a plan to build a cotton mill on Vickery Creek in what was then Cherokee land. He and his son purchased land lots, started recruiting investors, and began building the mill and other business concerns. James Bulloch invested in the company early in its conception.

It is believed that three slave couples joined James and Martha on the journey. These were most likely *Daddy* Luke Moumar, the butler and handyman whom Martha had taught to read and write, and his wife *Maum* Charlotte, the housekeeper, along with *Daddy* Stephen, the coachman. *Maum* Rose, the cook, *Daddy* William, and *Maum* Grace the nursemaid.[13] Taking along oxcarts of belongings, the family traveled first by sloop or steamship to Augusta, and then across eastern Georgia to the Chattahoochee River, and finally on to Roswell.

At first, the family lived in a small cabin, called Clifton Farm, while their new house was under construction. Located approximately four miles east from their new home site, this cabin had likely recently housed a Cherokee family. Willis Ball, a Connecticut skilled-builder, designed and built their new Roswell townhouse. Historic architects agree he based his work on the widely-used Asher Benjamin books such as *The Architect, or Practical House Carpenter* and *The American Builder's Companion*. With Tuscan columns across its wide verandah, the lovely home sat at the end of a long lane leading to the town square. At one time a captain's or widow's walk graced the roof.[14]

In late 1838 or early 1839, their family expanded with the birth of Charles Irvine. He was baptized by the visiting Reverend Nathaniel A. Pratt during his first visit to the colony on 20 October 1839, the same day the Roswell Presbyterian Church was organized. Two years later, in 1841, Charles Irvine Bulloch died at age two years and nine months. The family buried him in the new town cemetery, now know as Founders Cemetery. In 1842, Martha delivered her ninth and last child Irvine Stephens Bulloch.

The family worshiped at the Presbyterian Church, only a short walk down Mimosa Boulevard from their home. Anna, Mittie, and Irvine attended the Academy, Roswell's school, built directly north of the church. They socialized with the Colony's other prominent founders, the Barrington

King family, the Archibald Smith family, the Reverend Nathaniel A. Pratt family, and their cousins, the family of John Dunwoody. John had married James Stephens Bulloch's sister Jane in 1808. They raised five sons and one daughter. The Dunwoodys occupied Phoenix Hall (now called Mimosa[15]) directly adjoining the Bulloch property. The family frequently traveled to the coast to visit friends and relatives. The Bullochs were wealthy, well educated, and well traveled.

As Anna and Mittie grew to be young women, Martha sent them to Barhamville, South Carolina, to Dr. Marks' South Carolina Female Academy to further their education. Dr. Marks located his academy near Columbia, South Carolina, and named the area Barhamville. A physician by training but educator by choice, Dr. Marks opened his academy on 1 October 1828. His original idea was a place with "scale of economy" that would make it affordable to those of moderate circumstances.[16] The school offered four years of studies built on a collegiate basis and soon attracted the daughters of many of central South Carolina's wealthiest planters. The girls studied the ornamental arts, the Classics, music, dancing, and languages such as French, Italian, Spanish, and Latin. Marks and his wife, fellow educator Jane Barham (1788-1827), the school's namesake, thought studying these subjects would make a, so called, *accomplished lady*. After the death of Jane Barham, Marks hired and later married Julia Pierpont Warne, head of the flourishing girls' school at Sparta, Georgia.[17]

Mittie and Anna lived at the school for two terms each year. They were well attended with servants to draw baths, tend fires, and see to their needs. School rules required them to write home on the first day of each month. The staff inspected all incoming letters, and those deemed of a "trifling nature" were frowned upon. The girls were not even permitted to converse with a young man without the written permission of their parents. By the early 1850s, the school had well over 100 young ladies in attendance and bookkeeping had been added as a new course.[18] It is not clear how long the girls attended the Academy; however, the girls were in attendance in the fall of 1849.

The Roosevelt Family

Now that we have set the scene in Roswell, the much less confusing New York side of this love story needs to be told. Wealthy New York businessman, Cornelius Van Schaak Roosevelt (1794-1871) and his wife Margaret Barnhill (1790-1861) raised five sons, Silas Wier (1823-1870), James Alfred (1825-1898), Cornelius Van Schaak, Jr. (1827-1887), Robert Barnwell (1829-1906), and Theodore (1831-1878). By 1853, James, Robert, and Silas had married, however, only Robert had children. Theodore, who had just returned from the *Grand Tour of Europe* on the United States Mail Steam Ship *Arctic* on 19 April 1852, worked for Roosevelt & Sons, the family business.

The Roosevelts lived on the corner of 14th Street and Broadway in Manhattan. Theodore's father, Cornelius, was a glass merchant, an ultraconservative abolitionist, and a Quaker by birth. Cornelius' forefather, Claes Martenszen van Rosenvelt arrived in the New York area in 1644. Claes' son Nicholas' two sons established the two branches of the family. Johannes (1689-1750) established the Oyster Bay Roosevelts while Jacobus (1692-1776) established the line known as the Hyde Park Roosevelts. Each line would later produce an American president. During the intervening years, family members married into Welsh, English Quaker, Scottish, Irish, and even German families, creating an all-American blood line by the time of the American Revolution.

Theodore's 1851 passport application gave an accurate description of him as a 19-year-old man. The description stated he stood 6 feet tall, had a high forehead, blue eyes, and a thick nose on a long face. His mouth and chin are listed as large with lighter hair and a light complexion.[19]

Endnotes:

1. George White, *Historical Collections of Georgia: Containing the Most Interesting Facts, Traditions, Biographical Sketches, Anecdotes, Etc. Relating to the History and Antiquities, From Its First Settlement to the Present Time* (New York: Pudney & Russell, Publishers, 1855), 353-364: Rebecca McLeod, "The Loss of the Steamer Pulaski," *The Georgia Historical Quarterly* 3, no. 2 (1919): 88.

2. Walter E. Wilson and Gary L. McKay, *James D. Bulloch: Secret Agent and Mastermind of the Confederate Navy* (Jefferson, North Carolina and London: McFarland & Company, Inc. Publishers, 2012),16-17.

3. *Darien Gazette,* 22 September 1821.

4. Susan Ann Elliott, born 6 August 1820; Georgia Amanda Elliott, born 14 June 1822, and Daniel Stewart, born 20 November 1826.

5. *Savannah Georgian*, 11 September 1827. Obituary reads in part, "On the 8th inst. Charles Williams, son of the late John Elliott, age three." The "Savannah Georgia Select Board of Health and Health Department Records 1824-1864" listed his interment as 8 October rather than his death.

6. *Savannah Daily Georgian*, 1831.

7. In the antebellum period, a sister-in-law or brother-in-law was considered a brother or sister.

8. Mary Telfair wrote of Martha and James' relationship as it would have been recognized by the social community.

BettyWood (editor), *Mary Telfair to Mary Few: Selected Letters 1802-1844* (Athens: The University of Georgia Press, 2007),106-10.

9. Betty Wood (editor), *Mary Telfair to Mary Few: Selected Letters 1802-1844* (Athens: The University of Georgia Press, 2007),106-10: Charles Johnson, Jr., *Mary Telfair: The Life And Legacy of a Nineteenth-Century Woman* (Savannah, Georgia: Geor Frederic C. Beil Publisher, 2002), 93-94.

10. Ibid., 93-94.

11. Ibid., 93-94.

12. Roswell King and his son, Barrington King, established a cotton mill at Vickery Creek in upland Georgia in the mid-1830s. Roswell invited investors to his "Colony of Roswell" so as to establish a town with the social and religious values so desired by his social and economic status. By 1839, a number of prominent Savannah and Liberty County families had accepted King's offer and relocated to the village. A number of books on the subject can be found including Paulette Snoby's *Georgia's Colony of Roswell: One Man's Dream and the People Who Lived It*, published in 2015 by Interpreting Time's Past, LLC.

13. Southern slave-holding families often gave honorary titles to their beloved house slaves, such as *Maum* for Mama and *Daddy*. The slaves mentioned here were called by these titles in everyday speech and family letters by the Bulloch women.

14. Bulloch Hall is currently a house museum, owned by the City of Roswell, and funded in part by the Friends of Bulloch, Inc.

15. Mimosa Hall is, as of 2016, a privately-owned home.

16. Christie Anna Farnham, *The Education of the Southern Belle: Higher Education and Student Socialization in the Antebellum South* (New York: New York University Press, 1994), 65-67.

17. Mrs. I.M.E. Blandin, *History of Higher Education of Women in the South, Prior to 1860* (New York: The Neale Publishing Company, 1909), 260-263.

18. Lynn Salsi and Margaret Sims, *Columbia: History of a Southern Capital* (Charleston, SC: Arcadia Publishing, 2003), 41-42.

19. National Archives and Records Administration (NARA); Washington D.C.; NARA Series: Passport Applications, 1795-1905; Roll #: 36; Volume #: Roll 036-07 Apr 1851-22 May 1851.

These references are included in the book's bibliography.

Index

Mittie Bulloch Roosevelt, Thee Roosevelt, and Anna Bulloch are not indexed. All individuals are listed by their name as of 1860. Bold page numbers denote photographs.

Green, Benjamin 57
Green, Clara Glenda 18-19, 52, 56-57
Green, Jane 18
Green, Sarah 18-19, 41, 57
Gregory, Mrs. 247-248
Grosvenor, Miss 285
Guins, Mrs. 255
Gwin, Mrs. 258

Habersham, Frederick Augustus 15
Habersham, Susan Ellen 11, 14
Hand, Bayard 67
Hardee, Anna 286
Hardee, Elizabeth 286
Hardee, Sarah 286
Hardee, Sidney 280
Hardee, William 286
Hardee, Col. William Joseph, 280-283
Hart, Jessie 185
Hart, Mary 185
Heath, Mrs. 238
Hoge, Dr. 269
Holly Hill 81
Holmes, James 14
Hooper, Laura 284
Howland, Mrs. 258
Hows, John 173
Hoy, Mr., Mrs. and Miss 253
Hunter, Lydia 10, 14
Hunter, Martha 14
Hunter, Wimberly Jones 14
Hunter, Virginia 14
Hutchison, Corinne Elliott 5, 85
Hutchison, Ellen Laura Caskie 85, 211, 238
Hutchison, Mary Edmonia Caskie 5, 85, 211
Hutchison, Mary (b. 1849) 5
Hutchison, Nancy 5, 207, 211-212, 214, 217

Hutchison, Robert 4-5, 50-51, 83, 85, 89, 99-101, 107, 110, 112-114, 122, 125, 130, 175, 177, 210-212, 213, 217, 231, 236, 238, 290-291
Hyatt, Misses 284

Jackson, Nancy 143
Jefferson Medical College 166, 168, 177, 201, 257
Johnstone, Elliott 258-259
Johnstone, Joe 258
Jones, Alfred Mrs. 238
Jones, Rev. Charles Colcock 9, 12, 53, 157, 209
Jones, John 153-154
Jones, Dr. Joseph 157, 165-166
Jones, Mary 209-210
Jones, Noble Wimberly Jones 14
Jones, Sarah 14
Juniata River 172-174

Kermit, Mr. 108
Kermit, Mrs. 96
King, Anna Matilda 53, 64
King, Barrington 17, 24, 38-39, 46, 49, 74, 117, 130, 142, 228, 242
King, Barrington Simeral 39, 74, 76
King, Carolina Virginia Way 39, 49, 180
King, Catherine Evelyn 34, 38-39, 74, 82, 134, 143, 145
King, Catherine Margaret Nephew 24, 38-39, 49, 74, 133
King, Charles Barrington 39, 65
King, Clifford Alonzo 35, 38-39
King, Elizabeth Frances Hillhouse Prince 33-34, 39
King, James 33, 39, 100
King, Joseph Henry 39, 80
King, Mary Read Clemens 38-39, 155
King, Ralph 39, 228
King, Roswell 38, 67
King, Stephen 279

King, Thomas *Tom* Edward 22-23, 39, 100, 144, 155, 207, 226, 228, 232-233, 242?, 269
King, Dr. William Nephew 35, 38-39, 40, 47, 49, 64-65, 74, 178, 180
Knox, Ike 113, 118, 129
Kollock, Dr. Phineas 49-50

Ladson, George Whitefield 100-101
Langhorn, Mary 11
Lapierre House, 165, 167-**168**
Law, Henry 143
Lawton, D. 47-49
Lewis, Dr. 269
Lewis, John 81
Lewis, Mrs. John 80-81
Lewis, Margaret Adams King 81
Lewis, Mrs. 240, 290
Lewis, Robert Adams 81
Liberty County, Georgia 12-14, 38, 53, 100, 146-147, 157, 166, 210-211
Littlefair, Miss 247-249
Low, Andrew 14, 180
Low, Catherine Mackay 180
Low, Jessie 180
Low, Juliette Gordon 180
Low, Mary (b. 1859) 180
Low, Mary Cowper Stiles 10-12, 14, 179-180
Low, William Mackay 180

McAllister, Hall 52, 55
McCully (McCauley), William 165, 169-170
McCheyne, Robert Murray 162-163
Madison Springs, Georgia 34, **36**-37
Magie, Dr. 203
Markoe, Dr. Thomas M. 218-219
Maxwell, Laura E. 210
Mayo, Fitz-Hugh Mr. and Mrs. 238

Pittsburgh, Pennsylvania 164, 167, 169-170, 213
Planter's House 171, 173
Plaquamine, Louisiana 185-186
Poe, Frances 34, 38
Poe, Mary Prince 34, 38
Poe, Washington 38
Porter, Annette Cross 185
Porter, Ella 285
Porter, Mrs. 285
Porter, S. Grosvenor 185
Portsmouth, Virginia 149, 152-154
Potter, Sarah 10, 14
Poullaine, Dr. Thomas 11, 14
Poullaine, Mildred 11, 14
Powis, Dr. Terry 101
Pratt, Francis Lorinda 131
Pratt, Henry Barrington 129. 131, 134, 269
Pratt, Horace Southworth 58
Pratt, Isabella 147
Pratt, Jane Farley Wood 56, 58
Pratt, Laleah Georgianna 56-58, 202-203, 205
Pratt, Rev. Nathaniel Alpheus 17-18, 33, 38, 55, 58, 80, 100,
    131, 228-230
Pratt, Nathaniel 74-76
Prime, Mr. 241
Prince, Sarah Virginia 38
Proudfoot, Hugh W. 49

Rapello, Mr. 258
Rees, Elizabeth 13, 145, 147-148
Rees, Rev. Henry Kollock and wife 48, 145, 147
Rees, Matilda 9, 13, 25, 29, 145, 147
Reid, Johny 285
Renny, Tom 265
Richmond, Virginia 3, 85, 211-212, 231, 236-238
Robbins, Miss 256
Rockaway, New York 240

As few of the enslaved Africans' and northern servants' surnames are mentioned within the text, they are presented here by city and/or state of residence. Additional surnames were added, when possible, based on 1860 census records for Thee Roosevelt and Hilborne West.

New York

Listed in the 1860 Census are five Irish servants including Ann Demons (age 20) and her sister Betsy (28), Ann Butler (26), Dora Richards (40) and Margaret Dash (24)

Philadelphia *(see page 289 for census information)*

Georgia

About the Authors

Gwendolyn I. Koehler planned to write a book called *DSC*, better known as *Desperately Seeking Closure,* when she retired from teaching. Instead she and her husband left the cold and snowy North, and moved to Georgia, where she fell in love with historic Bulloch Hall and the fascinating lives of the Bulloch and Roosevelt families. At Bulloch, she trains docents, plans tours, and continually seeks new information about the family. She says the challenge of transcribing family letters and documents is irresistible.

As a child, **Connie M. Huddleston** loved history and dreamed about her future as an award-winning author. However, she got sidetracked and became an Army wife, a mother, an elementary school teacher, an archaeologist, and an historic preservation consultant, all before publishing her first book! As of 2016, she has published seven volumes, all dealing with her first passion (don't tell her husband and children) — our nation's past. She's even won her first book award for *Greg's First Adventure in Time.* Learn more at www.cmhuddleston.com.

Made in the USA
Columbia, SC
30 May 2018